Women in
Medieval England

Women in Medieval England

HELEN M. JEWELL

Manchester University Press
Manchester and New York
distributed exclusively in the USA and Canada by St Martin's Press

Copyright © Helen M. Jewell 1996

Published by Manchester University Press
Oxford Road, Manchester M13 9NR, UK
and Room 400, 175 Fifth Avenue, New York, NY 10010, USA

Distributed exclusively in the USA and Canada
by St Martin's Press, Inc., 175 Fifth Avenue, New York,
NY 10010, USA

British Library Cataloguing-in-Publication Data
A catalogue record for this book is available from the British Library

Library of Congress Cataloging-in-Publication Data
Jewell, Helen M.
    Women in medieval England / Helen M. Jewell.
        p.   cm.
    Includes bibliographical references and index.
    ISBN 0–7190–4016–7 (alk. paper). — ISBN 0–7190–4017–5 (pbk. :
alk. paper)
    1. Women—England—History. 2. Women—England—Social conditions.
3. England—Civilization—To 1066. 4. England—
Civilization—1066–1485. 5. Civilization, Medieval. I. Title.
HQ1147.G7J68   1996
305.4'0942—dc20
                                                            95–33401
                                                                CIP

ISBN 0 7190 4016 7 *hardback*
     0 7190 4017 5 *paperback*

First published 1996

00 99 98 97 96   10 9 8 7 6 5 4 3 2 1
Typeset in Hong Kong
by Graphicraft Typesetters Ltd, Hong Kong
Printed in Great Britain
by Biddles Ltd, Guildford and King's Lynn

Contents

Preface

A formidable sisterhood of Methodist great-aunts, born to no greater privilege than membership of a large, securely united and hard-working family, impressed forcefully upon me in my school and undergraduate days that individuals are very different from textbook generalisations. The small opportunities for ordinary English women in late Victorian and Edwardian England had not constrained their outlooks: they had patently wasted no time railing against their disadvantages, but had moved unselfconsciously and constructively where there were openings, and had grown up independently minded individuals with broad interests, good humour and the wisdom of experience. With them as role models, I could not fail to migrate towards the optimistic school of women's history, believing that women, even when they have legal, economic and social conditions stacked against them, are by no means as repressed as one might, from these constraints, expect them to be, and that they have contributed a lot more to society in the past than was acknowledged then or since. Unequal opportunities certainly characterised medieval English women; throughout society a woman would be at some disadvantage compared with a man in otherwise parallel circumstances. However, although inequality of opportunity was the lot of all women vis-à-vis their brothers or husbands, they had very little else in common, for there were wide variations in opportunities within the women's world, between slaves and their mistresses, villein women and the lady of the manor, the urban underclass and the mayor's wife, and thrifty gentry widows and conspicuously spending dowager duchesses.

The stance in this book is personal to me and no one else should be criticised for it. My great-aunts who did not conform to the textbook generalisations started me off in regarding with scepticism assumptions based on gender, itself a concept the implications of which are constantly redefined in the minds of commentators of different attitudes and experiences. Education at a single-sex school and a women's college before Oxbridge espoused coeducation brought me up in the belief that women can in many areas compete with men, and successfully, but it is my personal philosophy that to let this become bitter competition is totally counterproductive. I therefore do not find acceptable as interpretations of medieval behaviour some of the more extreme feminist expositions of recent years, which polarise by gender behaviour in the past according to feminist ideologies which belong to the transient present. But I hope I have in this book acknowledged fairly that such arguments have been put forward, for they stimulate debate, and contribute to the ongoing emergence of a better-balanced perspective.

In the particular preparation of this book, my thanks are readily offered to a number of work colleagues and other friends who have offered encouragement, supplied references and lent me books, notably Christopher Allmand, Elizabeth Danbury, Jenny Kermode and Richard Spence. I am most grateful for their help, but absolve them entirely from any responsibility for the views here put forward.

H. M. Jewell

Introduction

All historians face three problems: locating and selecting source material, interpreting it and presenting their findings. Writers about medieval women are particularly conscious of all three. Contemporary sources are much more informative about men; so would-be interpreters find obvious information about men, but little more than implications about women. In archival records women tend to be under-represented because it was normal for the male head of a household to be the recorded taxpayer, or the nominal tenant of land. In subjective source material, women may be berated, ignored, belittled, even idealised, by male writers, but all these attitudes indicate some degree of male consciousness of gender difference – that is the perceived social and cultural, rather than biological, differentiation between the sexes – and women could not reciprocate in equal volume. Comparatively few women left their own views either about men or about themselves on record. Consequently searching medieval sources specifically to find out about women often involves altering the perspective of the original sources. Lastly comes the challenge of presenting to today's readers a society very different from their own.

Because women have been disregarded so much in the study of history, this particular gap invites investigation, and much valuable work has been done with a selective focus on medieval women. But the goal should not be the production of separate studies about medieval women, any more than about medieval men. Society has always consisted of both sexes, and even where one sex is comparatively repressed – or may seem to have been, to another generation – it still influences the behaviour of the other. Women in England today have far greater freedom than their medieval forebears, but it does not advance our understanding of their situation to channel our reactions, on analysing it, into horror at what may seem repressive, or into hostility towards the apparent oppressors. Nor is it helpful to seize upon literary representations and interpret them as carrying subtle gender subversiveness which cannot be proved to have been understood at the time. It is healthy to want to know what women in medieval England did, and what they could do, but this will not be achieved by presenting them in isolation from the whole society in which they actually lived.

The historiography of the subject

The study of English medieval women illustrates particularly well how changing historiographical approaches are dictated by the changing interests of subsequent generations. In the medieval period itself, few writers found women as such intrinsically interesting, and there was no attempt to write their history, or even to accord them much place in the history of humankind in general. Not until the nineteenth century did any aspects of women's history receive more than cursory attention. Then contemporary legal arguments concerning the Married Women's Property Acts of 1860 and 1882 led to interest in women's legal status in the past. One of the early fruits of this was the handling of women and family matters in the classic *History of English Law to the Reign of Edward I*, first published by Sir Frederick Pollock and F. W. Maitland in 1898. It was firmly established that the married woman in the Middle Ages was dominated by her husband. Much of the discussion related to women and landholding, an area of activity which involved a wide range of women from dowager duchesses to the widows of manorial customary tenants. The common law conditions relating to land held in fee were uniform everywhere; socage tenure was basically similar; customary tenure varied more considerably, though still within recognisable lines. Dower within these various tenures was of early interest, and was discussed in countless introductions to editions of legal records. It was the law which was the focal point, not, at this stage, the social implications of it. Subsequently the social consequences have been probed, including the effect on landed families when estates were supporting more than one generation of dowered widows, and the effect of different dower conditions on widows' attractiveness in the remarriage market (see below, chapters 2 and 4). The legal history of women in medieval England is still a subject of interest and has particularly attracted a number of American historians in recent years. On the common law side, although no comprehensive history of medieval English law in its application to women has been attempted, work in such areas as rape, infanticide, property rights, marriage and widowhood has been done.[1] On the canon law side there has been valuable research by R. H. Helmholz and Michael Sheehan on marriage conditions and litigation, with actual practices illustrated from court records.[2]

From women's legal position in the land law, attention next turned to their legal position in trading, initially in London. The pioneering work here was by Annie Abram. For many years Marian Dale's work on London silkwomen and Sylvia Thrupp's work on the London merchant class have been the standard citations.[3] Recent writings in this field have come from Kay Lacey and Caroline Barron, and women's trading role elsewhere has also been taken up: for example in medieval Exeter by Maryanne Kowaleski (see below, chapter 3).[4] Comparatively recently women's criminal activities have come under the scrutiny of Barbara Hanawalt, and their court appearances in any capacity under Judith Bennett's, in her gender-orientated study of Brigstock (Northants) to 1348; this aspect will be treated in chapter 2.

From interest in the legal side of women's trading there developed interest in their earning power looked at in economic and anthropological terms. An early work was Alice Clark's *Working Life of Women in the Seventeenth Century* (1919), which, though focused on the early modern period, invites contrast with the Middle Ages, and is still influential on women's studies today. Economically, it has been realised that women tended to work in crafts where little capital was required to start up, or where the equipment would only be an extension of the household's normal requirements. Hence the almost imperceptible move from simply running an urban household, to taking a lodger or two, to running an inn, or from feeding the family, to selling a few extra pies or surplus ale, to baking and brewing as a major source of income. More anthropological is the study angled from the demands on the women: how the household workshop allowed her to combine domestic routines with minding the shop, or preparing yarn, or supervising the apprentices, whereas once manufacturing became more factory based, she lost out to men competitors, being unable to present herself at fixed hours to give undivided attention to the labour (see below, chapter 3).

There has come to light through these studies a gender-based distinction in both the life cycle and the work rhythm of the two sexes. Menarche and menopause have always divided a woman's life whether she marries or not. When a man married, for the first time or subsequently, he normally continued with his existing trade, but a woman marrying would leave, say, residential service to join her husband, and unless she had been employed in, or living at home in, a household related to his trade, she might have to pick up some new skills if she were going to be able to help him. Basic household skills and childcare she would have picked up from observation and involvement in her own or an employer's home. As her own children were born she would have to adapt to the needs of husband and children alongside any piecework or other sale of her labour. Thus the long-standing rhythm is there of the husband going out into the fields, or through into the shop, to work in sustained bursts punctuated by refreshment breaks until the end of his working day, when he expects thereafter to be at leisure, his work being done. This gender distinction was commented on in the fifteenth century, in Gill's speech in the 'Second Shepherds' Pageant' at Wakefield, and in the wife's comments in the later 'Ballad of a Tyrannical Husband'. The woman had to make meals to suit others' timetables. She had the basic housework to perform, fires to tend, any necessary shopping to do, and perhaps the feeding of a few poultry and animals. She might start spinning, and be broken off. It was the woman who had to down tools when a child rushed in bleeding, or the pig escaped. Nor was her day ever over. The baby may have needed breastfeeding during the night, and she would be the one to cope with sudden illness. All these conditions made the labour she had available for sale more amateur and haphazard than her husband's. Customers who wanted something done by a trained worker in a set time, generally needed a man, except in certain, very few, essentially feminised trades. So medieval women's labour for sale was marginalised and expected to yield to other demands. Once the children were off her hands, the mother's life changed yet again, more strikingly than the father's was affected by the same development.

[4]

The serious academic study of women's history has had from the first then two approaches, one legal and one socio-economic. With the opening up of career possibilities to women particularly during and after the two twentieth-century world wars, the interest in women as earners in the past was bound to increase. With modern woman going out to work, historians began to pay more attention to the place of women's earlier employment. The development of anthropological sciences has meanwhile brought the study of past social behaviour to attention, and the kinds of analysis which can be performed on census data almost instantaneously today prompt the asking of similar questions about the past, and the search for quantitative data to provide answers. Before the institution of parish registers of christenings, marriages and burials (begun in 1538 but rarely complete from so early a date) and decennial censuses (from 1801), databases for statistical analysis are lacking, but there are sufficient records, countrywide, from the poll taxes of 1377–81 to permit some conclusions to be drawn. For individual places, serial manorial court rolls provide data for attempting family reconstitution, so that such matters as the sex ratio of men to women, age at first marriage, family size and pattern of children's leaving, or staying at, home can be probed in some communities (see below, chapter 2). Inquisitions post mortem were used, by Josiah Russell in *British Medieval Population* (1948), to arrive at life expectancy and age at inheritance in the sphere of tenants-in-chief.

Up to the Second World War, histories of the family, childhood and women would have been viewed as facets of the same thing. The career woman was single, or widowed, and combining a profession with motherhood was rare. Since the 1960s women's behaviour has changed. The family unit has suffered challenge, and with more marriages ending in divorce, there has been a rise in interest in the history of separation and divorce. With the wide acceptance of contraception, revolutionised by the contraceptive pill, curiosity about earlier contraceptive methods has arisen, and the legalisation of abortion has altered the perspective on it, and infant exposure, in the past. With the greater openness in modern society about sexual intercourse, more attention has been paid to historical attitudes to this aspect of life. With the medieval church teaching that sexual relations even inside marriage were purely procreational and any enjoyment in the act sinful, one can hardly

[5]

expect much to have been written in contemporary sources that does not endorse condemnation of lust; however, much pleasure is hinted at in the lyrics about Maying and flirtations with parish clerks. Obviously modern society will view prostitution differently from the Victorian view of the 'fallen woman', and sexual abuse is a more open topic for discussion today.

Meanwhile, the study of medieval women and religion has been undertaken from a variety of angles. The classic work was Eileen Power's *Medieval English Nunneries* c. *1250–1500* (1922), now somewhat outdated. Sally Thompson's work *Women Religious: the founding of English nunneries after the Norman Conquest* (1991) offers excellent treatment of its more limited subject. English nunneries sheltered an astonishingly wide range of females from the wise Hilda of Whitby in the seventh century to the unchaste nun of Watton interviewed by Ailred of Rievaulx in the twelfth century (see below, chapter 5). Records of the nunneries are likely to leave a poor impression, for it was their backsliding which attracted attention at episcopal visitations, and it was their poverty and indebtedness which led to episcopal or royal intervention. Things going well passed unrecorded. The Reformation closed the nunneries in England, and because they were generally poorer and smaller communities than the monasteries, few of their ruins survive to capture the public imagination in the way that, for example, Fountains Abbey does. Roberta Gilchrist's work emphasises their architectural inferiority,[5] and no nunnery developed into a 'monastic' cathedral.

In recent years there has been a decline of Christian religious participation in England, and a furore in the Anglican church over women priests. Within the churches, there is today more tolerance and indeed encouragement of less-structured, unconventional worship. This may account for an increased interest in the less conventional side of medieval religion, the mystics, who while not wishing to challenge orthodoxy, believed in a more direct relationship between the soul and God, and the heretics (in England essentially these were Lollards) who attacked the established church, denigrating bishops and priests, denying transubstantiation, and rejecting pilgrimages and images. The study of heresy and the study of women have much to offer each other, for it is arguable that unorthodox religions were willing to accept women on more equal terms than women received from the established church.

[6]

Lollards could entertain the idea of women priests, and the orthodox mystic Julian of Norwich has recently received feminist attention for her concept of God/Jesus as Mother.

The legal, socio-economic and religious position of women in
the Middle Ages has thus been investigated by a wide range of
scholars using a variety of sources. Though the choice of subject
may have been influenced by changing legal, economic, anthropological or religious theories, the research has been based on medieval sources, either analysed texts or interpreted collected statistics.
Most of the interpretation has been intentionally historical, attempting to take account of the nature of the sources, and starting
from the traditional background perspective, whether subsequently
reinforcing it or challenging it. The work done on women in English
literature over the same period has been less firmly tied to the
historical past. From a historian's point of view, some of the
assumptions made in recent years seem anachronistic beyond serious belief. What may or may not have been in any writer's mind
is impossible to prove or disprove, but some of the attributions
seem extremely unlikely, and have been arrived at by starting from
a modern feminist perspective which may not be transferable to
the Middle Ages.

Source material

The advances in the overall study of medieval women in the past
century have not only come from changed perspectives inspired by
modern situations, but from the opening up of source material for
analysis. There is scarcely any evidence, other than archaeological,
earlier than the writings of Bede (d. 735), but there is a valuable
(though not complete) body of Anglo-Saxon law starting in the
reign of Æthelberht of Kent (d. 616), though many of the surviving texts were only written down several centuries after their original compilation. As will be shown, Domesday Book (1086) gives
some information about women as landholders, but their eleventh-
century position is not well evidenced. The twelfth century brought
some important developments: much sophistication of law, influencing England's emerging common law with Roman civil law
and canon law, and the hardening of rules on marriage, legitimacy
and inheritance. Visible twelfth-century emphasis on the Virgin

Mary and secular romance heroines was optimistically interpreted as indication of an improvement in women's status, or in attitudes towards them, but so simple an interpretation has rightly been found wanting (see Penny Gold's work *The Lady and the Virgin: image, attitude and experience in twelfth-century France*, 1985). From the start of the thirteenth century records become more abundant, providing source material concerning women in the feudal landholding world, women trading in London and provincial towns, and such women as appear in the manorial court rolls. Research into similar areas can be sustained from fourteenth-century records, from which the effects on both sexes of the drastic population drop after the Black Death of 1348 can be seen. By the fifteenth century more sophisticated tenurial developments, affecting the family, are recorded, and women of the landholding classes begin to speak for themselves, in the perhaps overquoted Paston letters and other less well-known correspondence, and in wills, and one woman, Margery Kempe, attempted her spiritual autobiography, though admittedly dictated to male amanuenses. Because of the later weighting of the evidence, the main concentration in this book will lie between 1100 and 1500, but the Anglo-Saxon background will be included, because it seems desirable to show the elements of continuity in women's position from the earliest recorded times, and the changes and contrasts brought about by political and economic developments.

As to the way historical evidence has been handled, up to the nineteenth century the academic study of history was a study of Latin sources, principally narrative chronicles, legal treatises and land charters, none of which is a particularly illuminating source for women's studies. The bulk of the chronicles came from monastic houses, abbeys and priories and later mendicant friaries. The writing of chronicles by laymen was a later development, and much tied in with civic chronicling. No chronicles were concerned with women, nor penned by them. The ecclesiastical chroniclers had little experience of the opposite sex. Their work was either centred on their house, or national in scope. Women only entered into either framework marginally, as patrons or patrons' wives and widows in the former type of chronicle, or as queens or more rarely other political influences in the latter. Female saints might make an appearance, and instances of women miraculously cured by a saint's relic. There is therefore incidental value for our subject in this type of source, but the genre is not generally rewarding.

Legal treatises and texts of law including custumals certainly embody information on women, but it needs seeking out and is not easy to understand. Charters provide women's names as landholders – often as wives or mothers of leading grantors, and as co-donors and witnesses rather than as the principal donor – but they need careful interpretation. The great vogue for publishing charter collections for localities and families, such as the *Early Yorkshire Charters* series, begun by W. Farrer and continued by C. T. Clay (1914–65), did not further the study of women. Charters and seals have begun to be studied in French sources as evidence for the place of women and this may be developed in England.

The value of legal texts and treatises, however, is much enhanced by the survival of comparatively huge quantities of secular and ecclesiastical court records showing the law at work, and the editing and calendaring of secular court records over the last century has made this activity more accessible. Court records sometimes permit quantification of the frequency, purpose and outcome of women's appearance in court. Particular records may be analysed to see how often women were plaintiffs and defendants, and whether they tended to be more successful in either capacity. It is possible to see how often they were involved in land litigation, alone or in the company of other women or men. In cases of debt and unjust detention the values involved may be assessed. In criminal cases, the crimes women were most prone to commit, or to suffer, can be indicated. Does it look as though women were done down because of their sex, in courts of law, or was there positive discrimination – if only out of pity? Men were the judges, and the jurors, and the clerks, but the legal record is supposed to be a matter of fact rather than opinion.

Records from secular courts have been sampled by historians rather than examined, for their bulk remains daunting. Much less work has been done on church court records, which are only just beginning to yield information. Government administrative records also are more suitable for sampling than total scrutiny, though the published, indexed, calendars of close, patent, charter, fine and liberate rolls, mainly published since 1900, are a help to students in research. Administrative records are not as good a source about women as legal records. The government's instructions were sent to men from men, and it is usually only if women were the beneficiaries of grants, or involved landholders, that anything of interest to the study of women emerges. The *Calendars of Inquisitions*

Post Mortem, for example, include the estates of deceased female tenants-in-chief, and where a deceased tenant-in-chief left only an heiress or coheiresses this factor comes to light there. Some proofs of age filed with the inquisitions give incidental recollections of memorable matters associated with the heir's birth.

Administrative records from private estates are not often illuminating in terms of gender: where the lord of the manor was a woman – as heiress or widow – the estate was run by her officials exactly as it would have been by a man's stewards and bailiffs. Household records, where they survive, are similar whether they are described as the lord's or his wife's or his widow's. *The Household Book of Dame Alice de Bryene 1412–1413*, a Suffolk widow, published in 1931 by Marian Dale and Vincent Redstone, is perhaps fairly feminised, in so far as there were many women among her friends and visitors, who may have been genuinely personal visitors rather than recipients of what one might call requisite 'status hospitality'.

From the household rolls it is only a short step to the family letters, and historians have certainly done their best to quarry from the Paston letters a picture of the home life of this family of East Anglian landholding lawyers. Due attention has been paid to the Paston womenfolk, but the other letter collections, from the Stonor, Cely and Plumpton families, have received far less attention.

Although monastic chronicles, which tell little about women, were the best-known ecclesiastical sources used in the study of medieval history in the nineteenth century, other writings from church circles have begun to prove rather more informative about women, namely the biographies of female saints, which have only surprisingly recently come to be appreciated (see below, chapter 5). What is of value is not the wild excesses of hagiography, but the incidental glimpses of the saint very much on earth, her family background, the attitude of her relatives to her vocation, what she endured in following it, how other people reacted to her at the time. There were many female saints, and books about their lives were in considerable demand. The best as historical sources are ones written soon after the saints' deaths by people who knew them. A valuable biography for the study of English religious women is that of a twelfth-century recluse and later nun who was not actually canonised, Christina of Markyate. Her life was written by a monk of St Albans who knew her, though the only extant manuscript is fourteenth-century. An even rarer work is the auto-biography of the laywoman Margery Kempe (*c*. 1373–*c*. 1439), though this was apparently orally communicated in two parts, the first to a layman, the second to a cleric who may have revised the first. Margery was not a saint, but she had the confidence to think her experiences should be communicated, on a par with the *Revelations* of St Bridget of Sweden (d. 1373).

Copious outpourings of religious men, theologians, canonists, homilists and other sermon writers, mostly untranslated from Latin or Old or Middle English, do not form a source attractive to modern readers, so are still largely untapped. A few items from this kind of literature have been translated and made better known, for example *Hali Meidhad*.[6] These writings form perhaps the most deliberate gender-conscious writing from the Middle Ages, making pointed contrast between the sexes, generally to the disparagement of the female. However, there were more kindly disposed spiritual counsellors who wrote for particular women or groups of them, nuns, anchoresses or worldly active but pious wives and mothers. Some works started out as private letters from the spiritual adviser, as Ailred of Rievaulx wrote to his sister *c*. 1162. One of the most widely circulated in England was the *Ancrene Wisse*, composed about 1220. Later Richard Rolle (d. 1349) and Walter Hilton (d. 1396) respectively wrote the *Form of Living* and the *Scale of Perfection* initially for specific women they knew.

There was also a range of behavioural teaching works for secular women's edification, at any rate by the fifteenth century. In 1483 Caxton printed a translation of the *Book of the Knight of the Tower*, a work which also exists in translation in a manuscript from Henry VI's reign, and which Caxton's publisher's blurb described as 'necessary to every gentlewoman of what estate she be'. This work had originated in France *c*. 1370, as advice from Geoffroi de la Tour Landry to his daughters. Whereas the Knight's Book was a full-scale book, 'How the Good Wife Taught her Daughter' was more of a broadsheet, aimed at a humbler level.

Alongside all this source material there exists the complex documentation of medieval literature. Contemporary literary sources should not be disregarded in the study of history, but they are harder for the historian to place in context. Historians and literary experts do not necessarily see eye to eye in their analyses: the historian wishes to relate the literature to the known history of the period of composition, the literary expert may be more interested in the analogous appearances of motifs, and is often happy to treat a literary episode as illustrable in real life citing an example fifty years later than the text. Moreover, much early medieval literature is anonymous, and borrows from still earlier work. The date and sex of the author remain unknown. However, given the educational imbalance which is shortly to be discussed, playing with words is more likely to be the work of men, even when the outcome represents a woman's situation, as in the case of the Old English poem 'The Wife's Lament'. Poetry is essentially a phrasing of generalised experience, and to appeal it has to reach out receptibly to imaginable emotions and reactions. Too individual an expression of too unique an experience would not be likely to survive in orally transmitted verse, or be copied out in the laborious reproduction by writing before the invention of print. So one may be reasonably content that the implications of marital companionship in 'The Husband's Message' and 'The Seafarer' (to use the modern titles given to originally untitled Old English verses) struck chords in their day, whilst in the epics and romances the roles of the heroines, as peace pledges, gracious patrons and objects of desire, fitted acceptable, if ambivalent, convention. From the later fourteenth century there are identified poets and assessment has been attempted for example of Chaucer's sexual poetics, but modern feminist criticism certainly warns one off taking literary figures too much at face value.

Fiction appears to have something to offer, but while textual allusions can be identified, the intentions of the writers, and their reception by their original audience/readership, remain open to changing interpretation. With his wife of Bath, to use a much discussed example, is Chaucer simply handing on the assimilated antifeminist literature of his age, or is he a feminist sympathiser criticising and poking fun at antifeminist arguments, or even positively subverting the misogyny of his culture?[7] What is plain is that many literary heroines were represented and read superficially as passive figures: Emily in 'The Knight's Tale' is a fair-haired doll, programmed to skip along picking flowers in the garden singing in the rising sun. She weeps and faints when tragedy strikes; there is no development of her character. This is quite often the case with medieval heroines: Guinevere is another who is presented more as icon than as participant in events. Apparently women were not expected to develop emotionally and intellectually. But victimised heroines like Constance, in 'The Man of Law's Tale', and most notably patient Griselda, in 'The Clerk's Tale', have dignity in their suffering. They illustrate and exaggerate the passive role approved by many men for women: women should suffer what happens to them, tolerate indignity, bear injustice and act throughout as patient, forgiving, sweet natured. Not for woman is the role of initiator, inventor, inspirer, doer. However, it is argued that some medieval heroines escape this characterless mould. Judith Weiss has noticed initiative and resourcefulness in heroines of Anglo-Norman romance.[8] Chaucer's Criseyde is a rather more complex character too.

Drama in medieval England, again for the most part anonymous and dateless, was largely religious – plays about saints' lives, Corpus Christi cycles, passion plays and moralities. Here the treatment of women is largely stereotyped: the representation of virtuous, or at least saved, women to emulate, from the Virgin to Mary Magdalene, and sinners to avoid, such as Eve and Noah's wife. It would be unwise to base opinion about the place of women in medieval England from dramatic sources, but they can be used for supporting illustration.

Any discussion of the opening up of source material and its interpretation must include advances deriving from recent archaeological studies, particularly environmental archaeology and the archaeology of gender. Before recorded history, archaeology is perforce the dominant supplier of evidence about settlements, technologies and the disposal of the dead. To illuminate the place of women in pre-literate societies, graves have to be studied and the sex of the deceased determined by analysis of the human remains or interpretation of the grave-goods. Neither process is straightforward. There are no equivocally sex-determining skeletal characteristics, though men tend to be more robust and larger, and there are differences in the skull and pelvis. Sexing by grave-goods tends to equate weapons and tools with males, and jewellery and domestic implements with females, but the categories are not exclusive and there are items common to the graves of both sexes, including pots, knives, coins and beads. Christian burial practices caused grave-goods to disappear, but the importance of archaeology does not diminish. Environmental archaeology of early urban sites tells us about diet and the pests and diseases to which medieval people were prone, from insects to arthritis. This type of evidence is not gender specific, and in reflecting the environment of both sexes treats women more impartially than gender-selective sources do. However, cross-gender samples may be used to illustrate aspects of gender, as the York Jewbury burial ground has been analysed to cast light on the distribution of the sexes, showing a slightly higher proportion of adult males.[9] Archaeology may also be used with deliberate discrimination to interpret aspects of women's position: in *Gender and Material Culture* Roberta Gilchrist writes of 'exploding androcentric traditions in monastic history and archaeology'.[10]

All the documentary source material is male dominated. A woman's own words may, on some occasions, be accurately reported by men, for example in records from both secular and ecclesiastical courts. The gist of her case must surely usually have been at least fairly accurately summarised in the Latin record, or women would have despaired of getting justice and not gone to court at all. It is tempting to believe the woman's actual words are preserved in what Jeremy Goldberg calls 'the immediacy of first-hand testimony' in the English phrases recollected by witnesses (of both sexes) in the York cause papers.[11] At other times words are put into a woman's mouth, some of which sound imaginatively suitable, and some of which are obviously the male saying what he would like to hear. The Wakefield plays illustrate both techniques. Gill's speech about her interrupted chores rings true, but Noah's wife is the blustering stereotype later developed into the pantomime dame.

Women's own silence: a matter of education

That medieval women so rarely speak for themselves is often attributed to their lack of education. Medieval women certainly did not normally have the education which would have enabled them to contribute to the international world of Latin scholarship. They did not normally have enough education to write, at a lower academic level, in such fields as narrative chronicling, from which historical study drew very heavily up to the twentieth century. Even when the growth of vernaculars as the media for written communication broadened access to reading and writing, the number of women represented by their own written words remained small. In most situations there are exceptions, and a few women writers did leave a distinguished mark. The tenth-century German canoness Hrotswitha of Gandersheim wrote metrical legends and plays, and the twelfth-century nun Hildegard of Bingen wrote religious and medical works. In the late twelfth century Marie de France wrote lays and fables prolifically in French, but it is a matter of speculation who she was and even whether she was a laywoman or nun. Much more is known about Christine de Pisan, an Italian widow writing at the fifteenth-century French court, called by Sarah Lawson, the first English translator of Christine's *The Treasure of the City of Ladies* (1985), 'the first professional woman writer in Europe'. Christine tackled, in French, varied topics including moral questions, education, the art of government, chivalry, and, remarkably given her sex, she was commissioned by the duke of Berry to write the official biography of his brother Charles V. No mean poet, she invigorated the contemporary controversy over the *Roman de la Rose*. There are no Englishwomen among this medieval authoresses' international superleague, and the best-known English female writers are not their intellectual equals. The anchoress Julian of Norwich wrote the brisk, optimistic, mystical *Revelations of Divine Love*, and Margery Kempe of Lynn communicated a far more amateur outpouring in English to successive male amanuenses. There were educated nuns in Anglo-Saxon England, such as Eadburg (abbess of Minster in Thanet) and Leoba, who corresponded in Latin with St Boniface in the eighth century, but by the later Middle Ages nuns had to be allowed French bibles because of their lack of Latin. Letters in the vernacular to and from English laywomen exist from the fifteenth century, but only Margery of the three corresponding Paston wives gives any indication of being able to sign her name (on letters written in three different hands).

So medieval women were not in a position to influence contemporary academic debate or religious or political thought by their own writings, nor even to chronicle their own times. They had scarcely any input into the expanding body of accepted authoritative writings and compiled traditions which formed the collective human experience, and set the parameters of contemporary behaviour. Without active part in the drawing up of the rules by which society was governed, they were not even in a position to record their feelings about what was expected of them. The picture of women in medieval England cannot therefore be based on their own words directly, and though their own words will be used when they can be found, the 'woman's point of view' from the Middle Ages is not one that is normally available.

To some extent, however, the lack of female education in the Middle Ages left its women much less disadvantaged than might be supposed, for the vast majority of the medieval population was illiterate, male and female alike. David Cressy estimates 90 per cent male and 99 per cent female illiteracy *c.* 1500.[12] Educational opportunity in the Middle Ages was very much a matter of class, and only within class was it a matter of gender. The peasant woman's views are no more unrecorded than the peasant man's. Certainly he could not pull the advantages of education over her. Though urban communities may have been more distinctively gender divided educationally, even this can be exaggerated, since the petty schools teaching only the vernacular were not closed to girls. Sons and daughters of artisan families were probably pretty equally uneducated like the peasantry; however, the more ambitious and successful urban classes must have gone along with a gender-divisive educational pattern, since the institutional evidence of town grammar schools for boys only is ubiquitous. There was no structured educational system for these boys' sisters. Nevertheless, there is plentiful evidence of their wives participating in their activities, and their widows continuing their trades and businesses.

In the aristocracy, the educational patterns for the two sexes were of a different tradition, the boys being trained, originally in households, in the military and cultural demands of knighthood, while the girls, equally domestically, learned the complementary skills of the lady, household management, embroidery, music. As time passed, the practical skills needed in this class changed more for the boys than they did for the girls. Military skill began to matter less than an understanding of the common law and estate management. Aristocratic institutional provision certainly drove a wedge between the sexes, with the development of boarding schools and inns of court and universities for boys, set against education at home, or in another higher-class household, or convent, for girls. But again the ultimate attainment gap appears narrower than might be expected. Geoffrey Gaimar's *L'Estoire des Engleis* was translated from Latin sources for Constance, wife of Ralph

FitzGilbert *c.* 1142; this lady paid a silver mark for a now lost 'Life' of Henry I commissioned by Adela of Louvain, 'and kept it and read it in her chamber'.[13] Robert Grosseteste's book on husbandry was written for the countess of Lincoln in the mid-thirteenth century, and a French–English vocabulary was compiled for Denise de Mountchesney to help her teach her children French at about the same date. Ultimately Lady Margaret Beaufort acquired a scholarly reputation and translated 'The Mirror of Gold for the Sinful Soul' and the fourth book of Kempis's *Imitation of Christ* from the French, though no institutional structure for the schooling of girls of her class existed, and her own childhood came to an early end when she bore her only child (Henry VII) at thirteen.

Women were educationally disadvantaged in the Middle Ages, and this is most clearly demonstrated institutionally by their absence from grammar schools, inns of court and universities. The professions for which these institutions were the training centres – the church, the law, medicine and teaching – were closed to them. But in terms of the overall population, these were rarefied career paths, so the deprivation for women in not having access to them must not be exaggerated. The church, to some extent, created a separate entry route and career path for women in its nunneries, so although women were barred from priesthood and office in the secular church, as nuns they could, like any ordinary monks, be picked out for office within their own religious community, not just as abbesses or prioresses, but also as cellarers, infirmarers and almoners. Marilyn Oliva's recent work on office holding in female monasteries in Norwich diocese will be considered in chapter 5.

Education leading to legal, medical and high ecclesiastical careers was not offered to women, but this was not so much to exclude them from these professions, as because no one had dreamed of letting them in. Women's exclusion from the highest educational echelons, into which only a tiny minority of the male population passed, is noticeable, however, because this small elite was naturally highly conscious of its own educational superiority and therefore inclined to exaggerate the importance of education, and to promote the continued monopoly of itself as the authoritative voice in theology, morality, philosophy, law and medicine. This voice was masculine, whether critical of women, indifferent, or genuinely sympathetic to them. That the written word was so dominated has to be understood, but it must be kept in proportion, because in the Middle Ages the vast majority of men were no more able than all women to enter this elite, and the pronouncements of the few were of no more significance to the peasant husbandmen, yeomen, rural landless labourers, urban journeymen and apprentices and probably their masters than they were to any of their wives, daughters and sisters. In many walks of life the menfolk were only marginally more educated than the women of their class, and are little more visible in their own written words. Thus in so far as women's lack of education was a disadvantage, it was one shared with many men too.

All this, however, perpetuated a society in which men wrote the records and communicated the opinions. Society expected this. It expected women to be passive, not independent: moderation, modesty and patience were feminine virtues. Where a woman had a husband, the law chose to deal with him. Her landed property came under his control when the couple married, his did not come under hers. She could not even make a will leaving her personal property (technically his) without his permission; he did not need her permission to leave his. In countless manorial courts, women brewers were fined for breach of the assize of ale not in their individual names but as the anonymous wives of their husbands. As women could rarely act independently, they were not encouraged to think for themselves. Some people thought it was dangerous to teach women to read, and certainly it was more widely believed that whereas reading was desirable for them as an aid to religion (at least the souls of either sex were arguably equal), it was unwise to teach them to write, since they ought not to be enabled to communicate the ideas from the weaker female mind. Widespread expectation of inferior female ability and capacity helped keep medieval women below their full potential.

As medieval English women wrote so little about themselves, what medieval English men, who compiled the records, wrote the sermons and preserved the opinions, thought about women must be carefully considered, and also how gender-conscious they were. Gender-consciousness is not a new phenomenon, though it is one which constantly redefines its terms with changing perceptions. Churchmen defined how women should behave, male lawyers worked out what they could do legally, and anonymous but presumably male entertainers developed a full range of situations focused on henpecked and cuckolded husbands, and male sexual desires. Tricks were played on women as less educated than men: a macaronic poem lists praiseworthy characteristics of women in English, for its female audience, then deftly contradicts itself in Latin, '*Cuius contrarium verum est*', for the amusement of the educated males.[14] There were undoubtedly many consciously misogynist writers.

The current expectation of assertive and even aggressive behavioural norms between and within the sexes makes it difficult to interpret medieval social attitudes. An expressed attitude might be interpreted as 'fatherly' by one cast of mind, as 'patronising' by another. Medieval men generally had a low opinion of women, believing them to be weaker, physically, emotionally and intellectually. The positive side of this conviction, for men, meant ruling their womenfolk, that is taking charge of their property, taking decisions for their welfare and protecting them physically, and the negative side meant avoiding their snares and wiles, constraining and correcting their capacity to do evil and, for some, keeping well away from the temptresses altogether. For women this state of affairs meant that they passed from control of father to husband, perhaps escaping into independence at widowhood. They were preached at by men, judged, if falling foul of the law, by all-male judges and juries, and had no access to higher education and naturally therefore to all the professions. But turning from theory to practice, these same supposedly domineering husbands are found time and time again leaving their wives as their chief executors with obvious confidence in their performance of this ultimate responsibility. So men's writing needs careful examination as evidence: not all cross-gender comment is what it seems, nor is the attitude of an identified male writer necessarily consistent in different situations or at different times in his life.

The origins of medieval attitudes, and developments within the period

Belief in the inferiority of women was not invented in the Middle Ages, and in the conditions of the time it had some appropriateness. Three major influences fed into the medieval attitude: physical anatomy, church teaching and law. Throughout history and before it, women have been physically smaller and less strong than men, and of course they bear and suckle children. In primitive times a natural division of labour would assign hunting, tree felling and soil turning to men. Women, spending a proportionately larger amount of their shorter lifespan pregnant or breastfeeding than their modern counterparts, would lead a less mobile life, preparing food for the family and rendering its home as comfortable as possible. Unsophisticated agricultural communities in Iron Age Britain, in Anglo-Saxon England and throughout the Middle Ages, retained some of this basic labour division between the sexes. Barbara Hanawalt's studies of the causes of accidental death in early fourteenth-century England showed her that women tended to die near the home in domestic accidents – drawing water and falling into wells, being scalded at the fireside, or burnt in thatch fires, whereas men tended to die further from home, in carting, or tree-felling accidents, at mills, or in the fields. However, Jeremy Goldberg has questioned Hanawalt's assumptions and methodology, drawing attention to the fact that not all tasks were equally hazardous. Some of the work men did in the fields was more dangerous than most of the work women did there, whereas some of the women's work around the home was more dangerous than most male household activities: this underlies the distribution of deaths but does not mean that necessarily women's chief sphere of work was the home and men's the fields and forests.[15]

As for the Christian church's attitude to women, this was imported into England already an amalgam of Jewish, Middle Eastern and Roman imperial attitudes. It contained many irreconcilables. There was the abysmal example of Eve, tempted and temptress, and the sublime example of Mary, the Virgin mother, and there were foolish virgins and wise virgins and impoverished widows. The church Fathers twisted this way and that following St Paul, speaking on the one hand of subordinate woman: 'the husband is the head of the wife' (Ephesians, V, 23) and on the other of equal woman: 'there is neither male nor female, for you are all one in Christ Jesus' (Galatians, III, 28). The effect on women of the coming of Christianity will be discussed in chapter 1, and the influence of religion on women after 1100 in chapter 5.

It was because of the influence of the Rome-centred church of the pre-Reformation period that old Roman secular law, lost on

English soil after the withdrawal of Rome and the influx of Angles and Saxons, came back into a position of influence, most notably during the twelfth-century renaissance, when it had some influence on the emerging English common law. (Roman civil law was not, however, as influential here as on the Continent.) Law essentially theorises and generalises about acceptable behaviour and its control. Law was written and administered by men, but not exclusively in their own interest. Indeed, an individual man's interest is rarely exclusive of women's interest, for even monks have mothers, and in the secular world the interests of the family and the more extended kin require protection for wives and widows, sisters and daughters, for the benefit of the whole. Laws from Anglo-Saxon, Anglo-Norman and later kings can all be used to throw light on the legal standing of women at various times. From individual laws something of women's practical capabilities within the law as a whole can be seen. The separate canon law of the Roman church, operative in England up to the Reformation, affected matrimonial and testamentary practices as well as matters of faith and contract.

So the ways in which men and women actually coexisted in English medieval communities were preconditioned by human physiology, by prehistoric practices which lingered on, by moral principles devised in the Mediterranean world, and by law influenced by the jurisprudence of the sophisticated Roman State. These inheritances were slowly adapted to different conditions, but women had very little influence on the changes. Some of the legal changes which effectively benefited them may have been of somewhat backhanded intention. Thus it is possible the church encouraged the strengthening of women's landed property rights because it foresaw female benefactors as a useful source of gifts and wished them to have full right to alienate their land to the church.[16] The church may have been helped in tightening the procedures for making a truly valid marriage, after a surprisingly long tolerance of informal and clandestine agreements, because of a landed society's growing anxiety to define the legitimate heir. Married women may have attained the right to trade in towns as *femes soles* to protect their husbands from liabilities for those wives' debts. In fact the position of women in towns will prove a major interest in this book, for it is arguable that there was far more change and variety in the role of women in towns, trade and industrial development

[21]

in the period 500–1500 than there was in their role in arable or pastoral farming, where evolution through continuity was the keynote. Although the Middle Ages did not invent towns, in the British Isles medieval people had to reinvent them, for Roman civic life had been practically totally eradicated here. The new towns they created were defensive burhs and outgrown villages, not modelled on the Roman concept of civic or municipal community. Thus English towns had to find their own way as they grew; neither the customs of the countryside nor the theoretical structure from Roman cities was a good fit. As towns were developing, they did not have a ready-made strait-jacket of convention to contain women, and it was possible for women to make some capital, literally, from this situation.

In all the areas of study, the place of medieval women in England proves full of contradictions and controversy. As has been indicated, women had an inferior position at law. The married woman, *feme covert*, was particularly subordinated to her husband. But the single woman was also disadvantaged – in feudal inheritance whereas an eldest son was heir to the main body of the estate even if he had younger brothers or sisters, by *c.* 1135 the eldest daughter was totally ousted as an heiress as soon as she had a brother, and if there was no brother, her inheritance was still diminished with the arrival of each younger sister, who became another coheiress. The widow, though technically more independent, was often unable to stand up for her rights. Political widows in the fifteenth century were particularly vulnerable, as will be illustrated in chapter 4. However, despite all this legal inequality, women were more active than might be expected during marriage, and were commonly made their husbands' executrices and proved competent at the trust. How could they be so effective, if they were as unpractised and downtrodden as otherwise appears?

It is another paradox that although women's education can be shown to be inferior institutionally, there is more evidence of female literacy than teaching opportunities can account for. Books were dedicated to women, and there is considerable testamentary evidence of their ownership of books, as testatrices and legatees. An etiquette market, moreover, was aimed at them, in manuscript in the early fifteenth century and in print by the end.

The contrasting pictures of women are nowhere clearer than in the church. Mary and Eve were the poles of medieval religious example, evidenced in church art as well as teaching and in the Bible itself. It would have been sacrilegious to hold Mary up as an example for imperfect human women to model themselves upon, and even Mary's name was long considered too holy for general use, only appearing in England as a Christian name at the end of the twelfth century. But stalwart matrons' position in the family may have been upheld by the image of a merciful interceder with the all-powerful Father, and the Magdalene repentant sinner held out hope for the remorseful prostitutes. In the hard world of the fourteenth and fifteenth centuries, though orthodox women did not aspire to the priesthood, and had only constrained opportunities within the church, individual women gained remarkable respect for piety and wisdom. Julian of Norwich and Margery Kempe are the most famous, but Ann Warren in *Anchorites and their Patrons in Medieval England* (1985) shows the scale of anchoresses' public image which led to their gaining support from so many lay and religious persons. Women anchoresses consistently outnumbered male anchorites in the periods for which records exist.

The last controversy to consider is whether women's position altered significantly over the period, in relation to law, to social expectations, or to economic realities. The key periods here are around the Norman Conquest and in the later medieval economic crises. Were Anglo-Saxon women more free than Anglo-Norman ones, who suffered from that premium on masculine fighting strength which feudalism fed into land tenure? Was women's labour relatively more highly valued because of the population fall after the Black Death? Did female labour fall in value as the population began to recover in the late fifteenth century? Did other economic developments, moving towards capitalism, undermine women's economic potential in diminishing the household unit of production even within medieval times?

There are several ways in which the arguments in this book could be presented. Women could be categorised according to the source material – looked at from legal, economic or literary sources. They could be looked at by life cycle: childhood, marriage, childbirth, middle age, death. They could be looked at by class, royal, aristocratic, gentry (if the term is not too anachronistic), mercantile, peasant. All would involve some forcing apart of what should go together, some repetition in the context of different sources or classes. The division adopted is derived from class but angled by what women did. To avoid repetition, subthemes are handled once, where they seem most appropriate in the light of available research: thus women and crime may be found in most detail in the countryside chapter, because most of the work on the subject has been from rural locations, but prostitution is treated in the chapter on towns, because, although it was not confined to towns, it is in urban communities that it has been most researched. Marriage, however, is treated in more than one context. The largest sector of women lived in the countryside, so will be treated first, following the background chapter on women before 1100. Next women from urban communities will be treated, and then women of the landholding class, a smaller but well-recorded stratum. The final chapter will look at women and religion, considering professionally religious women, conventionally pious women and those who joined Lollard conventicles.

Brief conclusions will underline the main changes of focus in recent times, and the advances in the overall subject brought about by interdisciplinary application of traditional historical methods, social science techniques and literary criticism to English and European sources.

Notes

1 Progress is discussed in J. S. Loengard, '"Legal History and the Medieval Englishwoman" revisited', in J. T. Rosenthal (ed.), *Medieval Women and the Sources of Medieval History*, Athens, Gia and London, 1990, pp. 210–36.
2 R. H. Helmholz, *Marriage Litigation in Medieval England*, Cambridge, 1974, and M. M. Sheehan, 'The formation and stability of marriage in fourteenth-century England: evidence of an Ely register', *Medieval Studies*, XXXIII, 1971, pp. 228–63; 'The influence of canon law on the property rights of married women in England', *ibid.*, XXV, 1963, pp. 109–24; 'Marriage theory and practice in the conciliar legislation and diocesan statutes of medieval England', *ibid.*, XL, 1978, pp. 408–60; 'Theory and practice: the marriage of the unfree and the poor in medieval society', *ibid.*, L, 1988, pp. 456–87.
3 A. Abram, 'Women traders in medieval London', *Economic Journal*, XXVI, 1916, pp. 276–85; M. K. Dale, 'The London silkwomen of the fifteenth century', *Economic History Review*, IV, 3, 1933,

pp. 324–35; S. L. Thrupp, *The Merchant Class of Medieval London [1300–1500]*, Chicago, 1948.

4 K. E. Lacey, 'Women and work in fourteenth- and fifteenth-century London', in L. Charles and L. Duffin (eds.) *Women and Work in Pre-Industrial England*, London, 1985, pp. 24–82; C. M. Barron, 'The "Golden Age" of women in medieval London', in *Medieval Women in Southern England*, Reading Medieval Studies XV, 1989, pp. 35–58, and C. M. Barron and A. F. Sutton (eds.), *Medieval London Widows, 1300–1500*, London, 1994; M. Kowaleski, 'Women's work in a market town: Exeter in the late fourteenth century', in B. A. Hanawalt (ed.), *Women and Work in Preindustrial Europe*, Bloomington, Ind., 1986, pp. 145–64.

5 R. Gilchrist, *Gender and Material Culture: the archaeology of religious women*, London and New York, 1994.

6 *Hali Meidhad* and parts of *Ancrene Wisse* are translated in B. Millett and J. Wogan-Browne (eds.), *Medieval English Prose for Women*, Oxford, 1990; see also A. Blamires (with K. Pratt and C. W. Marx), *Woman Defamed and Woman Defended*, Oxford, 1992, a useful anthology.

7 See E. T. Hansen, *Chaucer and the Fictions of Gender*, Berkeley, Los Angeles and Oxford, 1992, pp. 26–57.

8 J. Weiss, 'The power and weakness of women in Anglo-Norman romance', in C. M. Meale (ed.), *Women and Literature in Britain 1150–1500*, Cambridge, 1993, p. 13.

9 J. M. Lilley, G. Stroud, D. R. Brothwell and M. H. Williamson, *The Jewish Burial Ground at Jewbury*, York, 1994, pp. 333, 369–70.

10 Gilchrist, *Gender and Material Culture*, p. 1.

11 'I say to the fals harlot Selby wyf ...' sounds suitably insulting, P. J. P. Goldberg, *Women, Work and Life Cycle in a Medieval Economy: women in York and Yorkshire c. 1300–1520*, Oxford, 1992, p. 218.

12 D. Cressy, *Literacy and Social Order: reading and writing in Tudor England*, Cambridge, 1980, p. 176.

13 M. D. Legge, *Anglo-Norman Literature and its Background*, Oxford, 1963, p. 28.

14 R. T. Davies (ed.), *Medieval English Lyrics*, London and Boston, 1963, no. 123.

15 B. A. Hanawalt, *The Ties that Bound: peasant families in medieval England*, Oxford, 1986, pp. 145–6, 269–74; J. P. J. Goldberg 'The public and the private: women in the pre-plague economy', in *Thirteenth-Century England*, III, ed. P. R. Coss and S. D. Lloyd, Woodbridge, 1991, pp. 75–81.

16 J. Goody, *The Development of the Family and Marriage in Europe*, Cambridge, 1983, p. 95.

1

The background: women in England before 1100

A study which concentrates on the period after 1100 should first offer a review of how women had arrived at the position they occupied at this chosen starting point. Some six and a half centuries elapsed between the coming of the Angles and Saxons to Britain around 450 and the end of the eleventh century; within this period evidence relating to women is unevenly distributed, both chronologically and in terms of regional origin. Nor is the evidence in form or quantity as richly diverse as later medieval sources. Furthermore, Anglo-Saxon society was extremely hierarchical and the evidence tends to be drawn largely from sources reflecting upper-class interests. However, there is enough to indicate that there were elements of continuity from earliest times, whilst women's position did change in response to social, political and economic developments. The coming of Christianity, the Viking invasions and the Norman Conquest in particular had reverberations throughout society affecting the position of women.

The coming of Christianity to Anglo-Saxon England at the end of the sixth century was immensely important, for it brought not only a new religion but also entry into the civilised world of written communication and Latin literature. The new religion introduced new teachings about women and important rulings on marriage, from Judaeo-Christian traditions, and brought women the opportunities of a church vocation as a nun. Almost immediately individual elite women became recipients of Latin letters from churchmen, and more slowly they became writers of such letters, the best not stylistically inferior to men's. The churchmen quickly gave an impetus to recording legislation, both in the vernacular and in Latin, the first English laws being attributed to the first English Christian king, Æthelberht of Kent. More slowly, churchmen inspired the recording of land grants in writing, and the writing of wills, and they were authors of almost all the prose produced in English and Latin, as well as much of the poetry. So the coming of Christianity revolutionised the potential source material for historians, and established the types of evidence which dominate the rest of the Middle Ages: male-authored texts, government records, and documentation relating to private property.

As sources of information about women, the extant law texts are very valuable, though they are not complete, and often only survive in much later copies. Three codes originated with seventh-century Kentish kings, and one with the late seventh- /early eighth-century West Saxon king, Ine. The rest are of later West Saxon origin, from the reigns of Alfred and his successors. In particular the laws made a bold effort to restrain physical violence to women, and did not mince words about rape. They also laid down some protection for widows. One of the most important areas they illuminate is marriage. What form marriage took in pagan Anglo-Saxon England is not directly known, but certain features can be assumed from the early laws (before Christianity had had widespread impact on custom or behaviour). Early Anglo-Saxon marriage was planned, publicised and formal, though terminable before death. The woman was transferred from her natal family to her husband and received by him with certain formalities, though she did not sever links with her own family, and indeed her children's kin comprised relatives of both parents.

There was a state of being betrothed or pledged, and at this stage in early times a bride price may have been paid by the groom to the bride's father or other male guardian. Next came the actual handing over of the woman, and this should have been followed the next morning by the groom's gift to her of the *morgengifu*, which sealed his acceptance of his wife. The *morgengifu* was thereafter her own property. Seventh-century laws show these customs in operation. Æthelberht allowed a man to return a woman to her home in a case of fraud, and Ine required the bride's guardian to return the bridal price doubly if anyone bought a wife and the marriage did not take place. This particular law also compensated a third-party surety.[1] Æthelberht's laws acknowledge voluntary separation – a childless wife wishing to leave a marriage could do so; her father's kin would get her goods and *morgengifu*. A wife

[27]

wishing to depart with her children should have half the goods.[2] These are of course the proprieties of marriage in extant laws; how many people simply set up home together locally, or eloped elsewhere, is not known, nor how many Englishwomen may have been carried off by Viking invaders.

Ancient customs of betrothal, marriage and exchange of goods making provision for future security were not incompatible with Christianity, but Christianity brought additional definition to marriage. One of the most important, and for women most emancipating, developments was the idea that marriage must be entered into with free consent. This is recognised in Cnut's law: 'neither widow nor maiden is to be forced to marry a man whom she herself dislikes, nor to be given for money, unless he chooses to give anything of his own free will'.[3]

Supplementing the laws, charter evidence gives sight of women disposing of land, and wills, as we may loosely term them, also illustrate women's property rights. There are nearly two thousand entries in Peter Sawyer's *Anglo-Saxon Charters* listing charters granting land, or secular rights over it, purportedly from before 1066, whatever the date of the extant manuscripts (using the term 'charter' loosely to include wills, records of disputes and boundary descriptions). The vast majority record grants between men, and mostly by kings and bishops, in southern and western England. About eighty are grants or leases to or from lay women (including queens), alone or with a husband, and just over thirty refer to abbesses or communities of nuns receiving land, while another dozen or so refer to grants to individually named women described as nuns, religious women or *ancillae Dei*; only a handful of grants were made by such women. Statistically, therefore, the charter material on women as grantors or grantees is slight, but the variety of the circumstances revealed is impressive. Most of the women grantors acting alone were widowed queens; among those acting with husbands or another male were wives of kings, earls, ealdormen and a portreeve.[4] Individual woman grantees in royal charters include the king's mother, grandmother, sister and 'kinswoman', and women described as 'the faithful woman', or 'faithful lady', noble lady, and 'matrona' (?married woman) or 'faithful matrona'.[5] Among the bishop of Worcester's lessees were more than one 'dux' (ealdorman) and his wife, a king's minister and his mother, and Bishop Oswald's kinsman Osulf the cniht and his

wife and her brothers.[6] Christine Fell is impressed by the frequency of grants to husbands and wives among royal grants to lay
persons, and concludes, probably too optimistically given the comparative rarity of these charters, that 'women moved in the world
of landed property with as much assurance and also as full rights
as the men of their family'.[7] Similar interpretation lies behind
belief in a 'Golden Age' for women before the Norman Conquest.
The role of women as witnesses to charters should not be overlooked, and the warnings Penny Gold gives about using charter
evidence in her study of women in twelfth-century France is equally
applicable to English charters both before and after the Conquest.[8]

There are about sixty Old English wills known, mostly in later
copies. Dorothy Whitelock edited and translated thirty-nine in her
book *Anglo-Saxon Wills*. Of these, nine were wills of eight individual women (one in two versions), and in four wills women
were associated with a male testator, in three of these being expressly described as wife. All the wills in Whitelock's collection
date from between the mid-tenth century and the end of the Anglo-
Saxon period. The wills demonstrate women's ability to inherit
and to dispose of both land and personal property, as will be illustrated in citations below, but of course they come from the social
elite.

Because Anglo-Saxon society was so hierarchical, treatment of
women was not equal for all. It is clear from law and charter
evidence that women of the propertied classes, though in some
respects passing from the authority of father to that of husband at
marriage, had some property rights during the marriage, and not
merely residual entitlement but actual management. It is asserted
that the husband's gift to the wife at marriage, the *morgengifu*, be
it in money or land, went to her not her kin, and that she could
give, sell or bequeath it. It would be logical from this to assume
that women of these classes, that is freewomen upwards, could
receive compensation themselves for injuries done to them, and
Fell cites a law of Alfred using the pronoun 'her' in the phrase to
'compensate her'.[9] But whether women always enjoyed their own
compensation is not certain, and where a slave woman was raped,
the compensation went to her owner. The laws which offer the
praised protection of some women are capable of savagery towards others: consider Æthelstan's law 'in the case of a female
slave who commits an act of theft anywhere except against her

master and mistress, sixty and twenty female slaves shall go and bring three logs each and burn that one slave'. (The penalty for the male slave caught thieving was admittedly equally repulsive: sixty and twenty slaves were to stone him.)[10] The wills which demonstrate the lay testatrix's power can also show her wretched slaves' unfreedom. Class may have proved a more significant factor than gender in many a situation.

The priests in Anglo-Saxon England, as elsewhere, had to deal with women, and almost immediately Augustine was consulting Pope Gregory about them:

> should a pregnant woman be baptized? And when the child has been born how much time should elapse before she can enter the church? And after how many days may the child receive the sacrament of holy baptism so as to forestall its possible death; and after what length of time may her husband have intercourse with her; and is it lawful for her to enter the church if she is in her periods or to receive the sacrament of holy communion?[11]

Anglo-Saxon churchmen soon voiced their opinions on women in religious prose and verse. Alcuin (d. 804) wrote among other works a vast prose tract on virginity addressed to the abbess and nuns of Barking, and Bede, similarly disposed, wrote an elegant hymn to St Æthelthryth (Etheldreda). Bede's *Ecclesiastical History* and his *Life of Cuthbert* have been well trawled for vignettes of women playing particular roles. There are plentiful later Old English homilies which are less well known to readers today. Anglo-Saxon England produced many saints of both sexes: these were revered in their religious communities and in some cases inspired the writing of their lives; curiously a cluster of female Anglo-Saxon saints had their lives written (by men) soon after the Norman Conquest. King Alfred was the first English layman to have his life recorded for posterity, and two eleventh-century queens of England had a foothold in this field. Emma of Normandy, successively wife to Æthelred II and Cnut, commissioned the *Encomium Emmae*, and Eadgyth, wife of Edward the Confessor, was the dedicatee of *The Life of King Edward who Rests at Westminster*, and features in it with her husband and brothers.

Two hundred years after St Augustine's arrival, less welcome visitors, from Scandinavia, began appearing on English coasts. The Vikings attacked and plundered England sporadically for about forty years, then began longer campaigning involving wintering in England, and eventually the Great Army of 865 split up and began settling in Yorkshire and East Anglia. It is reasonable to suppose that the initial raiding expeditions were male, but the *Anglo-Saxon Chronicle*'s account of events in 893 tells of the English storming a fort at Benfleet, Essex built by Hæsten, the leader of a force which had arrived the previous year with eighty ships, and seizing everything inside it, 'both property and women and also children'. Hæsten's wife and two sons were among the captured, but Alfred returned them to him, because the sons were godsons of himself and ealdorman Æthelred. Two years later the *Chronicle* refers to the Danes as placing 'their women' in safety in East Anglia.[12] The racial origin of the Danes' women is unspecified, and their precise relationship to their menfolk unknown, but it seems unlikely that they would have been so distinctly identified if they were only transient native collaborators, willing or forced.

The Scandinavian settlement in eastern England, probably reinforced by colonists of both sexes in the tenth century, was populous enough to affect place-names, measurements, coinage, customs and dialect in the so-called Danelaw territory, north-east of Watling Street. Englishmen and women suffered from the depredations of the Viking warriors in the war years, and though church chroniclers and commentators were naturally hostile to pagan invaders, and may have exaggerated their viciousness, the ill-treatment of native women at the hands of the invading armies can be expected to have included rape. Judith Jesch sees 'more than a grain of truth' in the myth of Viking rapine and pillage.[13] The effect on women in religious houses was devastating. Monastic houses generally suffered destruction or damage in the ninth century, particularly outside West Saxon territory which alone was never totally overrun. Barking Abbey (Essex), for example, was destroyed by the Danes in 870.[14] Episcopal sees in the north and east suffered disruption and discontinuity. The ultimate outcome affected women more than men because when monastic reformation began in the tenth century, the previously successful double houses for men and women were not part of the revival. Nuns were thenceforth confined to single-sex houses which clearly were fewer in number, smaller and less well resourced than formerly. There were only nine or ten houses for women in 1066; the figure is obscured by what David Knowles called 'a few other groups of nuns of a semiprivate nature'.[15] Conventual learning did not again attain the levels of earlier scholarship, and the nuns' libraries were poorer. The abbesses had no longer the stature of their double-house predecessors. The whole picture of female monasticism in the later Anglo-Saxon period is one of comparative decline.

Late in the tenth century Viking attacks resumed, ending with the control of England by the Scandinavian king Cnut and his sons. For men and women this was a demoralising time. Wulfstan, the archbishop of York, described in his famous sermon *Sermo Lupi ad Anglos* (the sermon of the wolf (Wulfstan) to the English), which dates from about 1014, how the 'pirates' behaved: 'often ten or a dozen, one after another, insult disgracefully the thegn's wife, and sometimes his daughter or near kinswoman, whilst he looks on, who considered himself brave and mighty and stout enough before that happened'.[16]

Owing to the Danelaw settlements, and the installation of Cnut's followers as an aristocracy, there was a strong Scandinavian input into late Anglo-Saxon England. The Danelaw area appears from Domesday evidence to have housed a more free society than western England, with a distinctive class of sokemen (free peasants) and fewer slaves. Without going so far as to embrace fully the later northern sagas' portrayal of Viking women as strong-willed, independent and powerful, it would appear that the Scandinavian legacy in eastern England included women who were more independent within marriage than their counterparts in English England. It is from the eastern counties that there is evidence of wives not necessarily commended to their husbands' overlords, and one striking case of a woman who held on to her lands through marriage and separation will be described below. In Domesday Book female landowners bearing names of Scandinavian origin are most numerous in the eastern half of the country, particularly in Yorkshire and Lincolnshire. This area is ill-represented in Anglo-Saxon charters, but was studied into the twelfth and thirteenth centuries by Sir Frank Stenton, whose work shows peasant women sealing charters granting small properties – a toft and croft, ten acres and so on – with their own seals in the thirteenth century.[17]

The Norman Conquest of 1066 was in effect the final Viking invasion since the Normans were descendants of the Viking conquerors of northern France. Militarily aggressive, and muscular Christians, the Normans brought changes to society which had repercussions on laywomen and professed nuns. Believers in a 'Golden Age' see a setback here. The development of feudal land tenure made it more important to keep land in male hands and secure its descent to the eldest male heir. Domesday Book offers some information on women landholders in the time of Edward the Confessor as well as in 1086, and is the major source for the discussion of the effect of the Conquest on women in England. Long known as Domesday Book, this is not actually one composite text: Little Domesday Book, describing the counties of Essex, Norfolk and Suffolk, is thought to be a circuit return which was never further processed, whereas Great Domesday Book, describing the remaining counties surveyed, is the product of substantial editing beyond the Little Domesday Book stage.

Independent of the Norman Conquest, the Gregorian reforms in the Western church were separating the professionally religious from the laity, and within the ranks of the professed religious they were reducing the contact between men and women, elevating the former and depressing the latter. Although the Conquest facilitated the foundation of numerous new male monasteries, 'only a few women's communities were founded in its wake'.[18] For landed and professionally religious women these times were not propitious, but these were minority groups.

Women in the countryside

The vast majority of the Anglo-Saxon population lived in the countryside, in small communities pursuing arable and pastoral self-sufficiency. Some 13,000 place-names occur in Domesday Book, which indicates a sparse population (estimated 1.75–2.25m) widely distributed. Although Domesday Book is a registration of thousands of individual manorial surveys, and has predecessors on individual estates such as the survey of Tidenham, Gloucestershire (c. 1060), there is nothing from England to equal the ninth-century estate registers (polyptychs) from some ecclesiastical land-holders' estates in Carolingian realms. So our picture cannot start to match research there in terms of early population figures from estates, especially in terms of household size and the number and sex ratio of children. Between 4.5 and 5 is the range of the generally accepted multiplier for converting the Domesday population count into actual people, on the assumption that most of those counted were tenants and heads of households.

Anglo-Saxon society was stratified, fundamentally into nobles, free commoners (ceorls) and slaves, with intermediate gradations recorded in some legal sources. Social status dictated the *wergild* (literally man-price) which controlled the compensation paid for a killing, the fines due from an individual for certain offences, including the fine paid by women for fornication, and the value of an oath in court. There is no sign that women had lower wergilds than equivalent men. Angela Lucas assures us women were treated according to the status of their husbands, Fell finds no indication that a woman's wergild changed on marriage;[19] to tally, these assertions require marriage to take place within a class, as most probably did. Once married, the woman was in a degree of subjection to her husband. Indeed, a law of Ine's on theft states: 'if a husband steals any cattle and brings it into his house and it is seized therein, he is guilty for his part, but without his wife, for she must obey her lord'.[20] If she could swear that she had not tasted the stolen meat she could keep her third of the household property. This does underline the attribution of household property to the wife during the marriage, indicating that the couple's goods were not regarded as the husband's, or as held in common. Later Cnut specified that a wife was not guilty if property stolen by her husband was found in the home unless it was under her lock and key: 'she must look after the keys of the following: namely her store room, her chest and her coffer; if it is brought inside any of these, she is then guilty. And no wife can forbid her husband to place inside his cottage what he pleases.'[21] These laws are not specifically dealing with rural society, but that the society they deal with is predominantly rural can be seen from an early ruling on the support of widows and children: Ine states that the widowed mother was to keep the child, and have 6s a year maintenance, and a cow in summer, an ox in winter, the relations being responsible for keeping up the family home until the child reached maturity.[22] The kin group had important responsibilities for policing society, and in Anglo-Saxon England this group was cognatic (drawing on maternal and paternal kin), but weighted towards the male side. The normal weighting was two-thirds to the paternal kin, one-third to the maternal; thus anyone demanding redress for a slain thief needed three supporters, two from the father's kindred and one from the mother's.[23]

What happened to the ceorl's land on his death is not clear, though some form of partible inheritance seems to have been general. Widows clearly were provided for, though there was no standard provision set out in the various laws. Æthelberht's laws gave a widow who had borne her husband a child half his goods on his death.[24] As Pauline Stafford says of the widows in Domesday Book, the idea they should be provided for was constant, but the nature and extent of the provision varied immensely.[25]

Most Anglo-Saxon countrywomen were of the classes of ceorls and slaves. The laws tell more about class distinctions than occupational ones, though obviously some occupations were class concentrated. There is very little in the sources about any division of agricultural labour between the sexes. The only plainly female speciality seems to have been dairying, and a cheesemaker, who also made butter, is the only woman identified among the male workers in the tract *Rectitudines*, a description of estate running which dates from the half century before the Conquest.[26] There is nothing to suggest that techniques changed over the period in ways which would specifically affect women's participation in farming. Depending on the family's prosperity, it would live in conditions somewhere between those of Late Iron Age huts and stone-based farmsteads such as Ribblehead, a Viking homestead in Yorkshire.

Etymologically there may be a connection between the word 'wife' (wife or woman) and weaving; spinning was certainly a female occupation. Fine embroidery, especially gold threadwork, was of course a specialised skill, done for rich patrons, not the stitchcraft of hovels. Textile production need not have been exclusively rural, but equipment for it is listed in connection with the reeve in the Old English tract *Gerefa*.[27] The association of textile work with women is borne out archaeologically by the finding of thread boxes, spindle whorls and weaving battens in female graves.[28]

The servile population was in a sorry plight as the will of Wynflæd, a lady of some consequence, makes plain. She left a number of named slaves to be freed, and others were bequeathed to new owners, including 'a woman weaver and a seamstress'. Ecghelm and his wife and their child changed hands in this will, and were perhaps lucky to be kept together. 'Ælfhere's daughter' was left to Eadgifu, but 'Ælfhere's younger daughter' was left to Æthelflæd daughter of Ealhhelm.[29] Thus we see how one woman's property rights made a chattel of another woman's person.

Women in the towns

Towns were few in Anglo-Saxon England. Historians can only identify 112 places classified as boroughs in Domesday Book. Admittedly, borough is a more specific term than town, implying particular organisation and administration, but Susan Reynolds' attempt to distinguish Domesday towns from Domesday boroughs led to the consideration of no more places: 'most of the towns were centres of county government, most were bishops' sees and most were of Roman origin', qualifications severely limiting the number of places available for consideration.[30] The main characteristics of Anglo-Saxon urbanisation were small concentrations of population, denser than in agricultural communities, greater trading activity, shown in markets and fairs and in the provision of trading witnesses in law, varied manufacturing, the existence of mints, some form of fortification, and burghal tenure, which was a mortgageable, saleable, inheritable form of possession of real property in the town. None of these definitions created any conditions specific to women.

Towns developed most noticeably after about 800, some founded by the Viking invaders in their settlements, and some by the Anglo-Saxons in defending their areas. The Viking activity quickened the economic development in the eastern part of the country and the excavation of Viking Coppergate at York has thrown light on town life there. The crafts practised included amber and jet working, making glass beads, leatherworking, woodworking (Coppergate is coopergate in derivation), metalworking, stonemasonry, bone and antler working, and 'a well-established textile industry', but how much if at all women participated in some of these crafts is unclear. Presumably they were involved in domestic matters and archaeology tells us of a 'busy industrious people with a varied diet', living in a town 'which by modern standards would be regarded as intolerably squalid' but 'tolerable, even cosy, by the standards of the time'.[31] Some of the towns detailed in Domesday Book identify tenants, as at Oxford, where five women were listed among thirty-three named individuals, and Colchester, where twenty-three of 276 named holders were women. Stafford concludes from this that women formed a small proportion of urban tenants; clearly their sex did not disqualify them from tenantry.[32]

Women of the landholding classes

Women landholders are identifiable in Anglo-Saxon England from charter evidence, wills, writs and Domesday Book. At the apex of society sat the king and queen, and Anglo-Saxon queens (and royal concubines) are a comparatively well-evidenced section of society, frequently mentioned by churchmen.

Bede, in 731, wrote of queens in the early English tribal kingdoms; he described as queens Æthelberht of Kent's wife Bertha, their daughter Æthelberg wife of Edwin of Northumbria, Rædwald of East Anglia's unnamed wife, Eafa wife of Æthelwalh of the South Saxons, and Osthryth wife of Æthelred of Mercia. Asser, writing the *Life of Alfred* around 890, expressly explained that the West Saxons had not had queens since the tyrannous behaviour of Brihtric's wife Eadburh, daughter of the Mercian king Offa.[33] Alfred's father's second wife, Judith, daughter of Charles the Bald, was apparently the first West Saxon queen to be anointed, at her marriage. There is no proof of an English queen being anointed thereafter until Ælfthryth, wife of Edgar, in 973, in a period when the reformer Bishop Æthelwold was influential in church and court. Henceforward queens in Anglo-Saxon England were rather less obscure.

Bede allowed queens considerable influence. He portrays Christian queens of the conversion period uniquely graced as vessels of the faith. Pope Boniface V wrote to Edwin's queen, urging her to influence her husband's conversion. Bede acknowledged, in the tale of Edwin's period of exile in East Anglia, that Rædwald's queen could strengthen his resolve on a moral issue.

> 'When he secretly revealed to the queen the plan [to betray Edwin] ... she dissuaded him from it, warning him that it was in no way fitting for so great a king to sell his best friend for gold when he was in such trouble, still less to sacrifice his own honour, which is more precious than any ornament, for the love of money.'

Rædwald instead helped Edwin regain his throne. Rædwald was swayed by his wife on a further occasion, when he came home from Kent a wavering Christian. 'On his return home, he was seduced by his wife and by certain evil teachers and perverted from the sincerity of his faith.'[34] It is unfortunate for us that Bede has not indulged in any comment here which would indicate whether secretly revealing one's intentions to one's wife, and following her persuasion, was normal, or quite extraordinary practice. However, gnomic poetry, after dealing with the meadhall rituals, gives it to the woman to teach wisdom to her lord.[35]

Another royal wife presented as influential was Iurminburg, second wife of Ecgfrith of Northumbria. According to St Wilfrid's biographer Eddius, Iurminburg 'used all her eloquence to describe to Ecgfrith all St Wilfrid's temporal glories', and eventually 'the pair of them used their cunning to secure [his] condemnation'. Eddius takes the stock clerical misogynist standpoint. Iurminburg was a Jezebel. The devil 'chose his usual weapon, one by which he has often spread defilement throughout the whole world, woman'.[36] Ecgfrith and Iurminburg were well connected and Wilfrid found himself persecuted elsewhere through a royal ladies' network. He had to flee West Saxon lands because the king Centwine was married to Iurminburg's sister, and Æthelred of Mercia turned against him because his wife was Ecgfrith's sister.

Queens in one kingdom were often princesses from another; dispatched to other kingdoms as peace pledges or dynastic diplomats, they were expected to further the interests of both old connections and new: Wilfrid, thirsting in Northumbria to visit Rome, went to his queen Eanflæd, who sent him to Earconberht of Kent, her uncle's son, to further his plans. These stories from Bede and Eddius show more active, and intelligently active, roles than those allotted to the cupbearing queens in *Beowulf*, though even there Hygd seems to have had the practical power to dispose of the Geat kingdom to Beowulf when her husband died before her son was old enough to rule.[37]

Bede was interested in dynastic links when these furthered the church's interests, but marriages to create political alliances, or to settle tribal disagreements, were traditional. They were also traditionally ill-fated, as the *Beowulf* poet tells of the marriage of Hildeburh and Finn, and hints of in the case of Ingeld and Freawaru: 'when a lord is dead / it is seldom the slaying-spear sleeps for long – / seldom indeed – dear though the bride may be'.[38]

It took the church some time to tame barbarian marriage customs into approved monogamy between persons free to marry each other. Polygamous inclinations do not seem to have been a major problem in Anglo-Saxon England: where kings indulged in such leanings they seem to have been persuaded to accept one wife alongside concubines, or serial monogamy. Edward the Elder (d. 924) had a number of wives and concubines rendering the line of succession complicated. In Anglo-Saxon England suitability and some form of selection operated within the 'throne-worthy' circle of royal males. With offspring by successive wives, and also by concubines, available to succeed a king, who would become the next queen mother was open to manipulation. This uncertainty of the succession affected the position of Anglo-Saxon queens. Edward the Elder's widow Eadgifu bided her time, surviving under Æthelstan, who was not her son, to become influential again under her sons Edmund and Eadred and her grandson Edgar. But Æthelred the Unready's mother, Edgar's third consort, the anointed queen Ælfthryth who was the protectress of nuns in the *Regularis Concordia*, appears to have been fully involved in the murder at her home of Æthelred's older half-brother, Edward the Martyr, in 978.

Anglo-Saxon queens were in a position to do good or evil. Their reputations were much in the hands of contemporary churchmen, who might present them as conventional, pious, saintly innocents, or as cunning, ruthless and immoral Jezebels. One or two individuals left marks of character and action. Stafford describes Æthelflæd of Mercia as the greatest of the warrior queens. Contemporary sources called this daughter of King Alfred 'lady' or 'queen' of the Mercians (*hlæfdiga, regina*). Æthelflæd seems to have grown into power when her husband Æthelred, called in West Saxon sources merely 'ealdorman' of Mercia, became an invalid. After Æthelred's death she co-operated with her brother Edward the Elder in a drive against the Danes, fortifying Mercian burhs and defeating the Vikings in the north-west. It is interesting that later chroniclers attempted some comment on the intimacies of her life, claiming that she found her solitary experience of childbirth too horrible to repeat, even though the issue was only a daughter.[39] This daughter was deprived of authority in Mercia and taken into West Saxon territory after her mother's death, and disappears from view. Whether she was ever briefly regarded as a queen is obscure. Emma of Normandy, successively wife to Æthelred II and Cnut, his supplanter, bore sons by both kings and was obviously a survivor. Alistair Campbell, editor of the *Encomium Emmae*, which praises her and her Danish husband's dynasty, believes this work was written in Harthacnut's reign when Emma was at the height of her influence.[40]

Stafford points to a relationship between queens and women in society generally: societies which recognised and supported female rights offered most scope for queens, and tenth-century England was a favourable environment.[41] By the mid-eleventh century, conditions were becoming less encouraging. Women's rights to inherit and dispose of property were curtailed in the post-Gregorian feudal world. Primogeniture increasingly made succession clear, lessening women's opportunities to interfere influentially.

Right through the Anglo-Saxon period there is evidence of queens being endowed in some fashion with land in their husbands' kingdoms. Both Bede and the ninth-century writer long known as Nennius record Bamburgh (Northumb.) as named after Æthelfrith's wife Bebba, and Nennius asserts her husband had given her the place.[42] In the eleventh century, from at least 1002, when Emma is believed to have received Rutland on her marriage to Æthelred, there was a connection of Rutland, or parts of it, with the endowment of English queens.

Below the royal dynasties in early Anglo-Saxon England came a nobility, *eorlcund* and *gesithcund*, classes defined by birth and typified by service, and later there were earls and thegns. Little is known about the identity of the Anglo-Saxon ealdormen in the shires, and even the few regional earls are little more than names. Their wives are even less identifiable. There were intermarriages: King Æthelwulf's first wife Osburh, Alfred's mother, was daughter of ealdorman Oslac, the king's butler; King Edgar's wife Ælfthryth was the daughter of ealdorman Ordgar, and widow of ealdorman Æthelwold; Edward the Confessor's wife Eadgyth was the daughter of Earl Godwine.

Bede saw nothing amiss in deriving the place-name Bamburgh from a Queen Bebba, and place-names incorporating presumed non-royal Anglo-Saxon women's names are quite plentiful. F. M. Stenton commented that 'few ... can be closely dated; but as a group it is probable that they belong to the later rather than the earlier centuries of Anglo-Saxon history'; some however are pre-Alfredian.[43] Land could be given to a woman by her husband as morning gift, and by her family as dowry. It could be bequeathed to her, and granted to her for her own personal efforts. Fell cites a Worcester charter of 814 granting over 200 acres of land to a woman called Eanswith for the service of mending, cleaning and adding to Worcester's ecclesiastical vestments, and another

Worcester charter of 969 granting land for three lives, specifically describes a man called Ælfweard as the first man, and his daughter as the second.[44] Wills specifically left estates to women, both single and married, including women identifiable as the testators' widows, daughters, mothers, sisters and other blood kin, also their foster parents and godchildren. Over a quarter of surviving Anglo-Saxon wills are women's, and some dispose of sizeable acreages as well as personal property, including books. Wynflæd, whose bequest of slaves was mentioned above, had a clear understanding of property rights, leaving her daughter Æthelflæd 'her engraved bracelet and her brooch, and the estate at Ebbesborne and the title deed as a perpetual inheritance to dispose of as she pleases'. Besides leaving plate, men and stock, this will mentions remarkable items such as 'two buffalo horns, a horse and her red tent'. Among the household furniture and furnishings mentioned are 'two chests and in them a set of bed clothing, all that belongs to one bed', 'two chests and in them her best bed curtain and a linen covering and all the bed clothing which goes with it', 'a long hall-tapestry, and a short one and three seat coverings', 'two large chests and a clothes chest and a little spinning box and two old chests'.[45] Bedclothes and other household furnishings, characteristic features of later medieval women's wills, thus feature in pre-Conquest ones too.

Wills are a restricted source, and the outstanding ones have been much cited and may have too much read into them. The will of Wulfric (Spott), who left estates to his unnamed daughter, to a god-daughter and to her father and, separately, his wife, among others, is a much quoted example.[46] Similarly, a unique lawsuit from Cnut's reign entered in a Hereford gospel book is frequently cited: here an anonymous mother, outraged by her son's suing of her, declared before witnesses, who were to report to the county court, her bequest to a kinswoman of her land, gold, clothing and all her possessions.[47] So we know this could be done, but have no idea how commonly or rarely.

Grants of land were made jointly to husbands and wives, and grants by them have been interpreted as reinforcing the picture of the wife having right in the common possessions of the couple. However, it is also possible to interpret joint gifts as showing how little power of disposal the married woman had over what were her lands during her husband's lifetime. The husband may have had to be associated with her in order to give effect to what might really be her gift, and she may have had to be associated with his gift, of possibly her land, to secure the donee against her reclaiming alienated property on widowhood. The wills and charters give us probably the most elevated of the possible perspectives on landed women's property rights in Anglo-Saxon England, but Stafford, writing of the eleventh and twelfth centuries, issues warnings: women did inherit but often only a life interest with the long-term future controlled by the testator's will, in a family where the kin was 'strongly patrilineal and male dominated'. Furthermore, Stafford believes that marriage settlements made on brides were usually in the husbands' hands during their lifetimes, and she points out that most of the women will-makers were widows.[48]

Women do appear as landowners in Domesday Book, both in 1066 and 1086, but this source is not exactly an open book. The women who appear in it must be treated as individuals whose cases show what could happen, but not necessarily what was commonplace, and certainly not what should be asserted as typical.

Domesday Book is a registry of land possession, listing for each county the estates held by the king and his tenants-in-chief in 1086, describing their resources, and generally noting who held each estate in 'the time of King Edward'. The text was compiled by the royal administration with the identification and preservation of royal rights and dues as a primary purpose; this dictated the selection of information required in the survey and later preserved in the records. Setting aside the institutional female tenants-in-chief in 1086 (the abbesses of eight English and two French abbeys) there were only some twenty women tenants-in-chief. They have a low ranking in the county tenant lists (which are strictly hierarchical, beginning with the king, then any bishops and abbots, followed by abbesses, other clergy, then the leading Norman laymen, then lesser Norman male tenants, women tenants, and finally groups of small landholders holding directly of the king). Countess Judith, for example, the king's niece, widow of Waltheof, earl of Huntingdon, and the most important woman landowner in England in 1086, was fortieth of the forty-four landholders listed in Leicestershire, forty-first of forty-four in Cambridgeshire, and fifty-third of fifty-seven in Bedfordshire.

Of the women landowners with only small estates, many are to be found in the group entries, often in association with a son or other relative. Some were clearly survivors from 1066, or the widows of English holders in 1066. In Bedfordshire, in the hundred of Stodden, Thorgot and his mother were holding half a hide which Thorgot's father had held as a king's thegn.[49] One Leofgeat held three and a half hides at Knook (Wilts.) in 1086, which her husband had held in 1066. In her case the text adds the information that she pursued her own skilled career, as she did gold embroidery for the king and queen before and after the Conquest.[50] Women could of course be subtenants, often in a small way. Shelton (Beds.) was held in 1086 as a subtenancy of the bishop of Coutances. The Domesday entry states that in 1066 'Wulfeva held this manor under Burgred; she could not grant or sell without his permission'. At Holme, in the same county, in 1086 a subtenant, Wulfric, held three virgates from William of Eu; they had formerly been held by Ælfeva, Askell's man (*homo*), and she could assign to whom she wished.[51]

There had been individuals whose cases were complex enough to require statements of their particular rights and standing. Stafford cites the case of Asa, an East Riding woman who had been married and separated. According to the claims' section of the Yorkshire Domesday, she held her land separate and free from the rule and control of Bjornulfr her husband, even when they were together, so that he could neither make gift nor sale of it, and after their separation she withdrew with all her land and possessed it as 'lady'.[52] Both parties to this broken marriage had Scandinavian forenames and came from Danelaw territory, which may explain some of this freedom, or the Normans' uncertain grasp of it. Stafford points out that the fuller entries in Little Domesday Book, also Danelaw territory, contain statements that show husbands and wives could be commended to different overlords. It is clear from the comparison of Little Domesday Book with Great Domesday Book that the former contains more information about women, which was presumably edited out from the final stage of the text, though social conventions may well have varied regionally too. Countess Gytha's lands, worth over £580, spread over ten counties in the south and south-west of England, are all recorded in Great Domesday Book, but as Godwine's widow and King Harold's mother she was a special case.[53] Women in many cases are likely to have been under-recorded as holders in 1066, since it would probably have seemed to the 1086 male tenant more secure to claim a male antecessor, particularly if the woman holder in 1066 was a dowered widow temporarily sandwiched between her husband and a male successor in the history of the estate.[54]

In her analysis of women in Domesday, Stafford argues that the entries underline how dependent women were on familial landholding: they came by land as widows and daughters, occasionally as mothers and sisters. Precision mattered: thus the Bedfordshire entries distinguish between the dower (*de dote*) and marriage portion (*de maritagio*) of Azelina, widow of Ralph Tallboys.[55] The distinction between dower and dowry is important but often confused. Dower (*dos*) was provided by the husband, and its institutionalisation will be described below (chapters 2 and 4). The dowry, or marriage portion (*maritagium*), came from the bride's side of the family. The confusion is compounded because *dos* meant dowry in Roman law. Important men had an interest in women landholders: Stafford points out that both before and after 1066 the kings exercised rights of wardship over at least some noble widows, and that surviving Anglo-Saxon lords gave tenants' daughters with the land in marriage between 1066 and 1086.[56] Judging from Domesday Book there was probably not much more of a 'Golden Age' for women before 1066 than after it: 'Domesday does not suggest extensive female landholding for any stage in the eleventh century'.[57] It can be argued, however, that 1086 is really too soon after the Conquest to take stock. Less than twenty years of possession by the vigorous victors of Hastings had not been long enough for the full consequences of widowhoods, forfeitures and deaths without male heirs to play havoc with the male-dominated first generation of the Norman settlement. Moreover, the argument that male primogeniture became more important after the feudalising of social relationships, and that this was to the disadvantage of women, cannot be expected to be demonstrated as early as 1100, for the heritability of tenure was only slowly defined. If there were disadvantages accruing to landholding women as a result of the Norman Conquest, and on balance it seems that there were, these were not instantly observable but gained hold in the twelfth century. By 1185 Henry II could have a valuation drawn up of those feudal victims, widows and minor heirs and heiresses in the king's gift, and by Magna Carta (1215) we can see King John being restrained from profiting out of forcing feudal tenants' widows to remarry, and disparaging in marriage heirs of either sex.

Women and religion

The pagan Anglo-Saxons had female gods in their pantheon, the most famous being Frig the wife of Woden. No source makes it clear whether they had female priests or prophets, but that women might have distinctive ritual roles is suggested by the performance of the dirge for Beowulf by 'a woman of the Geats'.[58]

When Christianity was brought to the English at the end of the sixth century it was for women something of a mixed blessing. Negatively, the church had a gender-repressive side, teaching women to submit to their husbands, and condemning them to an inferior, largely passive, role in public worship. No one doubts that women were capable of very great piety and that laywomen's influence on the early training of their children in the Christian faith was of great importance. Asser's *Life of Alfred* contains a vignette of maternal influence on early education: he tells of the king's mother showing her children a book of English poetry, saying 'I shall give this book to whichever one of you can learn it fastest'.[59] But one has to admit doubts about the provision of Christian teaching for the generality of women in this period, and indeed in much later times.

In the early days of Anglo-Saxon Christianity, according to Bede, conversion was effected by missionaries such as Paulinus (d. 644), whose crusade at Yeavering (Northumb.) is described in the *Ecclesiastical History*. Paulinus is said to have come to the king and queen at this royal residence and remained there thirty-six days, catechising and baptising. 'During these days, from morning until evening, he did nothing else but instruct the crowds who flocked to him from every village and district in the teaching of Christ.'[60] Nothing sexist here, one may think. But who was likely to 'flock' from surrounding villages and countryside when the king (and queen) came round on tour with a new bishop? Surely it would be the men who traditionally turned up at such gatherings, for renewal of homage, payment of tribute and performance of guard service. In 'gathering', would they slow themselves down by dragging a perhaps pregnant wife and some children with them? Would they bring their elderly mothers? That they did not may be inferred from the story cited above of Rædwald, the East Anglian king, who was led into apostasy on his return from conversion in Kent by his wife and evil teachers. Furthermore, provision for even professed women evidently lagged behind that for men: Bede tells us that Earcongota, daughter of Earconberht of Kent (640–64), became a nun at Faremoûtier-en-Brie because there were few monasteries in England, so girls of noble family were sent to the Frankish realm or Gaul for education and 'to be wedded to the heavenly bridegroom'.[61]

However, positively, conventual life offered royal and aristocratic women, virgin and widow, an honourable career in a protected environment free from the hazards of political marriages and childbearing. It does not seem to have tried to attract women from the lower social classes, but it offered highly born women a new career opening in a structured profession which peaked with the abbesses of mixed communities. Some nuns proved capable of real scholarship, and benefited from their institutional libraries and became as learned as monks in Latin composition. Professed religion allowed some of them to travel far afield. Abbess Haeaburg (Bugga), St Boniface's correspondent, consulted him about making a pilgrimage to Rome, and eventually fulfilled it. Leoba (d. 780), another of his correspondents, joined Boniface in Germany as abbess of Bischofsheim, and had her biography written by Rudolf of Fulda.

The first flush of female monasticism in England began around 630. The royal family of Kent was associated with the founding of Lyminge, Folkestone and Sheppey.[62] In the north, the famous abbey of Whitby in the North Riding of Yorkshire was tied in with the Deiran dynasty. Its founder, Abbess Hilda, formerly abbess of Hartlepool, was a great-niece of King Edwin. Eanflæd, Edwin's daughter and the first Northumbrian to be baptised, became abbess there after the death of her husband Oswiu, sharing rule with her daughter Ælfflæd, who had been Oswiu's thank-offering to God when he defeated Penda of Mercia in 654. Æthelthryth, daughter of King Anna of the East Angles and for twelve years of unconsummated marriage the wife of Ecgfrith of Northumbria, retired to conventual life and built the convent at Ely (Cambs.).[63] These pre-Viking English nunneries were all double houses, mixed communities of nuns and monks or priests, with separate living-quarters but not total segregation. Since in England these houses were under the abbess's control, an abbess like Hilda or Ælfflæd was an important executive figure of considerable influence in the world, not just within the walls. By 664 Whitby was capable of hosting an important church synod, and although Hilda and her community, being on the Celtic side (despite Hilda's baptism by Paulinus), had been defeated, she remained in respected charge until her death in 680: Bede says 'so great was her prudence that not only ordinary folk but kings and princes used to come and ask her advice in their difficulties'.[64] No other career would have placed a seventh-century Anglo-Saxon woman, even of royal birth, in such an influential role. That others achieved it also is clear from Eddius's tale of Ælfflæd's incisive intervention on Wilfrid's behalf at the synod near the River Nidd (W. R. Yorks.) in 706; Stephanie Hollis attributes to her a 'quasi-episcopal eminence'.[65] In the pioneering period religious women may have been less segregated and restricted than later male writers imply, and by the late Anglo-Saxon period the church was arguably more markedly misogynist.

However, the close association of nunneries and royal dynasties in the Anglo-Saxon period also provides some support for the modern cynical view that they were useful for the disposal of surplus daughters and royal widows, and indeed unwanted wives and even discarded mistresses. Certainly some were dispatched there, and the royal families behaved proprietorially with their foundations. Barbara Yorke has recently written of the political consequences of Anglo-Saxon nunneries being regarded by kings as royal possessions, which may have proved more destructive to their survival than the Vikings.[66]

No rules of early houses survive. Only in the case of Coldingham (Berwickshire) does Bede hint, in the *Ecclesiastical History*, at any irregularity, attributing a fire to the 'worldliness of its members, and in particular of those who were supposed to be in authority'. Abbess Æbbe (King Ecgfrith's aunt) was warned by a pious Irishman there that a vision had revealed to him the forthcoming destruction of the house because of its laxity, and a lurid picture is painted of sloth and sin, feasting, drinking and gossip in the cells.[67] Such was the picture of Anglo-Saxon nuns misbehaving. But what should they have been doing? There are no rules known before the *Regularis Concordia* (*c.* 970), which prescribed a regular regime for male and female houses alike. By this time the pre-Viking houses had been destroyed, and the tenth-century refoundations and new foundations did not resume the double monastery pattern. This seems to have worked to the detriment of women's scholarship, and to the diminution of stature for abbesses and their communities. Resumed foundations did continue the pattern of royal dynastic connection. Alfred founded Shaftesbury (Dorset) for his daughter Æthelgifu, and his widow Ealhswith established Nunnaminster at Winchester. Romsey (Hants) and Wilton (Wilts.) were founded in the reign of Edward the Elder, probably for members of his family. Ælfthryth, Æthelred II's mother, founded Amesbury (Wilts.) and Wherwell (Hants). Some of these houses maintained royal connections for centuries. Edward the Confessor's wife Eadgyth was sent to Wherwell during her family's disgrace in 1050–1. Wilton is described as a favourite monastery of the Confessor and his wife.[68] Christina, sister of Margaret of Scotland and aunt of Henry I's wife Matilda, was at Romsey and Wilton, and had her niece in her charge.

The early evidence of the devout ideals of Anglo-Saxon female monasticism is indirect. Bede refers to 'virgins vowed to God' at Ely, and approves of Hilda establishing at Hartlepool 'a Rule of life in all respects like that which she had been taught by learned men'. The emphasis is on the regular life: at Barking the nun Torhtgyth helped 'to keep the discipline of the Rule by teaching or reproving the younger ones'.[69] As to the degree of segregation within double monasteries, a poem by Aldhelm (*c.* 639–709) indicates separate choirs of monks and nuns at the unidentified monastery of King Centwine of Wessex's daughter Bugga, where male and female lectors read the lessons, and Rudolf of Fulda's *Life* of Boniface's kinswoman and correspondent Leoba tells of a strict regime at Wimborne (Dorset), but the *Life* was written on the Continent after Carolingian rulings on segregation and claustration and may have exaggerated the proprieties of the earlier scene.[70] So too may the *Lives* of Anglo-Saxon female saints written after the Norman Conquest: Goscelin's of Eadgyth of Wilton and Wulfhild of Barking, and Osbert of Clare's of Eadburg of Nunnaminster. Anglo-Saxon nuns were expected to pray for the souls of founders and intended beneficiaries, including political murderers and their victims, thus neutralising sin. They kept monastic hours like the men, and of course needed men for priestly functions. In the later Middle Ages their day still revolved round the Divine Office. In their lives, charity and humility were highly valued.

The *Regularis Concordia* treated male and female houses alike, and Bishop Æthelwold made a translation of the Rule of St Benedict into Old English; a version intended for nunneries was in use in the tenth and eleventh centuries, indicative that the tenth-century sisters were not as adept at Latin as their seventh- and eighth-century predecessors.[71] As Heloise later pointed out in her correspondence with Abelard, the Benedictine rule really required some amendment for application to women's institutional life.[72] Some women effected adaptation, before and after the Norman Conquest, by living the life of a canoness or vowess, under an ameliorated form of the Rule allowing retention of private property.[73]

From its arrival in Anglo-Saxon England, the church was male dominated and had long subscribed to a collection of doctrines which assumed that men were the stronger sex and that sexual activity needed purification; hence Augustine's questions to Pope Gregory, cited above. From the start the church pronounced on the closest intimacies and continued to be the authority on these matters, from Gregory's disapproval of women refusing to breast-feed their own children to later medieval episcopal statutes against the overlaying of children in the maternal bed.[74]

The Anglo-Saxon church brought ideas on marriage which urged its permanence but recognised that couples could find themselves in impossible, for example unconsummated, unions, or shakily founded ones, across religions, or irreparably damaged ones, where one partner committed fornication. Bede quotes a letter from Pope Boniface V to Æthelberg of Northumbria, hinting that her very marriage might be invalid while King Edwin remained a pagan, and so urging her to influence her husband to adopt Christianity, 'so that you may thereby enjoy the rights of marriage in undefiled union'.[75] The nature of the gesith's forbidden marriage referred to in Bede's story of Sigeberht II of Essex is not known, but he tells us that Bishop Cedd, 'being unable to prevent or correct' it, excommunicated the man and forbade anyone to enter his house or eat with him. The king ignored the ban, and was subsequently murdered by the gesith and his brother.[76] The story shows nicely the church's ability to define rules but powerlessness to enforce them in the 650s. The problem may have been one of consanguinity and affinity, where the church actually complicated matters. King Eadbald of Kent, Æthelberht's son, married his stepmother, which was contrary to Christian regulation. More surprisingly, because much later, Alfred's brother Æthelbald married his young stepmother Judith.

Bede tells how Æthelthryth, wife of Ecgfrith of Northumbria, lived with him for twelve years in resolute virginity, though Ecgfrith promised Bishop Wilfrid estates and wealth if he could persuade her to consummate the marriage.[77] At length Ecgfrith let her enter the life of religion, and he himself married Iurminburg. Archbishop Theodore (archbishop of Canterbury 668–90) only required mutual consent for the dissolution of lawful marriage.[78] Over dissolution more of a culture clash was looming. Lucas sums it up: 'divorce by mutual consent was recognised by the Germanic peoples . . . and for some centuries . . . the church was not able to interfere too deeply in such secular practices'. From the ninth to eleventh centuries the Anglo-Saxons went on following their relatively lax rules about divorce.[79] The complications of marriage between Christian and pagan became a declining problem, but consent and consummation remained at the heart of the validation of marriage. The church did not in Anglo-Saxon times (nor much later) claim to offer the only validating marriage ceremony. Spousal services were available: Lucas cites eighth- to eleventh-century ones, but these were purely religious and of no legal significance.[80]

The bulk of the source material for the study of Anglo-Saxon women and religion relates to nuns, some of whom had been married women with children before entering the church either willingly or under pressure. For laywomen, the church's teaching on marriage and sexual morality may have been where it touched them most markedly. Archbishop Theodore's *Penitential* prescribed three years of penance for a man committing adultery, seven years for a woman.[81] In the Anglo-Saxon polity, morality flavoured the law, and the law enforced morality. So Cnut condemned as wicked adultery fornication with a single woman, and worse with another man's wife or a nun. But the errant wife had the worst of it: 'if a woman during her husband's lifetime commits adultery with another man, and it becomes known, let her afterwards become herself a public disgrace and her lawful husband is to have all that she owns, and she is to lose her nose and ears'.[82] From the earliest days of Christianity laws had put a higher price on violating and harassing nuns than laywomen, but despite the protection of the cloister, women in religion remained vulnerable. Alfred ruled: 'if anyone in lewd fashion seizes a nun, either by her clothes or her breast, without her leave, the compensation is to be double that we have established for a lay person'.[83] King Æthelred of Mercia was condemned for adulterous behaviour in convents; Edgar (d.

975), in other respects a 'priests' king', for abduction and viola-
tion of nuns, and King Harold Godwineson's brother Swein had
to return the abbess of Leominster after a year.[84] It is naive to
believe the laws tamed even the lawmakers that much.

Laywomen's personal piety is a seriously underevidenced subject in the pre-Conquest period. Obviously piety was one motivat-
ing factor when Anglo-Saxon secular women gave land to the
nunneries and other ecclesiastical foundations. The will of Æthelflæd, widow of King Edmund, granted Damerham (Hants) to Glas-
tonbury Abbey 'for King Edmund's soul, and for King Edgar's and
mine', and Ham (Kent) to Christchurch Canterbury, for Edmund's
soul and her own. Several estates were left in reversion to churches,
after the life interest of ealdorman Brihtnoth and the testator's
sister Ælfflæd, or this sister alone. Ælfflæd herself, who was conscious of her ancestors' gifts to holy foundations, begged her lord
in her will to protect 'the holy foundation at Stoke [probably
Stoke by Nayland, Suffolk] in which my ancestors lie buried'.[85]
Some testatrices gave chapel furnishings: Wulfwaru left St Peter's,
Bath 'two gold crucifixes, a set of mass vestments with everything
that belongs to it, and the best dorsal that I have and a set of bed
clothing with tapestry and curtain and with everything that belongs to it'.[86] This will ends with arrangements to provide Bath
with a food rent, and the words: 'whichever of them shall discharge this, may he have God's favour and mine; and whichever
of them will not discharge it, may he have to account for it with
the Most High, who is the true God, who created and made all
creatures'.

Conclusions

It is surprising how much can be pieced together about women
who lived a thousand years ago, and the nature of what can be
learned about them proves in many ways similar to the nature of
the findings in the next five centuries too. Already the main types
of written evidence are male-composed narrative, government archival record and private documentation, wills and charters. Not
surprisingly what we learn is mainly the top people's view – the
learned ecclesiastics' rumination on women, the law enforcers'
attempts to control breakdown in traditional social order, the
government's interest in exploiting resources, the concern of the

propertied classes for the disposal of their assets, especially after death. It can all look deceptively settled and comfortable, which may be why a mythical 'Golden Age' for Anglo-Saxon women has had appeal.

There is no law of progressive enlightenment, and no point at which it can be said that specific conditions must represent improvements on earlier times, or will in turn be ameliorated later. The coming of Christianity brought both new opportunities and new repressive attitudes. The coming of the Vikings seems to have breathed more freedom, for both sexes, into eastern England, but only after terrifying earlier generations, and it certainly had a devastating effect on the nuns in England. The coming of the Normans, while not ending any 'Golden Age' at a blow, did usher in some changes which affected for the worse those most privileged in the earlier regime, namely the landed women. So it may be seen how historians approaching the distant past expecting it to be primitive received a pleasant surprise in the sophistication of Wynflæd's will, the elegance of Leoba's letters and the eminence of Hilda of Whitby, and for this reason may have credited Anglo-Saxon women with more status than they probably, individually, had. To historians who absorbed this perspective, the Norman Conquest seemed to offer a cold douche. But all these interpretations, as far as the place of women is concerned, tend to pay too exclusive attention to the political side of history, with its concern with who ruled and how. For the vast majority of Anglo-Saxon women the centuries between 450 and 1100 were a round of mainly domestic chores, agricultural tasks, childbearing and rearing, and caring for the sick and injured. The same routine went on occupying most of England's women in the next half millennium, as we shall see. Inevitably the unique or rare illustrations of women acting probably extraordinarily arouse more interest than any consideration of their daily chores, but these continuous, unremarked contributions of the mass of women amount in themselves to a vastly undervalued underpinning of the medieval English economy.

Notes

1 *English Historical Documents I*, c. *500–1042*, ed. D. Whitelock, London, 1955, pp. 359, 367.

2 *Ibid.*, p. 359.
3 *Ibid.*, p. 429.
4 P. H. Sawyer (ed.), *Anglo-Saxon Charters*, London, 1968, nos. 1201, 1211, 156, 1232, 1188, 1200, 1119.
5 *Ibid.*, nos. 489, 811, 45, 460, 593, 762, 600, 703, 754.
6 *Ibid.*, nos. 1273, 1298, 1326.
7 C. Fell, *Women in Anglo-Saxon England*, London, 1986, pp. 94–5.
8 P. S. Gold, *The Lady and the Virgin: image, attitude and experience in twelfth-century France*, Chicago and London, 1987, pp. 117–44.
9 Fell, *Women in Anglo-Saxon England*, p. 63.
10 F. L. Attenborough (ed.), *The Laws of the Earliest English Kings*, Cambridge, 1922, p. 151.
11 *Bede's Ecclesiastical History of the English People*, ed. B. Colgrave and R. A. B. Mynors, Oxford, 1969, p. 89.
12 *The Anglo-Saxon Chronicle*, trsl. and ed. G. N. Garmonsway, revised edn London, 1954, p. 86.
13 J. Jesch, *Women in the Viking Age*, Woodbridge, 1991, p. 1.
14 J. T. Schulenburg, 'Women's monastic communities, 500–1100: patterns of expansion and decline', *Signs*, Winter, 1989, xiv, 2, p. 275.
15 *Ibid.*, p. 275, citing D. Knowles, *The Monastic Order in England*, Cambridge, 1940, p. 101.
16 Quoted in H. R. Loyn, *The Vikings in Britain*, London, 1977, p. 91.
17 Jesch, *Women of the Viking Age*, p. 76; F. M. Stenton, *The Free Peasantry of the Northern Danelaw*, Oxford, 1969, for example nos. 96, 112, 124, 125, 126.
18 Schulenburg, *Signs*, p. 269.
19 A. M. Lucas, *Women in the Middle Ages: religion, marriage and letters*, Brighton, 1983, p. 65; Fell, *Women in Anglo-Saxon England*, p. 83.
20 *English Historical Documents*, I, p. 370.
21 *Ibid.*, p. 430.
22 *Ibid.*, p. 368.
23 *Ibid.*, p. 383.
24 *Ibid.*, p. 359.
25 P. Stafford, 'Women in Domesday', in *Medieval Women in Southern England*, Reading Medieval Studies, XV, 1989, pp. 84–5.
26 *English Historical Documents*, II, ed. D. C. Douglas, London, 1953, pp. 813–16.
27 Fell, *Women in Anglo-Saxon England*, p. 43.
28 *Ibid.*, p. 40.
29 D. Whitelock (ed.), *Anglo-Saxon Wills*, Cambridge, 1930, pp. 11–15. Whitelock dates this will to *c*. 950.

30 S. Reynolds, 'Towns in Domesday Book', in J. C. Holt (ed.), *Domesday Studies*, Woodbridge, 1987, pp. 295–309.
31 A. MacGregor, 'Industry and commerce in Anglo-Scandinavian York', in R. A. Hall (ed.), *Viking Age York and the North*, Council for British Archaeology, London, 1978, pp. 37–57; H. K. Kenward et al., 'The environment of Anglo-Scandinavian York', *ibid.*, pp. 65, 68, 67.
32 Stafford, 'Domesday women', p. 92, n. 18.
33 'Asser's Life of King Alfred', in S. Keynes and M. Lapidge (eds.), *Alfred the Great*, Harmondsworth, 1983, pp. 71–2.
34 Bede, *Ecclesiastical History*, pp. 181, 191.
35 Fell, *Women in Anglo-Saxon England*, p. 36.
36 'Life of Wilfrid', trsl. J. F. Webb, in *The Age of Bede*, ed. D. H. Farmer, Harmondsworth, 1983, pp. 129–30.
37 *Beowulf*, trsl. M. Alexander, Harmondsworth, 1973, lines 2369–72.
38 *Ibid.*, lines 2029–31.
39 P. Stafford, *Queens, Concubines and Dowagers: the king's wife in the early middle ages*, London, 1983, p. 118; J. Stevenson (ed.), 'Book of Hyde', *Church Historians of England*, London, 1853–8, ii, ii, p. 514.
40 *Encomium Emmae Reginae* ed. A. Campbell, Camden Third Series, LXXII, 1949, p. xxi.
41 Stafford, *Queens, Concubines and Dowagers*, p. 141.
42 Bede, *Ecclesiastical History*, pp. 231, 263; Nennius, *British History and the Welsh Annals*, ed. and trsl. J. Morris, London and Chichester, 1980, p. 38.
43 F. M. Stenton, 'The historical bearing of placename studies: the place of women in Anglo-Saxon society', *Transactions of the Royal Historical Society*, 4th series, XXV, 1943, pp. 1–13.
44 Fell, *Women in Anglo-Saxon England*, pp. 42, 17.
45 Whitelock, *Wills*, pp. 11–13.
46 *Ibid.*, pp. 47–51.
47 *English Historical Documents*, I, p. 556, discussed in H. R. Loyn, *The Governance of Anglo-Saxon England 500–1087*, London, 1984, pp. 139–40.
48 P. Stafford, *Unification and Conquest: a political and social history of England in the tenth and eleventh centuries*, London, 1989, pp. 164, 167, 175.
49 Domesday Book, fo. 218d.
50 Stafford, 'Domesday women', p. 76.
51 Domesday Book, fos 210a, 212a.
52 Stafford, 'Domesday women', p. 76; Domesday Book, fo. 373a–b.

53 P. Clarke, *The English Nobility under Edward the Confessor*, Oxford, 1994, pp. 204–5.
54 Stafford, 'Domesday women', p. 81.
55 Domesday Book, fo. 218a.
56 Stafford, 'Domesday women', pp. 80, 87.
57 *Ibid.*, p. 89.
58 *Beowulf*, line 3150.
59 'Life of Alfred', p. 75.
60 Bede, *Ecclesiastical History*, p. 189.
61 *Ibid.*, p. 239.
62 B. Yorke, '"Sisters under the skin"? Anglo-Saxon nuns and nunneries in southern England', in *Medieval Women in Southern England*, Reading Medieval Studies, XV, 1989, p. 96.
63 Bede, *Ecclesiastical History*, pp. 407, 429; 391–3.
64 *Ibid.*, p. 409. S. Hollis, *Anglo-Saxon Women and the Church*, Woodbridge, 1992, is critical of Bede's treatment of monastic women, which she calls 'an artifact of his own bias', p. 243.
65 'Life of Wilfrid', p. 172; Hollis, *Anglo-Saxon Women*, pp. 181, 163.
66 Yorke, 'Sisters', p. 99.
67 Bede, *Ecclesiastical History*, p. 425.
68 Yorke, 'Sisters', p. 98; S. Elkins, *Holy Women of Twelfth-Century England*, Chapel Hill London, 1988, p. 21.
69 Bede, *Ecclesiastical History*, pp. 393, 407–9, 361.
70 Yorke, 'Sisters', p. 97; see too Hollis, *Anglo-Saxon Women, passim.*
71 M. Gretsch, 'Æthelwold's translation of the *Regula Sancti Benedicti* and its Latin exemplar', *Anglo-Saxon England*, III, 1974, p. 138.
72 *Letters of Abelard and Heloise*, ed. B. Radice, Harmondsworth, 1974, p. 160.
73 Yorke, 'Sisters', p. 108.
74 Bede, *Ecclesiastical History*, p. 91; one example among several may be found in F. M. Powicke and C. R. Cheney (eds.), *Councils and Synods with other documents relating to the English Church*, Oxford, 1962, II, i, p. 136.
75 Bede, *Ecclesiastical History*, p. 173.
76 *Ibid.*, p. 285.
77 *Ibid.*, p. 393.
78 J. Scammell, 'Freedom and marriage in medieval England', *Economic History Review*, 2nd series, XXVII, 1974, p. 532.
79 Lucas, *Women of the Middle Ages*, pp. 70, 77.
80 *Ibid.*, p. 71.
81 Hollis, *Anglo-Saxon Women*, p. 59.
82 *English Historical Documents*, I, p. 426.

83   Ibid., p. 376.
84   J. T. Schulenburg, 'The heroics of virginity: brides of Christ and sacrificial mutilation', in M. B. Rose, Women in the Middle Ages and Renaissance, Syracuse, 1986, p. 43.
85   Whitelock, Wills, pp. 35, 39. These wills are c. 980 and c. 1000.
86   Ibid., p. 63. Dated c. 984–1016.

2

Women of the medieval countryside

The women of the medieval countryside are here classed as a group which is defined by residence and occupation, not by legal status. The discussion includes villein women and their free socage neighbours within the manorial tenantry, shading up into the women of the small landholding class later known as the yeomanry, but it stops short of the wives and daughters of the higher landowning classes, who will be treated in chapter 4.

The women in focus in this chapter had in common fixed residence in the countryside and employment, paid or unpaid, in farming communities. Approximately 90 per cent of the population was rural in the Middle Ages, so the vast majority of women fell into this category, which is why they attract attention first. There is some suggestion that the balance of the sexes, or sex ratio, varied between town and countryside, being higher (that is, more men to women) in rural than in urban areas, at any rate after the plague; Goldberg's study of 1377 poll tax returns reveals a sex ratio of 92.7 men per 100 women in Hull, 89.7 in Carlisle, but 103.5 in rural Rutland.[1] The imbalances are not high, and must not be supposed to have remained constant.

Contemporary sources contain references to countrywomen, but scarcely proportionate to their numbers. The main written source materials are manorial court rolls, manorial extents, surveys and accounts, records of royal justices, especially justices of the peace, and poll tax records. These may be supplemented by works of art, mostly in the form of illuminated manuscripts, and archaeology. There are several well-known representations in literature.

Manorial court rolls are not found before the 1240s and are not widespread before the 1270s; they are of less significance after about 1350. They are probably the best single source for the history of rural women in the Middle Ages, but they are limited to matters relevant to the manorial court, which dealt with manorial tenure, petty crimes such as breaching the assize of ale (and more rarely, bread), illicit gleaning and damaging woodlands, and more sophisticated civil disputes within the tenantry such as breach of contract and unjust detention of goods or animals. The women who appear in the court rolls of the manor of Wakefield between 1348 and 1350 constitute 27 to 30 per cent of the total of people appearing, some 600 out of just over 2,000. There may be imbalance within the representation, since arguably richer male tenants appeared more frequently, partly in their capacity as manorial officials and pledges, whereas, brewing offences apart, it was women of poorer families who appeared for offences such as illegal gleaning and taking wood. Women may have been more active than the record implies, since the activities of married ones may be concealed in entries apparently concerning only their husbands. The identification of individual women named in a series of court rolls is problematic, complicated by changes of name on marriage. Patronymic and occupational surnames seem even less likely to be accurate in relation to women than the same names applied to men. For example, in the 1348–50 Wakefield court rolls the brewsters included Margery Clerk, Beatrix Lorimer, Agnes Smith and Juliana Spicer; Margaret Orfeour was amerced for offences to vert, and Annabel Waynwright's lands featured in the list of decayed rents.[2] It seems more than likely that some of these surnames at least reflected these women's fathers' or an unspecified husband's occupations, or may have been derived from a still earlier relative.

Manorial extents, surveys and accounts begin earlier, but in England are not much more than spasmodic before the thirteenth century. Women had much less reason to appear here, only as tenants or occasionally as paid employees on the estate, or as the cause of the levying of merchet (the fine due to the lord on a villein woman's marriage). The censuses of bond inhabitants on three Spalding (Lincs.) priory manors *c.* 1268–9 are unique. Like the court rolls, the estate records decline in value in the late fourteenth century as demesne farming gave way to leasing. But it is about this very time that the records of the king's justices of the peace become interesting, especially with regard to the labour legislation following the plagues of 1348–50, which the justices enforced. These records provide valuable information on country-women as wage earners, both in agriculture and textile crafts. The justices also dealt with rape and assault.

The returns of the standard lay property taxes of the thirteenth and early fourteenth centuries noted women payers – at Thornbury (Glos.) in 1327 women tenants formed eighteen per cent of the taxpayers.[3] Unfortunately, this source of information disappears in 1334, when the separate assessment of individuals each time a property tax was granted gave way to the levying of such taxation as a negotiated, and thereafter fixed, sum chargeable on the local-ity. The poll taxes of 1377–81, being on heads, male and female alike, are a more useful source of information on women, and have allowed work to be done on sex ratios in both households and communities.

Artwork is a fairly dubious source for the countrywoman, for although reapers and wool carders and suchlike are represented, their appearance in luxury manuscripts for the upper classes may have had a touch of the Arcadian about it: the peasants depicted about their tasks seem rather too well dressed. Archaeology has a more sophisticated role to play in gender studies now that medical evidence is being extracted from human remains. That the women of Wharram Percy (E. R. Yorks.) suffered from post-menopausal osteoporosis was disclosed by Simon Mays to the British Associa-tion Science Fair at Loughborough University in 1994.

Two famous late fourteenth-century literary passages are par-ticularly apt as they reflect respectively agricultural and pastoral societies. The first comes from an alliterative satirical poem, *Pierce the Ploughman's Crede*, wherein a graphic description of a ragged ploughman with his toes out of his shoes and in mud up to his ankles, driving four scraggy oxen, ends with the description of his wife walking beside him, with a long ox goad, in a ragged coat cut short to the knee, wrapped in a winnowing sheet to keep out the weather. Their children cry piteously at the edge of the field.[4] The second is Chaucer's impoverished elderly widow in 'The Nun's Priest's Tale'. 'Litel was hir catel and hir rente', and she kept herself and two daughters by husbandry. She had three large sows, three cattle and a sheep named Malle, and in an enclosed yard, fenced with sticks, a cock and seven hens. Her diet was largely milk and brown bread, with bacon and sometimes an egg or two. Chaucer calls her a dairywoman.[5]

From other literature of the late fourteenth, fifteenth and sixteenth centuries come some particularly valuable sympathetic descriptions of women's roles. In the C text of *Piers Plowman* (*c.* 1385–7) Langland has a passage about the poor, with too many children and rack-renting landlords. He says what they save by spinning they spend on house rent, and on milk and (oat)meal to make gruel to feed their children, clamouring for food. He sees them often famished and wretched with the miseries of winter, and writes of cold sleepless nights when they get up to rock the cradle, rise before dawn to card and comb wool, to wash and scrape and wind yarn, and peel rushes for lights. He comments that the miseries of the women living in cottages are pitiful to read or describe in verse.[6]

In the 'Second Shepherds' Pageant' of the Towneley Corpus Christi play cycle, Gill, roused in the night by her returning husband, complains that she is spinning and it is not profitable to get up from this. A. C. Cawley paraphrases: 'any woman who has been a housewife knows what it means to be got up from her work continually. I have no work to show because of such small chores.' Later Gill boosts herself. 'Who brews? Who bakes? . . . it is ruth [pity] to behold, now in hot, now in cold, full woeful is the household that wants a woman.'[7] A fuller description comes from the 'Ballad of a Tyrannical Husband', whose nineteenth-century editors attributed the text to Henry VII's reign (1485–1509). In his construction of a battle between the sexes, the poet sets up the housewife as having much to do, and no servant but many small children. Her husband's first words on his homecoming are to ask if dinner is ready. ' "Syr", sche sayd, "naye;/ How wold yow have me doo mor then I cane?" ' In the ensuing argument he says that she ought to try ploughing all day, and she rejoinds that if he followed her day he would be weary.

> 'Wery! Yn the devylles nam!' seyd the goodman,
> 'What has thou to doo, but syttes her at hame?
> Thou goyst to thi neybores howse, be on and be one
> And syttes ther janglynge . . .'[8]

The wife then describes her day, in a text which will be further cited below. The interesting point made in these last two extracts, both designed for popular consumption, is the recognition of what modern sociology defines as a different rhythm of work based on gender. In terms of the chronological distribution of these sources, there is very little evidence for women's role in the countryside before the twelfth and thirteenth centuries.

In so far as countrywomen have attracted the attention of historians, they did so at first almost entirely in the legal areas of landholding, inheritance and dower, and only later in the spheres of physical labour in and away from the home, and most recently in the area we might call 'women as members of the community', that is particularly in their connections and coexistence with people outside their immediate families.

Women, law and landholding on the manor

Domesday Book provides us with a satisfactorily ubiquitous sighting of the classes of rural society in 1086: freemen (*liberi homines*), socmen (*socemani*), villeins (*villani*), bordars (*bordarii*), cottars (*cotarii, cotsetlas*) and slaves (*servi*). In numbers slaves were in decline, and villein status, not at this date pejorative (*villanus* means man of the vill), was beginning to subsume lesser distinctions and create a large category of people more free than the slave but more bonded than the truly free. During the twelfth century the codifiers of law distinguished free and villein tenure, but whatever the theory or origins of the distinction it became blurred, leaving it possible for freemen to take on villein tenures, and villeins free ones. Villeins themselves began a noticeable upwardly mobile movement in the thirteenth century by asserting themselves as property owners, will-makers and holders of land by charter, even if only 'by the custom of the manor'. Zvi Razi estimates that 64 per cent of the families he reconstituted from Halesowen (Worcs.) court rolls 1270–1349 were of unfree status.[9] By the end of the fourteenth century there was social tension caused by an outmoded legal theory being upheld against real practices of mobility, money rent and wage earning. The Peasants' Revolt (1381) reflects this tension, but villeinage was not formally ended spectacularly: it withered into insignificance in the fifteenth century. The tenure itself became known as copyhold because the copy of the entry of the tenant's admittance on the court roll served as a title deed.

Villeinage had consequences for women, not only as landholders, but for their personal position. Villein tenure was defined by manorial custom, a custom fixed enough probably on the manor, but varying from manor to manor and region to region, though it shows similarities to frée socage practices. In open-field farming districts impartible inheritance customs generally passed the patrimonial holding intact to the eldest son (primogeniture), but sometimes to the youngest (ultimogeniture). In default of sons a daughter or daughters could inherit.[10] Partible inheritance was, however, quite widespread, especially in Kent, East Anglia and the north and north-west, outside the main open-field arable zone. The prevalent inheritance pattern affected the structure and mobility of the population. Anywhere, however, prospering peasants might enlarge their holdings sufficiently to divide up acquired lands between several children before, or to follow, death, and incoming heirs seem to have responded to some responsibility to help siblings settle. Both these factors make the difference between partible and impartible inheritance less clear cut.

The predecease of one partner to a marriage was inevitable, and social custom prepared for it. As soon as the wife bore a child, by both common and customary law the husband's interest in her lands strengthened: the birth assured that he had life tenure. When the surviving husband died, the wife's lands could revert to her heirs. As an example of this may be cited Jan Titow's identification of the descent of a holding in Hampshire: Alice, daughter of Isabella Bodenham, paid 30s in 1361 to have a messuage and a virgate of bondland and eight acres of purpresture in Hoo, which belonged to her mother, and which John le Parker, who had married Isabella, held for the term of his life. Roger le Clerk of Upham paid 40s to have Alice and this land, and was left a widower within three years, but unlike John le Parker, Roger forfeited the holding according to the particular custom of that manor 'for he had accepted another wife'. Alice's uncle paid 50s to enter the lands in 1364.[11]

If the husband died first, his widow was entitled to dower. Dower was the responsibility of the husband to provide, at the outset of the marriage, hence the concept of being dowered at the church door. But it soon became so basic an entitlement that it could be assigned fairly mechanically, within forty days of the death, by the heir or guardian. Dower of one-third of the husband's lands probably originated in feudal tenures and spread into socage (non-military freehold) tenure, where the dower was not to exceed half the lands,[12] but villein dower was not as uniformly fixed. It could be more than a third of the copyhold lands of which the husband had been seised, in some places at the time of his death, in others at any time during the marriage. This was regardless of whether the lands were subsequently alienated or not, except where they were alienated with the wife's consent. Out of the complexities of these conditions dower disputes not unnaturally arose, but are not as frequently recorded as one might expect. Usually the widow did not have to pay an entry fine to enter her dower, but this was not always the case. Where there was no fine, it suggests the widow was being treated as the survivor of joint tenure, and where there was, that she was regarded as an heir. Whereas the widow at common law held on to her dower, increasing it perhaps through successive marriages, in some places the widowed villein could only hold her dower if she remained unmarried and/or kept herself chaste. However, marriage to landed widows was a prominent means of access to manorial land for some males, especially in the early fourteenth century, and custom varied as to whether second husbands could or could not claim the property if they outlived their wives.[13]

It is not clear when dower customs were established, but they follow from tenure being a relatively secure phenomenon. Widows' rights seem to have been by far the most durable and firmly established of all inheritance customs, but conditions were far from static. Richard Smith noted 'a significant transformation of manorial justice' between 1280 and 1310, bringing the customary tenants into the increasingly sophisticated world of land conveyancing.[14] The requirement (derived from final concord procedure in the royal courts) that a married woman's consent be obtained in court before her husband could alienate land is found in manor courts at the very end of the thirteenth century. If the wife concurred in the surrender, she could make no later claim to dower from the land alienated.

The tenants at Wakefield (W. R. Yorks.) in 1348–50 were well aware (or astutely advised) of the significance of turning in their holdings to the manorial lord to get them regranted promptly on different terms, perhaps jointly, or with specific descent to one or other of a couple's heirs. They were quite able to manipulate legal conditions to suit their family requirements. So at Wakefield on 5 May 1349 Adam son of Robert of Castleford, of Wakefield, surrendered by the bailiff an acre and three roods in Alverthorpe, which were then granted to the same Adam and Margaret his wife to hold to themselves and the heirs procreated between them, according to the custom of the manor. If they died without such an heir, the whole land was to remain to Adam's nearest heir. However, on 10 June 1350, when William del Morehouse and Alice his wife, she being examined for her agreement, surrendered seven acres and a messuage in Crigglestone to Peter Whitlof to hold to himself and his heirs according to manorial custom, this was clearly only a half-way stage in the proceedings, for Peter immediately surrendered the same property which was then granted to William and Alice to hold to whichever of them lived the longer and to Alice's heirs. Alice would have benefited from this change, for she would have the whole holding not just a dower portion, if she were the survivor, and her heirs were to benefit, whichever party died first. In a third example of the rearrangements possible, on 1 July 1350, John son of John de Emlay and his wife Matilda paid heriot (the fine due to the manorial lord on a tenant's death) for land previously held by her sister, of whom she was the heir. Husband and wife apparently paid the heriot, but the land was initially to be held to the wife and her heirs. However, the couple surrendered the land immediately, and the holdings were granted to the wife's mother for the whole of her life, an example of familial provision for the elderly.[15]

The heiress or widow in possession of a manorial holding excited Eileen Power's pity: she thought women manorial tenants 'perhaps the most hardworked class of all', and Ambrose Raftis thought it virtually impossible for a widow to maintain the larger tenements.[16] The extent of Littleton in Hampshire from 1265/6 identifies services due from six virgators (holders of about 30 acres) regardless of sex – 5s a year rent, plus specified amounts of the following labour services assessed as worth 12s 2½d: ploughing twice a year, harrowing, weeding, lifting hay, planting beans, washing and shearing sheep, making a haycock, carrying services to Andover and Ludgershall, reaping, boonworks, carrying the lord's corn, gathering nuts, and churchscot. Among the virgators was Rosa de la Putte, 'and she shall perform the same services, besides the aforementioned money rent', says the extent about her as about the other virgators. Among the half-virgators, charged with amounts of similar services totalling 10s 3d, was Isabella the widow of le

Bloware, charged uniformly with the rest. A third category of tenant, holding ten acres of land and performing services worth 4s 7¹/₂d, included Juliana the widow of Ralph, and Emma the widow of William Maideus.[17] Josiah Russell found women forming 15 per cent of the landholders in a representative catalogue of pre-plague manors.[18]

Agricultural labour services had to be performed or commuted, so women tenants had to make arrangements with a man to perform them if they could not do so themselves, or they had to buy off the responsibility. Ploughing seems to have been normally done by men, and references to women ploughing by no means specify 'in person'. Everywhere, the tendency towards commutation of services must have rendered the woman's inferior physical strength less relevant, though she would need cash to commute services. Such commutation might take care of the performance of the services due as rent, but what happened if an elderly widow grew too feeble even to provide her own food? Some made arrangements of a corrodial kind with their own kin or strangers. Thomas Bird of Romsley, taking over a cottage from his mother in 1281, promised to maintain her for the rest of her life in a 'competent dwelling' he would build, 30 feet long and 14 feet wide, with corner posts, three new and competent doors and two windows. Her food and fuel allowances were stipulated.[19]

Farming history is too often dominated by arable activities. It should be remembered that particularly in the higher areas of the country, most notably the north and west, pastoral farming predominated. Pastoral communities had two differences from arable ones: they tended to favour partible inheritance among males more, for most of the Middle Ages and into early modern times, and they provided comparatively more employment opportunities for women as herdswomen, dairywomen, and spinners and carders of wool.

Only her own biological limitations made the physical demands of manorial tenancy, villein or socage, harder for a woman. But the most distinguishing female physical characteristic, childbearing, opened the villein woman, but not the woman of the free manorial tenantry, to more insidious personal disadvantage. Based on the premise that villeins were the lord's chattels, came the idea that the lord had to be compensated if the chattel became less valuable. A villein woman's marriage could have repercussions for

[65]

her lord, most obviously if she married an outsider and if giving her a dowry dispersed her family's resources, particularly if the family was comparatively well placed. The lord, therefore, had to be paid to agree to the marriage. He did not, apparently, in England enjoy *ius primae noctis*.[20]

The marriage payment to the lord appears in records by the eleventh century as merchet. It was paid most commonly by the bride herself or her father, but could be paid by the groom, or other persons. Judith Bennett's analysis of 426 merchets recorded in twenty-nine Ramsey Abbey manors between 1398 and 1458 reveals that the woman herself paid in 33 per cent of the instances, her father in 33 per cent, the groom in 26 per cent and others in 8 per cent, and Bennett believes the records can be trusted: 'both quantitative and written evidence indicates that the record speaks accurately when it mentions women as paying their own merchets'.[21] Widows generally paid their own merchets for remarriage, though William Baildon thought Wakefield widows only needed licence to remarry if they were moving away from the manor.[22] There must have been many more peasant marriages than there are recorded payments of merchet, and on the whole it seems to have been the better-off villein tenants who paid it. It was resisted, and at Halesowen the abbot had to stop the exaction in the 1380s.[23] It was certainly in decline after the Black Death. Whether the payment was in advance of the marriage, for permission, or after it as a fine for marrying without licence was not significant: in Wakefield in 1348–50 both types of payment were termed merchet.

If a villein woman did not marry but cohabited, she was fined leyrwite (alias legerwite, lecherwite) for her fornication. This fine has been somewhat diversely interpreted. It was of Anglo-Saxon origin, and since there existed the separate fine 'childwite' (the fine for bearing a bastard child), leyrwite would seem in origin to be a fine variously described as for cohabitation, fornication, incontinence or adultery, whether or not pregnancy resulted. However, childwite as such is rarely recorded, whereas leyrwite is much more common, and the record of its incidence may actually specify that the woman is 'deflowered and made pregnant', or 'deflowered and has given birth'. Razi tries to use the incidence of leyrwite as a guide to illegitimacy in Halesowen.[24] Tim North notes that it was frequently associated with pregnancies, which, as they became impossible to conceal, brought the matter to light. North suggests that

[66]

between the eleventh and thirteenth centuries the fine changed character from one for the moral lapse to one for its legal consequences – the manorial offence of causing a matter arising on the manor to be brought into the church courts. (The principle is that for villeins to pay fines to the church court was alienating the lord's property since their chattels were the lord's.)[25] The woman was not the only guilty party in these sexual lapses, yet leyrwite seems originally to have been applied only to women, and rarely ever to have been applied to men.

Leyrwite used to be treated somewhat salaciously by historians, but has begun to be handled with much more sensitivity in the light of known economic backdrops in terms of both class and chronology. Where it has been studied, it seems clear that leyrwite and childwite fell most often on the poorer women on the manor, ones whose parents could not afford to help them start married life with even a small dowry in land or kind. In Halesowen, Razi estimated the fornication rates at 5 per cent of rich families (that is 25–30 acre yardlanders), 11 per cent of middling families (that is half-virgators) and 16 per cent of the poor families (those with a quarter virgate or less). In the poorer families, more members of the family fornicated than in the rich. After the plague, conditions eased and leyrwites diminished; this suggested to Razi that 'poverty rather than licentiousness' lay behind the earlier situation at Halesowen.[26] The Wakefield evidence suggests a surge of leyrwites and fines for marriage without licence in 1316, a time when the area had suffered the national famines of the teens of the century, Scottish invasion after the battle of Bannockburn (1314), and local disruption owing to the feud between the earl of Warenne, Wakefield's lord, and the earl of Lancaster. Warenne's difficulties may have led him to seek tighter enforcement of his rights at this date, and it must be remembered that changes in court procedure may always be matters of recording or policy as much as changes of people's habits. However, it seems likely that the common pattern of premarital cohabitation, vague troth-plighting and unsolemnised marriage among peasantry would lead to more women being fined if particularly hard times prevented the fulfilment of promises of matrimony they had been given, by making it much more difficult to set up a new household.[27] Neither merchet nor leyrwite seem to have been levied very tightly, and both dwindled markedly after the Black Death.

Women and rural toil

When Eileen Power described women manorial tenants, free and villein, as so hardworked, she commented, 'no doubt they hired men for the heavy ploughing, but performed other services in person'.[28] Some women certainly employed hired labour. The wives and daughters of male tenants presumably shared out some of the manorial services and contributed labour to any plots the family tilled. Women made good sowers, weeders, reapers and gleaners, at appropriate seasons. Obviously they could tend vegetables and herbs, which formed an important part of the medieval peasant diet. In *Piers Plowman* Piers has soup, beans and bacon but does not claim to eat meat from the larger animals, beef and mutton. The animals of Chaucer's widow in 'The Nun's Priest's Tale' gave her access to limited amounts of shorn wool, milk and eggs, and presumably, by arrangement for breeding, piglets and calves. She lived with two daughters, and it is not hard to imagine that while the husband lived, the women of the family had tried to keep sickly runts alive, fed and milked animals, and made cheese and butter, turning their hands in appropriate ways on a subsistence holding of about ten acres (the minimum size for an average household).

There has been a good deal of argument about the size of a household, the universality of marriage and the age at first marriage in the Middle Ages.[29] Obviously the opportunities for sons and daughters to marry and set up house even during their parents' lifetimes varied with local custom and parental wealth. Familial involvement in children's marriage was probably greater among more substantial tenants than among the poor, where the daughters may have had more freedom of choice and less supervision of courtship.[30] Generally speaking the better off were able to marry at an earlier age, but Razi's interpretation of the age at marriage at Halesowen, where he calculated 49 per cent of 285 three-generation families had a son or daughter married between the ages of eighteen and twenty-two, has been subjected to severe criticism of the presumptions behind it.[31] The sooner couples married, the more children they were likely to produce. Two distinctive marriage regimes have been postulated: a medieval one in which marriage was universal and embarked on young, and a modern one, operative in sixteenth-century England and pushed back into the fifteenth or earlier, where many married late or not at all. Before the keeping of parish registers the data on age at first marriage is not strong and generalisations are risky. Obviously the life cycle of women would be different if they almost all married, and youthfully, or married late with some not marrying at all. Furthermore their life style would be different according to whether a nuclear or extended family was the norm. Herbert Hallam argued from the Spalding serf lists, where partible inheritance was common, that 'the nuclear household was overwhelmingly predominant' and much of the evidence reads this way.[32]

Simply keeping such a peasant household (estimated at four to five persons) running must have been a physically demanding task. In the home, fires had to be lit and tended, to provide both domestic warmth and cooking power. Water had to be fetched from wells and springs, and disposed of. 'A woman is a worthy thing, she doth the wash and doth the wring', says a fifteenth-century poem.[33] Barbara Hanawalt's search of coroners' rolls for causes of accidental death shows peak danger periods for women in the morning, leading up to midday, early evening and night. The dangers came from drowning fetching water or in laundry work, scalding or burning relating to cooking, and house fires at night. Though Goldberg has perceptively criticised the presumptions and methodology of this study, he agrees drawing water and cooking over an open fire were hazardous activities.[34]

There were various maintenance tasks such as caring for straw pallets or the luxury of a feather bed, and keeping the family clothed and covered. Archaeological evidence from Wharram Percy shows the sweeping of earthen floors was frequent enough to wear the floor to a 'U' shape over time.[35] Out of doors, wild fruits would be harvested, for food and possibly dyes. Rushes would be fetched and laid, and replaced. Firewood and kindling had to be gathered, and there were uses for brushwood for fencing in animals (Chaucer's widow's yard was fenced with sticks), and reeds for basketry.

Once the still picture from the illuminated manuscript showing rather too clean a female peasant gathering fruit or cutting sheaves is animated, and the pattern of her day's work examined, the constantly broken concentration which was the woman's lot emerges. In what Judith Bennett termed the work aspect of the 'conjugal economy', both husband and wife worked vigorously to support the household, but her work was less autonomous and less focused: she had to show the flexibility; he had the superior status from his more continuous and specialised labour. Hanawalt argues that within the marriage partnership 'gender ordinarily determined the division of labour, but the goal of both partners was the survival and prosperity of the household unit'.[36] Where the two worked is significant: Hanawalt terms the women 'homebodies'. The daily routine was endless, one task after another. The 'Tyrannical Husband' goes off to plough demanding dinner betimes. The wife's defence case in the ballad includes the claims that she has but small sleep, that her husband will get her up early in the morning even though their child may have woken her in the night, and that she has milked the cows and turned them out in the field while her husband stays asleep. She goes on to make butter and then cheese, comfort the children, feed the chickens, hens, capons, ducks and goslings, bake, brew, handle flax and tow, card and spin wool, feed the beasts, and get the meat ready for human consumption. Chiding her that a good housewife would do all this long before prime, the husband resolves they exchange tasks next day.

> 'To morow with my lade to the plowe thou shalt gone;
> And I wylbe howsewyfe, and kype owr howse at home,
> And take myn ese as thou hast done, by God and Seint John.'

Even after this insult, the wife volunteers to get up earlier and leave things ready, and the husband does prepare the animals for her. She starts giving him instructions about steeping the meat, childcare, the malt kiln, the geese and so on, and is cut short:

> 'Dame' seid the goodmane, 'hy the to the plowe,
> Teche me no more howsewyfre, for I can i-nowe.'[37]

The poet tells us they were busy all day, but the version breaks off before we hear how they got on. Even women's daily chores were interrupted by the unforeseeable but inevitable emergencies which beset all those who look after small children, or sick or elderly persons, and were still further disrupted by animal intrusions: the penned getting out, or the fenced-out breaking in. On top of all this, the wife was often carrying out this labour pregnant or nursing, more of the time than one would suspect from the size of the family successfully reared, since child mortality was high. Razi estimated the mean number of offspring of rich tenants at

Halesowen 1270–1349 as just over 3.5, of middling peasants around 2.2, of poor peasants just over 1.6, but the calculations are problematic.[38]

One should not regard medieval country housewives or their adolescent daughters as economically unproductive simply because they were not regularly employed by an external employer and in receipt of wages. In unpaid works in the home or holding women 'earned' because they performed necessary tasks in families which could not afford to 'pay' others to do them. The wife in the 'Ballad of a Tyrannical Husband' makes precisely this point:

> 'Yefe a pece off lenyn and wolen I make onys a yere,
> For to clothe owre self and owr cheldren in fere;
> Elles we shold go to the market, and by het ful deer.'

If the family unit also had other activities such as weaving, or baking or brewing beyond home consumption, for sale, then wives and daughters who spun yarn, or carded wool, or darned loose threads in, or roasted the malt, or even ran round the village selling the pies, all used their labour productively, though they were not individually 'paid'. However, some of these women did earn real money in piecework rates for extra labour hired at harvest time. Extra harvestworkers had to be fed, and among the temporary cooks and baking staff on New College's Hornchurch estate in Essex, one woman was paid to disembowel capons for the harvest, and another washed the napkins and other cloths used by the cooks and harvesters.[39] This might be a nice little earner for six to ten weeks.

Where rural women were in regular paid employment, how did their wages correspond to men's? In the thirteenth century Walter of Henley advised employment of a woman to tend animals, sift and winnow, since her wage would be lower than a man's. But as much of the work done was different, it is difficult to compare wage rates: the dairyworker's 6*s* a year in 1388 corresponded to swineherds' and ploughmen's rates, while carters and shepherds got 10*s* a year. Certainly in harvestwork after the Black Death there seems to have been parity of pay for the same job, regardless of sex.[40]

The keeping of servants penetrated well down the social strata, and the unfortunate skivvies had to be worth their keep. The

[71]

proportion of servants in rural areas was lower than in towns: Goldberg assesses servants as forming 20 to 30 per cent of urban poll tax payers, but only 10 per cent of rural Rutland's in 1377. More of the artisan household's children, especially the girls, remained in those households in the countryside, however, in preference to employing servants.[41]

Childhood and adolescence spent at home, or in domestic service, provided both daughters and servants with the basic skills for coping with their own domestic roles later. Hanawalt argues that most rural women married, having little long-term alternative.[42] The inadequate registration of marriage is a failure of record. The parish register was only introduced in 1538, and early survival is somewhat hit and miss. Merchet fines only ever applied to the villein population, and however completely they may have been collected in earlier periods, by the time court records become plentiful the incidence of merchet is often surprisingly low. At Wakefield there were only nine recorded payments over the 1348–50 rolls, and at Halesowen Razi observed 202 merchet payments in the years between 1293 and 1348, fifty-six or seven between 1349 and 1385/6 (his figures for both totals and years covered are discrepant), and only one payment between 1386 and 1400.[43] But thirteenth-century confessors' handbooks show parish clergy taking sexuality and marriage seriously for all elements in the population: marriage was clearly an institution for villeins and free socagers as for their superiors.[44]

Outside of domestic labour and agricultural work, women apparently did most of the brewing in medieval England. Brewing was a frequent activity because ale did not keep well before hops were introduced in the late fourteenth century. The scale of operations varied from merely selling the excess over home needs, to brewing regularly for retail sale. The 'Tyrannical Husband' tells his wife she need not bake or brew more than once a fortnight, but this is thought to be a late fifteenth-century or early sixteenth-century source. Women's brewing activity is well recorded because of the fines for breach of the national regulatory assize of ale recorded regularly in manor court records. However, the distribution of brewing offences between the sexes varies considerably between manors and it is likely this may reflect different procedural and recording conventions as well as different brewing practices. At Alrewas (Staffs.) there was no five-year period between

1331 and 1375 in which more than 33 per cent of those presented for brewing offences was female. At Wakefield between 1348 and 1350 brewing was almost entirely a female preserve, only a handful of men being presented for it. A further procedural and recording difference is that at Wakefield these fines arose from the twice-yearly tourns, but at Brigstock and Alrewas amercements arose in the normal three-weekly court. Of the 600 women identified in the Wakefield Court Rolls 1348–50, 185 were there for brewing offences. The fact that the women were often identified as the unnamed 'wife of' a named male may suggest, however, that the court would hold him responsible for paying amercements: 122 of the Wakefield brewsters were recorded without their own forenames. When men appear to brew, it may be they were only paying their wives' fines. On the other hand, Goldberg has argued that many of those identified as the wife (*uxor*) of a person were really his widow.[45] It certainly appears that most brewsters were married or widowed, probably only an established household would have the capital and resources to invest in sufficient equipment to trade regularly. A single woman would be unlikely to manage to set herself up, but an already equipped widow could of course carry on brewing.

Evidence of rural women's involvement in other trades is scarce. Baking on a large scale required more expensive equipment. At Havering (Essex), M. K. McIntosh found two-thirds of married craftswomen were wives of men who farmed, and concluded that women's craftwork was not just a side-effect of their husband's involvement in such activities.[46] However, it is likely that wives and children contributed to the textile industry in those parts of the country where farming and textile work were combined, for example the Calder valley (W. R. Yorks.); while in Derbyshire, cloth, lead and quarrying activities were developed alongside an agrarian base. The labour laws of 1349–51 enforcing wages at pre-plague rates and forbidding contract workers to leave their employment prematurely, created new offences. These can be followed up in the Wakefield court rolls: the tourn at Halifax in June 1352 saw five vills present workers for refusing to serve in their own neighbourhood, or seeking work outside; three of the presentments included women. The rolls of the justices of the peace are, however, a better countrywide source for this kind of offence: Bertha Putnam's *Yorkshire Sessions of the Peace 1361–64* reveal women presented for labour offences as servants, reapers, spinsters and weavers.[47]

Women as members of the manorial community

It was as members of their communities that medieval countrywomen were most seriously disadvantaged. Positions of authority excluded them completely. Although they did most of the brewing, men were almost always the aletasters. Women were never reeves, and from Wakefield evidence it seems women holders of land liable to this service had to pay a male deputy. They were not foresters, woodwards or haywards. In medieval conditions there were good reasons for the male monopoly of these offices, and little sign of female grievance about the situation, but the outcome for women was that they never, in their own right, penetrated the manorial elites, those groups of active office holders and mutual pledges identifiable from the records. In some places, and on certain conditions, women were allowed to stand as pledges, but this remained rare whereas it was a normal contribution to community life for men making their way in the social hierarchy of the manor, until it died out in the late fourteenth and fifteenth centuries. When Amabel of Bootham was sued for 10s as a pledge in Halifax in 1298, she argued that she could not be a pledge for anyone while her husband was alive. The plaintiff was fined 6d for false claim because it appeared that the liability was incurred during the lifetime of Amabel's husband.[48] Women apparently could be pledges when widowed or single, but not while married.

Women were never sworn as jurors of presentment or to resolve the justice of a case, and jurorship was therefore another key communal activity where women had no place. They were only called together as a jury when it was necessary to summon a jury of matrons to examine and report on the condition of a woman who pleaded pregnancy as a side issue to judicial proceedings. They were not included in the frankpledge tithings because they were seen as legal dependants within their households. Nor were they acceptable as compurgators or fellow oath helpers. A Wakefield plaintiff argued in 1285 that the court should proceed to judgment because the widowed defendant had waged her law with women, and ultimately she was to be distrained until she satisfied the plaintiff, as she could not find pledges.[49]

Women might become court suitors, through holding land burdened with suit. Their sex did not alter the obligation. In October 1349 Agnes de Bretton essoined of common suit at Wakefield along with three men, all in apparently the same way. In September 1348 Agnes de Dronsfield paid 18*d* fine for respite of suit for the year, and 12*d* for the same in 1349; that payment was the same as Thomas Culpon paid for a year's respite in October 1349.[50] But as they were not normally going to become jurors or pledges, women's participation was restricted. Pollock and Maitland summed up the situation clearly enough: 'private law with few exceptions puts women on a par with men, public law gives a woman no rights and extracts from her no duties save that of paying taxes and performing such services as can be performed by deputy'.[51] Ninety years later this distinction is upheld by Bennett as the concept of private wives and public husbands.[52] Brigstock's local politics were a male affair, as everywhere else.

Office was burdensome and it is unlikely that many women on the manor coveted it. Admittedly if they did, they did not get it. A recent attempt to level them up by suggesting that 'informal influence' can be significantly powerful as well as 'sanctioned authority' does not seem very convincing.[53] If exclusion from office had been women's only disadvantage their 'second-class citizenship' might not have felt too restricting. But Bennett finds that in Brigstock the custom of the manor followed the common law in limiting women's contractual capabilities, and she feels that they were further disadvantaged in always depending on male attorneys, essoiners, pledges and compurgators, for whom they could not reciprocate. Marriage increased the gap between the sexes, for the married woman, *feme covert*, lost independence to her husband, while marriage (reinforced by her assets) increased his chances of local office and respect.[54] This is of course a contrast of husband and wife, rather than male and female *per se*. Widowhood brought the wife out into the world again.

Because women were restricted in their public role, there is little evidence of their activities in the community. The patterns of association in pledging which can tell us what circles menfolk moved in are just not there for women. But they lived in the community, none the less, and perhaps were not as confined to the house, or as dominated by their husbands, as earlier historians assumed. Britton considers that Broughton (Hunts.) wives were by no means wards of their husbands in landholding, business affairs and in the home.[55] They held land and pursued legal pleas. Opinions differ as to whether they got an impartially fair deal in court as land-holders, or as plaintiffs and defendants. Bennett argues that at Brig-stock suing for male violence seems discounted or disregarded; at Wakefield in 1348–50 thirteen occasions when women raised hue and cry (the outcry to pursue an offender) on men led in nine instances to the amercement of the men, and only in four to the amercement of the woman for unjust raising of the hue. In civil litigation there in the same period eighty-nine women appeared as plaintiffs, only ten jointly with other persons. Of the cases which can be followed to a conclusion in the rolls, ten plaintiffs failed to prosecute, and six were adjudged to have made false claim, but some fifty-six successes are recorded in different ways. Of eighty-five female defendants (thirty-five jointly with others), forty-four lost cases or admitted defeat, ten were saved by the plaintiff failing to prosecute, and fourteen were definitely successful.[56]

Bennett considers non-householding men were nearer to women in status, and householding women most nearly emulated men. This indicates some room for manoeuvre in status, the variable being a gender-neutral quality: householding (in practice, of course, more frequently male). Householding women might be pledges for members of their households, even for male servants. For example at Wakefield, Juliana, widow of Richard Pykard, pledged for Alkoc, her husband's servant.[57] Widows were often householders and may have been quite a powerful sector of society. Peter Franklin re-minds us they were a substantial proportion of the tenantry and not inactive; he believes widows played a significant role in peas-ant movements, taking part in male-led labour offences, refusals of service, badly done services, and so on.[58]

Women were born into families and married into others. If they are found acting with siblings or inlaws it is not surprising and shows no startling initiative. Godparents could offer alternative association but it is rare to be able to identify them for these levels of society. Women must have communicated with other, unrelated members of society: they were seen by men as particularly prone to gossip.[59] Perhaps servanthood had some significance in social-ising medieval women. Female servants entered others' homes, and had to adapt to them and make what new friends they could. The employer's family had to take in the newcomer and train her in its ways and wants. Girls may only have remained in service until they married, but they might change employer in the meantime. Girls from rural families might migrate to nearby towns in search of domestic or other work. However, there was more mobility than used to be thought on manors too, which the lords tried to rein in after the Black Death. That the wanderers included women was frequent enough for the lords to be concerned to chase them for merchet.

One perhaps surprising service to the community that some women performed was moneylending. Rodney Hilton described peasant women's activities as moneylenders in their communities as 'a badly documented element in medieval village society'.[60] Lending at interest was usury, frowned on by the medieval church and condemned in the public utterances even of the business world. In the crisis years of the early fourteenth century at Wakefield, in 1316, William son of Richard of the Haghe was amerced 40*d* because he lent 20*s* to Alice the Stinter, taking every week 10*d* in usury. The APR on this sum works out at 216 per cent.[61] Lending lurks in court rolls in unjust detentions and recognised debts, though occasionally the noun *mutuum*, a loan, is used. In May 1350 at Brighouse (W. R. Yorks.) Thomas Gilleson admitted detaining 2*s* 2*d* from Margaret daughter of Ellen from a loan, and was to satisfy and was amerced 2*d*. Here was a man borrowing from a woman. Some of the lenders were widows, as were some of the borrowers, which seems the less surprising, since one might expect their needs to be more acute. However, the degree of freedom married women had to enter contracts was restricted, and making loans in their own right during their husbands' lifetimes was probably not strictly possible. It certainly appears, however, that some women were agents of their husbands, in both lending and borrowing. The widow Margery Gunne was accused of detaining 27*s* 3*d* from Robert Wolf which he had lent her through his wife on several occasions: the inquiry resolved that she was detaining 20*s* from Robert, but it was a debt of her husband's.[62]

Women's activity in the community was not always to the community's advantage. In her study of the female felon in fourteenth-century England, Hanawalt worked out from gaol delivery records that there was 1 woman for every 9 men (the equivalent figure in the 1970s was 1 to 7.4). Were women less criminal or less often caught? The fact that 83.7 per cent of them were acquitted, compared to 70.3 per cent of the men, suggests the female alleged felon was treated more leniently. In 64.4 per cent of the homicide cases the woman had another person with her, and in 84.2 per cent of the robberies; in over half the homicides and over 80 per cent of the robberies the associates were male. Mostly women committed property crimes, and were hauled up for larceny, burglary or receiving. In Hanawalt's study they committed 12 per cent of the burglaries (compared with 3.3 per cent in the 1970s), and in nearly half the cases they had accomplices, usually male. They specialised in taking foodstuffs, livestock and household goods.[63] Hanawalt's sources are not restricted to country people but it is likely many of the felons were of such a group. Indeed, the lesser criminalities in manor court rolls (lesser because the jurisdiction was more limited) tell a similar picture. Foodstuffs, cloth and clothing were most commonly taken at Wakefield in the years 1274–1313, but almost all the stealing involved food in 1315–17.[64] Assessing the proportion of women who were victims is less clear cut, since the charge may often content itself with words such as 'took from the house of' a named male, even a deceased one, 'the late William Bothes'. When a woman is named as the victim it is more likely that she is a widow or unmarried. One seems to have been a single woman living in her father's house: Joan daughter of Thomas of Tothill successfully accused Richard del Rode of coming to Thomas's house in Fixby and burgling his chamber, but breaking her coffer and carrying off jewels, a silk garment and other valuables. This thief was hanged.[65] But women may have been more involved than they appear, with debts and damages actually due to them appearing in the records as though only a matter between their husbands.

One of the vilest crimes against a woman is rape. Later medieval law had difficulty in distinguishing ravishment (abduction) from rape (forcible intercourse), but Anglo-Saxon law had been quite definite about the offence of 'lying with' a woman. Ravishment was defined as a felony in 1285.[66] In 1363 in the East Riding peace sessions the presenting jurors said Elias Warner of Malton had lain with Ellen Katemayden of Malton at Norton against her will, assaulted her, and so injured or crushed her – the verb is *conculcare*, to tread under foot, bruise by treading, which corresponds pretty closely with the modern phrase 'to put the boot in' – that she died within three days. However, another jury found him not guilty. In 1363 jurors of Langbaurgh wapentake (N. R. Yorks.) presented John son of Thomas clerk of Wilton for taking Robert Penok's wife Alice at Lackenby and beating, wounding and ill-treating her, and crushing her 'wishing to have raped her in the field there'; then he beat, wounded and ill-treated Alice wife of John Smith of Lackenby when she went to Alice Penok's aid. He eventually paid fines of 20*d* for each of these offences.[67]

Conclusions

Clarification of what it really meant to be a woman in rural England in the Middle Ages has gained considerably in recent years from the application of anthropological and social science techniques to the evidence, particularly from court rolls. The picture which the legal historians painted was very much the letter of the law, and the portrait presented by the earlier social and economic historians was not critical enough. In her writings on medieval women, Eileen Power's work is rather less substantiated than is now required. Her perspective is still accepted, but the filling out of it post-humously edited by her husband Michael Postan in 1975 lacks buttressing illustrations. The contrast of biological and work rhythms in the sexes has most obvious applicability in rural soci-ety where hard physical work was the order of the day for both sexes. As the Tyrannical Husband's wife summed it up:

'I ame as bessy as I may in every [yere].'

Notes

1 P. J. P. Goldberg, *Women, Work and Life Cycle in a Medieval Economy: women in York and Yorkshire c. 1300–1520*, Oxford, 1992, p. 343.
2 H. M. Jewell (ed.), *Court Rolls of the Manor of Wakefield 1348 to 1350*, Yorkshire Archaeological Society, Wakefield Court Roll Series, II, 1981, pp. 177, 245, 34, 183, 260.
3 P. Franklin, 'Peasant widows' "Liberation" and remarriage before Black Death', *Economic History Review*, 2nd series, XXXIX, 2, 1986, p. 188.

4   Paraphrased from *Pierce the Ploughman's Crede*, ed. W. W. Skeat, Early English Text Society, London, 1867, pp. 16–17.

5   Chaucer, 'Canterbury Tales', *The Riverside Chaucer*, ed. L. D. Benson, Oxford, 1988, p. 253.

6   Paraphrased from *Piers Plowman by William Langland: an edition of the C text*, ed. D. Pearsall, London, 1981, p. 164.

7   A. C. Cawley (ed.), *Everyman and Medieval Miracle Plays*, London, 1967, pp. 92, 96.

8   'Ballad of a Tyrannical Husband', in *Reliquiae Antiquae*, ed. T. Wright and J. O. Halliwell, II, London, 1843 reprinted 1966, pp. 196–7.

9   Z. Razi, *Life, Marriage and Death in a Medieval Parish: economy, society and demography in Halesowen, 1270–1400*, Cambridge, 1980, p. 10.

10 G. C. Homans, *English Villagers of the Thirteenth Century*, New York, 1975, p. 110.

11 J. Z. Titow, *English Rural Society, 1200–1350*, London, 1969, p. 187.

12 R. M. Smith, 'Women's property rights under customary law: some developments in the thirteenth and fourteenth centuries', *Transactions of the Royal Historical Society*, 5th series, XXXVI, 1986, p. 167.

13 R. J. Faith, 'Peasant families and inheritance customs in medieval England', *Agricultural History Review*, xiv, 1966, p. 91; J. Ravensdale, 'Population changes and the transfer of customary land on a Cambridgeshire manor in the fourteenth century', in R. M. Smith (ed.), *Land, Kinship and Life Cycle*, Cambridge, 1984, p. 197; J. M. Bennett, *Women in the Medieval English Countryside: gender and household in Brigstock before the plague*, Oxford, 1987, p. 163.

14 Smith, 'Women's property rights', p. 173.

15 Jewell, *Wakefield Court Rolls*, pp. 106, 243, 253.

16 E. Power, *Medieval Women*, ed. M. M. Postan, Cambridge, 1975, p. 71; J. A. Raftis, *Tenure and Mobility: studies in the social history of the medieval English village*, Toronto, 1964, p. 40.

17 Titow, *Rural Society*, pp. 148–50.

18 J. C. Russell, 'Demographic limitations of the Spalding serf lists', *Economic History Review*, 2nd series, XV, 1, 1962, p. 143.

19 G. C. Coulton, *The Medieval Village*, Cambridge, 1925, p. 99.

20 P. R. Hyams, *King, Lords and Peasants in Medieval England*, Oxford, 1980, p. 187; E. Ennen, *The Medieval Woman*, trsl. E. Jephcott, Oxford, 1989, p. 92, sees little evidence anywhere for this 'law of the first night', the supposed right of the feudal lord to deflower his tenants' brides.

21 J. M. Bennett, 'Medieval Peasant Marriage: an examination of

marriage licence fines in *Liber Gersumarum*', in J. A. Raftis (ed.), *Pathways to Medieval Peasants*, Toronto, 1981, pp. 197, 205.

22 W. P. Baildon, *Court Rolls of the Manor of Wakefield*, II, Yorkshire Archaeological Society Record Series, XXXVI, 1906, p. xix.

23 L. R. Poos and R. M. Smith, '"Legal windows onto historical populations"? recent research on demography and the manor court in medieval England', *Law and History Review*, II, 1984, pp. 144–8; Smith, 'Women's property rights', pp. 170–2; Razi, *Halesowen*, p. 132.

24 Razi, *Halesowen*, p. 64; for criticism see Poos and Smith, 'Legal windows', pp. 148–50.

25 T. North, 'Legerwite in the thirteenth and fourteenth centuries', *Past and Present*, 111, 1986, pp. 7–8.

26 Razi, *Halesowen*, p. 69.

27 S. J. Stratford, 'Women before the customary courts: the manor of Wakefield, 1274–1352', M.A. thesis, University of York, 1994, pp. 42–5.

28 Power, *Medieval Women*, p. 71.

29 Goldberg, *Women Work and Life Cycle*, pp. 204–15, is an accessible summary of the arguments.

30 *Ibid.*, pp. 244–50.

31 Razi, *Halesowen*, pp. 63, 137; Poos and Smith, 'Legal windows', pp. 144–5.

32 H. E. Hallam, 'Some thirteenth-century censuses', *Economic History Review*, 2nd series, X, 1958, p. 353; Titow, *Rural Society*, pp. 83–93.

33 C. and K. Sisam (eds.), *Oxford Book of Medieval English Verse*, Oxford, 1970, p. 521.

34 B. A. Hanawalt, *The Ties that Bound: peasant families in medieval England*, Oxford, 1986, pp. 145–6; Goldberg, 'The public and the private: women in the pre-plague economy', in *Thirteenth-Century England*, III, ed. P. R. Coss and S. D. Lloyd, Woodbridge, 1991, pp. 75–81.

35 M. Atkin and K. Tompkins, *Revealing Lost Villages: Wharram Percy*, London, 1986, p. 24.

36 B. Hanawalt, 'Peasant women's contribution to the home economy in late medieval England', in *Women and Work in Pre-Industrial Europe*, ed. B. A. Hanawalt, Bloomington, 1986, p. 17.

37 'Ballad of a Tyrannical Husband', pp. 197–8.

38 Razi, *Halesowen*, p. 75; Poos and Smith, 'Legal windows', pp. 137–9.

39 M. K. McIntosh, *Autonomy and Community: the Royal Manor of Havering, 1200–1500*, Cambridge, 1986, p. 149.

40 S. Shahar, *The Fourth Estate: a history of women in the middle ages*, trsl. C. Galai, London, 1983, p. 242; S. A. C. Penn, 'Female wage-

earners in late fourteenth-century England', *Agricultural History Review*, XXXV, 1987, pp. 9–10.

41 Goldberg, *Women, Work and Life Cycle*, pp. 159, 166–8.
42 Hanawalt, 'Peasant women's contribution', p. 4.
43 Razi, *Halesowen*, pp. 48, 132–3, 138.
44 M. M. Sheehan, 'Theory and practice: the marriage of the unfree and the poor in medieval society', *Medieval Studies*, L, 1988, pp. 484–5.
45 H. Graham, ' "A Woman's Work …": labour and gender in the late medieval countryside', in *Woman is a Worthy Wight: women in English society c. 1200–1500*, ed. P. J. P. Goldberg, Stroud, 1992, pp. 136–44; H. M. Jewell, 'Women at the courts of the manor of Wakefield, 1348–50', *Northern History*, XXVI, 1990, p. 61; Goldberg, 'Female labour, service and marriage in the late medieval urban north', *Northern History*, XXII, 1986, p. 30.
46 McIntosh, *Havering*, p. 174.
47 C. M. Fraser, Introduction to *The Court Rolls of the Manor of Wakefield 1350–2*, ed. M. Habberjam, M. O'Regan and B. Hale, Wakefield Court Roll Series, VI, 1987, pp. xv–xvi; B. H. Putnam (ed.), *Yorkshire Sessions of the Peace 1361–64*, Yorkshire Archaeological Society, Record Series, C, 1939, especially pp. 50–5, 58–9, 69–72. One group of recalcitrants is classed as 'whelespinners', p. 76.
48 Baildon, *Wakefield Court Rolls*, II, p. 36.
49 *Ibid.*, I, pp. 194, 212.
50 Jewell, *Wakefield Court Rolls*, pp. 146, 3, 155.
51 F. Pollock and F. W. Maitland, *History of English Law*, 2nd edition, reissued Cambridge, 1968, I, p. 482.
52 Bennett, *Brigstock*, pp. 6, 22.
53 M. Erler and M. Kowaleski (eds.), *Women and Power in the Middle Ages*, Athens, Gia and London, 1988, p. 2.
54 Bennett, *Brigstock*, pp. 104–5.
55 E. Britton, *The Community of the Vill: a study in the history of the family and village life in fourteenth-century England*, Toronto, 1977, p. 33.
56 Bennett, *Brigstock*, pp. 26–7; Jewell, 'Courts', pp. 66, 73–4.
57 Baildon, *Wakefield Court Rolls*, I, p. 140.
58 Franklin, 'Widows' "Liberation" ', p. 196.
59 See, e.g. R. T. Davies (ed.), *Medieval English Lyrics*, London, 1963, nos 96, 123.
60 R. H. Hilton, *The English Peasantry in the Later Middle Ages*, Oxford, 1975, p. 103.
61 Jewell, 'Courts', p. 77.
62 Jewell, *Wakefield Court Rolls*, II, pp. 250, 152, 154, 161.
63 Hanawalt, 'The female felon in fourteenth-century England', *Viator*,

5, 1974, reprinted in S. M. Stuard (ed.), *Women in Medieval Society*, Philadelphia, 1976, pp. 126–33.

64 Stratford, thesis, pp. 68–70.

65 *Wakefield Court Rolls, 1315–17*, ed. J. Lister, Yorkshire Archaeological Society, Record Series, LXXVIII, 1930, p. 150; *1331–3*, ed. S. S. Walker, Yorkshire Archaeological Society, Wakefield Court Rolls Series, iii, 1983, p. 202.

66 S. S. Walker, 'Punishing convicted ravishers: statutory strictures and actual practice in thirteenth- and fourteenth-century England', *Journal of Medieval History*, XIII, 3, 1987, p. 237; Welsh law, preserving fossilised regulations, was clear about rape, see D. Jenkins and M. E. Owen (eds.), *The Welsh Law of Women*, Cardiff, 1980, p. 139.

67 B. H. Putnam, *Yorkshire Sessions of the Peace*, pp. 46, 48, 109, 117.

3

Women in medieval urban communities

About 10 per cent of the medieval English population lived in towns, and the group examined in this chapter is defined by residence alone. It comprises all women whose habitual residence was in a town, deliberately excluding women of the landholding class who might have town houses and connections but were not essentially town people. The women in focus in this chapter range from members of aldermanic families to their humblest servants and suppliers, and the beggars at their doors. As shown above, in chapter 2, the sex ratio in towns, at any rate after the plague, seems from poll tax evidence to have been lower than in the countryside, but the imbalance is not great, nor necessarily constant. In the late fourteenth century it may particularly reflect the attraction of female labour to towns in a time of labour shortage.[1]

Medieval townspeople embraced a wide range of wealth and poverty, compacted together in close proximity with startling contrasts in comfort and squalor. Within the urban community there were localised pockets of prosperity and impoverishment, richer and poorer parishes, specialised concentrations of craftworkers. However, though the environment may have been pleasanter or more squalid in different quarters of even a small town, fire and disease were great equalisers, and the physical as well as the economic health of the community was a unifying interest and a constant preoccupation of each generation of 'City Fathers'. (The gender-specific term is used here deliberately, for all urban government and administration was firmly in male hands, which is strongly reflected in the available sources.)

Contemporary sources for the study of urban women include court records, custumals, tax records and rentals, gild records and wills. The court records include borough court rolls and ecclesiastical cause papers, the tax records include the particularly valuable poll taxes of 1377–81, the gild records include ordinances, and with them it is sensible to consider admissions to the freedom of the borough. Useful discussions of these sources may be found at the end of the Introduction to Goldberg's *Women, Work and Life Cycle*, and in Maryanne Kowaleski's article 'The history of urban families in medieval England' (in the *Journal of Medieval History*, xiv, 2, 1988). There is rather less to be gained in the urban sphere from art and literature, which suggests that the patrons of these arts did not find artisans and traders an attractive subject.

In borough court records women's trading activities do emerge quite prominently, but, as Goldberg remarks, only when the women fall on the wrong side of borough law, for example by forestalling and regrating.[2] Furthermore, where a married woman was not trading as *feme sole*, the record may name her husband when the activity was really hers. Custumals, revealing a great variety of customs in different places, are most useful for indicating the differences between burgage and manorial tenures, affecting women as heiresses and widows. The poll tax records, being concerned with men and women over a varying minimum age – 14 in 1377, 16 in 1379, 15 in 1380–1 – are more informative than any taxation records tied to heads of households, which, like rentals and leasebooks, reflect the male dominance in householding.

Gild records are particularly informative for showing the contrast between women's full participation in the social, charitable and religious aspects of gild membership, and more limited participation in the trade practices' side. Gilds which were purely socio-religious accepted their 'bretheren and sisteren' on equal terms and provided the same type of social security, small subsistence allowances and funeral provisions, for both sexes. Gilds of merchants and craftsmen, however, though they might well on their charitable and religious wing concern themselves with the souls, and even with the bodies, of their brethren's wives and widows and orphans, were sometimes restrictive in the participation they allowed females in the husband's or father's livelihood. Goldberg senses an 'observed chronology of gild regulation against women', born of economic recession, from the mid-fifteenth century. He sees little evidence before then of actual prejudice against women learning or engaging in particular crafts or trades, but calls attention to the Coventry Weavers' ruling of 1453, which regarded a master setting 'his wyffe or his doughter or ony woman servaunt to weyve in the brode loom' as 'a geyn all goode order and honeste'.[3] The observation of a chronological significance is worth noting, but precision is often lacking since some gild ordinances may have been already in operation before the earliest date they are evidenced. Furthermore, even in times apparently more 'generously' disposed towards women, there were still gild restrictions on gender lines, for the rules allowing the participation of wives, daughters and sometimes female servants of craft members, did not allow other women to enter the trade.

Wills of urban women are plentiful and informative. Well over 600 women's wills, for example, are extant fom York alone before 1500, and Caroline Barron has recently engagingly described some London widows' wills as 'verbose, bossy, disorganised, affectionate and anecdotal'. Both Goldberg and Barron have used wills as evidence of female networks.[4]

Very few urban archives contain documentation earlier than 1300 and municipal records only become really full in the sixteenth century. Historians naturally focus their researches on specific places which have a good run of a particular type of record, so the same towns provide their examples – London (which has to be accepted as unique), York, Coventry, Southampton, Bristol, Exeter and Norwich. These places were towns of first rank; York, Exeter and Norwich were positively regional capitals, certainly rather more than county towns. Southampton and Bristol were developing as national ports. Coventry was a manufacturing and commercial centre. Urban centres such as these had, as appropriate, a traditional place in the county administration and visitations of itinerant justices, developing bureaucracies of marketing controls and revenue collection, sometimes defence priorities, and sometimes importance as ecclesiastical centres – as the seat of a bishopric, or the site of an important collegiate institution or dominating monastery, or a place with all four mendicant orders active. Some twenty-seven towns, which were then the principal Jewish centres in the country, had *archae* (chirograph chests) for the registration of Jewish debts in the thirteenth century, though this number had shrunk before the expulsion of the Jews in 1290.[5] The existence of some or all of these variables affected the community structure and atmosphere.

Towns of lesser ranking are rather more difficult to separate distinctly from overgrown villages – and the translation of 'vill' as 'township' underlines the lack of distinctiveness. Nevertheless, Rodney Hilton has made a strong case for the functional differentiation of even small towns of under 500 inhabitants from the agricultural hinterland, with what he called the 'tempo of the market' replacing the agricultural rhythms of the villages.[6]

Towns may indeed be very generally defined as concentrations of people living not primarily by agriculture. The inhabitants lived by servicing wider communities with credit and trading facilities, craftwork and manufacture, and professional skills, for example the services of lawyers and scriveners. Goldberg suggests from poll tax returns that about 20 per cent of the working population was occupied in victualling, and a further 60 per cent in leather, textile, clothing, mercantile and metal trades.[7] A town is thus best defined in relation to economic function, but it was also a concentration of population at a higher physical density than that normally found in the countryside. The legal distinction focuses round borough status, and one test of a borough is a charter, from the king or a secular or ecclesiastical lord. Because of the strong legal input into early academic history, historians have tended to contrast borough and manor, rather than simply urban and rural communities. Borough history as such need now hardly attract attention in our pursuit of urban women, beyond acknowledging its contribution in the collection and display of comparative borough charters and customs, which can form a useful introduction to understanding the tenure of burgage plots, and their inheritance, mortgage, sale and gift. From extracts from charters and written borough custumals one may learn roughly what was general and what was exceptional in borough practices, and depending on the level of judicial activity granted and exercised locally, one may locate surviving court records illustrating these practices. At Exeter, for example, the inheritance laws were favourable to women and they could inherit on equal terms with men, regardless of marital status. Widows controlled the property and chattels formerly shared with their husbands. Trading wives there could avail themselves of *feme sole* status.[8]

Mary Bateson's subsection on 'Husband and wife' in the seigniorial and family law section of her *Borough Customs* volume II (1906) deserves to be better known, but for the most part urban women did not attract historians' attention until the First World War. Annie Abram's article 'Women traders in medieval London' in the *Economic Journal* (xxvi, 1916) was the first published investigation of the subject, directly related to the contemporary entry of women, in response to the demands of war, into trades usually carried on by men. This was rapidly followed by Alice Clark's *Working Life of Women in the Seventeenth Century* (1919), which is relevant because the contrast between medieval and early modern situations (and where the division should be drawn) is still a central issue.[9] No great progress had been made thereafter when Marian Dale wrote her article on the fifteenth-century London silkwomen, 'to illustrate the usual practices among female participants in trade and industry at this time, and to show that although this mistery was not recognized as a definite gild, it was pursued on the lines of the craft gilds of male workers'.[10] When Sylvia Thrupp wrote *The Merchant Class of Medieval London* in 1948, she gave four and a half pages specifically to 'The woman's role', though women do appear elsewhere in the book.

Recently there has been a wide broadening of the investigations to other cities, though Caroline Barron and her associates have also kept up the focus on London. Welcome variety comes from Diane Hutton's work on fourteenth-century Shrewsbury, Jeremy Goldberg's on women in the late medieval urban north, and Maryanne Kowaleski's on Exeter. Martha Howell's research on urban women on the Continent, in Leiden and Cologne, may also be beneficially considered here.

Women in trade

Before the Industrial Revolution and the shift to large-scale factory output, towns were more markedly centres of trade than of manufacture, and distinction between trade and manufacture was in any case unreal. The actual production was carried on in small domestic workshops, and goods were processed through a number of specialists rather than made from start to finish under one roof. The sales tended to be direct from the producer to the purchaser, and the retailing of items deliberately bought in for sale was a feature of the lower end of the market, the selling of items in small quantities that were beneath the attention of the more prosperous traders. In the contrast between town and country it is the woman trader who attracts the focus of attention, because it appears to be the career option which most distinguishes urban from rural women. Brewing apart (this in many cases being merely a sale of surplus domestic production), there were few trade opportunities for women of the countryside. But the towns were essentially trade centres, and the evidence shows clearly that women were involved.

The modern distinction between trade and manufacture is not appropriate to the Middle Ages, and the study of women as traders is also the study of them as manufacturers. Thus Dale's survey of the London silkwomen embraced the throwing of the yarn, the weaving of ribbons, laces and corses (unfinished banding for later embroidery), the making up of goods, and also the purchase of silk goods wholesale from Italian merchants, and the supply of silks, for example to the queen's household. A parliamentary petition in 1482 could take a united tone on behalf of 'men and women of the whole craft of silkwork', but in fact the craft brought together very diverse individuals from sizeable capitalists to the much poorer throwsters who probably worked in their own homes, either working others' material put out to them, or buying the raw material, preparing it and selling it on to the weavers. Throwing and weaving may have taken place under one roof in larger workshops. The only factor these various participants in the 'whole craft of silkwork' had in common was handling a particular product, and not surprisingly sometimes their interests, far from being united, were in conflict. Dale cited a case where a former mistress sued an ex-apprentice, who successfully petitioned the chancellor with a counter-claim.[11]

Given Dale's intention, it was relevant to show that the apprenticeship system followed the male pattern, being indentured, of seven years' duration, and with the usual kind of conditions binding the parties to mutually acceptable behaviour. It is interesting to learn that girls were apprenticed to London silkwomen from as far afield as Yorkshire and Warwickshire. In two examples cited by Dale, girls were apprenticed to both a husband and his wife, but to learn her craft.[12] A similar example cited by Barron shows a woman apprenticing her son to Robert Sampson, cordwainer, and Isabel his wife, tailoress, to learn her trade.[13] This is a more interesting example, since whereas the silk trade was monopolised by women, there were presumably plentiful male tailors to whom a boy could have been apprenticed, but his mother chose to attach him to a married woman.

Dale was also able to show that the silk craft involved capitalist women who could trade in large quantities, and that certainly some London silkwomen opted to operate sole (more in fact than are formally recorded as having so declared themselves), but others remained covert. Darcy's now lost custumal of London of the 1340s stated clearly:

> where a woman, *couverte de baron* [covered by her man, that is, married], follows a craft of her own in the city in which the husband does not intermeddle, such a woman shall be bound as a single woman as to all that concerns her craft.[14]

In this way a woman escaped the common law disadvantages of wifely status. As Barron sums it up: the married woman acting as *feme sole* 'enjoyed a measure of economic independence and could, in effect, run her own business, rent a shop, accumulate money (and debts), contribute to taxation and train her own apprentices and servants'.[15] The women who took up the advantage included embroideresses, clothweavers, upholsters and hucksters. Their husbands, of course, benefited by losing liability for their debts, which may have been the greater advantage in the eyes of the City Fathers. Worcester's 1467 ordinances spell it out:

> yf eny mans wyf becom dettor or plegge, or by or sylle eny chaffare or vitelle, or hyre eny house by hur lyf, she to answere to hym or hur that hath cause to sue, as a woman soole marchaunt; and that accion of dette be mayntend ayenst hur, to be conceyved aftr the custom of the seid cite, wtout nemyng hur housbond in the seid accyon.[16]

Dale concluded that the silkwomen followed the usual industrial and trade practices although not organised as a regular craft gild. She pointed out that without a gild, the craft lacked ordinances which would have effected quality control and supported a religious and social infrastructure. She tried to minimalise the significance of the lack of a gild by suggesting that regulations tending to standardise quality and price were inappropriate for silk manufacture – 'more of an art than a craft' – and that the participants' religious and social needs were satisfied by the gilds or companies to which their husbands belonged.[17] But this surely emphasises how households took status from the male. The silkwomen were an attractive focus, because their trade was both feminised and a luxury one, and their involvement in so prestigious a trade looked a promising opening for women. But the key point about the silkwomen is surely that their craft was not exercised in serious competition with men. (The reference to men in the 1482 petition Dale considered to be only to 'an occasional corse weaver'.[18]) Theirs was a craft largely consigned to women. So it cannot illustrate how women fared in the more usual situation of participating in trades or crafts where men were dominant in numbers and influence.

Goldberg's analysis of townswomen's occupations between *c.* 1300 and 1520 treats victualling trades first, as being those where women were most conspicuous. Retailing ale, bread, fish, poultry and dairy products was a female speciality, attested in records from places as far apart as Exeter, Norwich and York. Women were not, apparently, into butchery, but the making and selling of black puddings appear to have been women's work.[19] In turning next to textiles, Goldberg finds women were involved in all stages of the industry, but especially in the primary processes of spinning and carding. These tasks required little capital investment in equipment, and were paid at piece rates, a system 'ideally suited to the needs of domestic and family responsibilities'.[20] The York weavers' ordinances of 1400 forbade a woman (*mulier*) to work in the trade unless skilled. Wives and daughters of weavers certainly assisted, and many independent women weavers may have been weavers' widows. The York dyers' ordinances of 1472 refer to women workers, but in the undated ordinances in the 1376–1419 Memorandum Book they only allowed a widow to trade for one year after her husband's death, unless her servant, performing the craft for her, was enfranchised. An ordinance in the 1389 gild returns from the gild of fullers at Lincoln (a gild with 'brothers and sisters') reads: 'none of the craft shall work [that is, walk cloth] in the trough, and none shall work at the wooden bar with a woman, unless with the wife of a master or her handmaid'.[21] In the clothing trade, seamstresses were ubiquitous, many being unmarried and able to finance this low-capital investment craft; there were also women dressmakers, tailoresses, embroiderers and capmakers. At Exeter in 1531 tailors' widows were allowed to keep as many servants as they liked so long as they paid their full dues.[22] At a higher social level, women did market textiles. Of the

454 individuals dealing in cloth in the York aulnage (cloth duty) accounts of 1394–5, 113 were women, far higher than the 7 per cent so recorded at Winchester that year.[23]

It is perhaps more surprising that Goldberg finds women 'moderately active' in metal crafts, citing late fifteenth-century London blacksmiths' company accounts showing quarterage payments by female members. The York founders' ordinances of 1390 allowed members to instruct their wives and one master was allowed a second apprentice because he had no wife. Not surprisingly pin-making was the most feminised area in metalworking; more unusually, two enterprising London bell-founders' widows are known to have taken over their husbands' businesses.[24] In leatherworking, in London the skinners' craft was male dominated; however, William Penne's widow Matilda carried on his craft in the 1380s. The York curriers' ordinance of 1423–4 forbade the employment of women assistants other than wives, but whether this was a new imposition or old custom is not known. Women were rarely found in building, but were active in second-hand clothes dealing (uphalding) and tallow chandlery.[25]

Where there was employment for both sexes in trades, it is pretty clear that women generally had the less prestigious, lower paid and more 'domestic' tasks. In Shrewsbury Hutton finds the women in textile work preparing the raw material, while the men had the more prestigious finishing. In the retailing sector, women tended to be found in the occupations associated with domestic labour, and with selling low-priced goods in small quantities. Twenty-two of thirty-five regrators presented at the view of frankpledge in Shrewsbury in March 1400 were women, and it is Rose the Regrator who personifies the practice in *Piers Plowman*.[26] Regrating – buying in order to sell again quickly in the same locality, forcing up the price – is often associated with hucksters, that is hawkers and peddlars dealing in small wares, and the feminine *-ster* ending, as with brewster, kempster and spinster, suggests widespread female participation in this trading. In London half the women sued as *femes soles* among the original bills of the Mayor's Court in the fifteenth century were trading as hucksters.[27] Hucksters probably peddled in the surrounding countryside, and at Shrewsbury many of the regrators were apparently single women and from out of the town, so it is a moot point whether these traders were generally townspeople working outwards, or countryfolk merely dependent on towns for gathering supplies. In Exeter women were trading in poultry, dairy products, oats, salt, flour and ale, but the men controlled the dearer goods such as spices, and the skilled processing of bread and meat.[28]

Hutton considers that what she calls cheap female labour boosted the profits of the cloth export trade, but there is the age-old problem with comparative wage rates: were women paid less for the same job, or paid less because they only had access to the less remunerative employments? Did wage rates tend to lag behind in areas employing both sexes because of women's participation? There is more information about agricultural wages than urban ones. Christopher Dyer's work on *Standards of Living in the Later Middle Ages* offers little information on specifically urban female rates. He merely remarks that before 1349 women's and children's rates of pay were markedly below those of men (but does not give details), and that afterwards differentials narrowed to the benefit of female and child labour.[29]

As serious for women as low pay, and perhaps more divisive on gender lines, was the insecurity of work. It appears that gilds may have encouraged wives' work when trade was good, but discouraged it when times were bad. Sue Wright cites Bristol weavers' regulations in 1461 (a time of decline) and 1463 (a time of revival) to illustrate this point.[30] Moreover, as is now frequently recognised, it was women who had to redirect their skills in ways not generally expected of men. Goldberg sums it up: 'herein lies a particular point of gender-difference in terms of work identity. Whereas a man might follow the same trade all his active life, a woman might have to change hers on leaving service, on marriage, and even after marriage.'[31] Abram's interpretation of the 1363 Artificers' Act that it put women in a better position than men by ordering men to keep to one trade, but leaving women to follow as many as they chose, now looks naive.[32] In fact it surely reflects the contemporary perspective that women's work was comparatively casual and amateur, and that they would have to be the flexible workers in any marriage partnership, turning their hands to different trades as opportunity arose or desperation drove. Naturally a jill-of-all-trades was likely to be offering herself at the unskilled or less skilled end of the market. This is borne out at Exeter, where Kowaleski finds women worked intermittently whereas men stuck at one trade, and women more often practised more than one trade, reflecting their marginal and low position in the workforce.[33]

It is clear that women could be individually paid-up members of both social and craft gilds, but the recorded numbers in specifically craft gilds are small. In 1418 thirty-nine women were among the 234 members of the London brewers' company.[34] Given the variety of ordinances about the assistance of wives and daughters, and provisions for widows carrying on trading, one suspects that many of the women members in their own right may have been widows of former members. Gild ordinances extend their charitable and pious work among wives and daughters: they are patently not expecting a situation where their benevolence would normally be expected to extend to the husbands of female members. Nevertheless, the already cited case of Isabel Sampson's apprentice shows a married woman following a trade different from her husband's, and fully enough recognised in it to take an apprentice.

Women's association with the gilds was more frequently alongside their husbands, working within gild regulation as the family of male gildsmen. As Hutton remarks, it is often 'impossible to distinguish between the paid work done by the craftsman and the unpaid labour of his family'.[35] The family unit was contributing to the household prosperity this way; it was usefully training younger members of the family, if only informally, and the wives were familiarising themselves with various aspects of the business which enabled them to carry on in widowhood.

Another very small class of urban women sometimes managed to carry on their husbands' businesses in widowhood: the Jewesses. Jews first took up residence in England in any significant numbers in the wake of the Norman Conquest. For some 200 years until their expulsion in 1290 the Jews were an urban phenomenon, but only reaching an estimated 4–5,000 in the early thirteenth century, the total Jewish population was never large. Barrie Dobson recently made the point that 'it is as a businesswoman that the English Jewess of the thirteenth century tends to be known to us at all'.[36] Cecil Roth commented that Jewesses played a significant part in economic life. 'Every roll of English Jewry mentions the names of women who contributed important sums to the Exchequer, not always the widows of dead financiers, but frequently wives or even spinsters in business on their own account.'[37] The Jewish women's judicial and social status compared very favourably with that of Christian Englishwomen, though they shared their menfolk's disadvantages as property of the king ('serfs of the royal chamber').[38]

Before moving on to women's domestic role in the urban family, it is worth glancing into the northern European situation. Recent study of women in north European cities has looked hard at the changes brought by the advent of more sophisticated methods of technology and distribution. In Leiden, Martha Howell concludes that women gained access to high-status work through the family, which provided training and opportunity, but they lost out as what she calls the 'family production unit' (characterised by its control over the economic resources of production) declined in the face of tightening rules under Leiden's *ambacht* (gild) system. In the fifteenth and sixteenth centuries middling women were driven into domesticity or low-status work. In Cologne there were specialised women's gilds, but these had no political power in the city, and the women of the gilds did not run them. In the traditional craft gilds women were increasingly excluded or restricted by the fifteenth century. As at Leiden, Cologne women lost out as the family production unit declined, and as work took on rhythms incompatible with family life. Howell suggests a general rise in women's legal status from 1200 to 1500 was a response to their need for legal capacities for the work they were doing, but after 1500 patriarchy restricted them.[39]

Domestic occupations of urban women

Medieval towns retained many rural characteristics, so the urban housewife should not be completely contrasted with her rural counterpart. With the burgesses' rights to pasture their beasts on Port Meadow or Town Field, and the complaints about 'swine going at large' rooting about in the streets, and what Thrupp called the custom of keeping poultry and saving a small stretch of the yard for a garden,[40] there must have been some overlap with the rural housewife's dairying and animal-tending activities. Nevertheless, for most urban housewives the environment was very different.

York's well-surviving walls bring home forcefully the small circuit of the defences and the sense of containedness which must have united those secure within. Such towns expanded by adding extra-mural suburbs running up to – or out from – the walls. The layout of the medieval towns is still clear in the centre of York, Chester, Norwich and Winchester. In these four cities streets were narrow and small parish churches numerous. The town housewife, therefore, generally lived in close proximity to her neighbours, and in cramped conditions. Space was at a premium, leading to the design of narrow-frontage properties, often with shops on the street front, and a house extending backwards, or even built sideways on to the street, and extending on the upper floors over the shops.

Towns had regular markets, the larger ones having specialist markets on different days of the week, in different places. The town housewife therefore knew where she could get particular provisions, regularly, only a few hundred yards from her home. The markets specialised mainly in raw materials – poultry, fish, butter. Butchery was generally ongoing in fixed shops, and often in a specific quarter or street, for butchery was a noisome trade with a disposal problem, and best kept contained. Any trade requiring the heating of substances was a fire hazard, and this also applied to domestic heating and cooking, especially in timber houses with no enclosed hearths. A sensible arrangement for the better off was a separate kitchen at the back of the house, across a rear courtyard. But the less prosperous could not afford their own kitchens. The oldest identified urban terrace housing surviving is Our Lady's Row (Lady Row), Goodramgate, York, dating from 1316, built in timber, with bays about 16 feet by 13 feet, with a slightly deeper room jettied out on the upper floor. Anthony Quiney describes these as modest houses, offering 'the comforts of substantial quarters, however small'. He supposes of the inhabitants: 'presumably they kept warm with winter braziers, for a fire in an open hearth was out of the question, and took their food to York's bakeries to be cooked'.[41] These conditions help to explain the ubiquity of cooks and bakers offering customers a ready-made loaf, a hot pasty or indeed their own food cooked for them. It must be realised that the medieval town housewife was not always in a position to be self-sufficient in a matter as basic as feeding her family.

With no water piped to private houses, the better off collected rain-water in cisterns, running gutters into their kitchens, and some had their own wells. For the less fortunate, water had to be fetched from conduits or river banks. Thrupp believed the sanitation in late medieval London was better than in later centuries (which brought greater overcrowding). Larger houses had their own cess-pits, smaller properties shared privies, and there were street privies for the poor; however, one must not be too confident of their proper use. What housewives and servants emptied into open street gutters was doubtless noxious. All washing done inside the home used portable basins and tubs. Public bathhouses served the less well provided – Thrupp remarked that early fifteenth-century London had 'at least three respectable ones for women and two for men'.[42] Household servants and professional laundresses washed bed and table linen and clothing, and not just for the master's comfort – apprentices had to be provided with clean clothes and bedding.

Household fabrics were treasured and bestowed in wills, where references to beds, coverlets and cushions testify to their value. Tables, clothespresses, chairs and stools were simple; Thrupp estimated the pots, pans and pewter dishes of the London merchant class were worth more than their wooden furniture.[43] Obviously there was an enormous scale of variation between the furnishings of a mercantile palace and of a house like those in Lady Row.

If Lady Row offered substantial quarters, there were far worse hovels, single rooms in alley tenements, and at the other extreme grander establishments, the urban equivalent of manor houses. Brick chimney stacks began to become common in the later fifteenth century, in timber-framed shops, large inns and prosperous private housing such as Thomas Paycocke's house at Coggeshall (Essex), built shortly before 1505. This was the top end of the mercantile property market, as is the older stone hall house originally built in Bishopsgate, London, by Sir John Crosby in 1466. Crosby's house was palatial: Richard III lived in it for a time just before his accession. In literature, Chaucer's Criseyde is portrayed at the start of the poem living very comfortably in Troy in her widowhood. At various points in the poem Chaucer tells of her paved parlour, her closet, a sizeable garden, and a green cedar under the chamber wall where the nightingale sings. This pretty establishment suffices for Criseyde, her 'folk', her three nieces and women in attendance.[44] One wonders how the English audience visualised it. Chaucer's contemporaries would remember John of Gaunt's Savoy palace, consigned to the flames in the Peasants' Revolt, and for later Londoners the bishops' houses in the Strand might offer models. Elsewhere more effort of the imagination may have been needed. Many houses were extremely lacking in privacy. A grocer's inventory of 1390 lists only one bedroom for the master, his wife, and five children, two of whom were daughters.[45]

England has unfortunately nothing like the Ménagier of Paris's book, written *c*. 1392–4 for his young wife, a comprehensive manual of domestic economy dealing with supervision of servants, airing, mending and cleaning clothes, pest control and menus and recipes.[46] No single source takes us inside an English house for a daily breakdown of activities. The only glimpses into the medieval town house are offered when something was going on which made the incidental events a matter of record, be it the circumstances of a subsequently broken contract, or a death.

In her autobiography, itself an extraordinary source from a medieval woman, Margery Kempe of Lynn in Norfolk provides some insight into the life style and expectations of the upper bourgeoisie in a thriving provincial town, though this was not the purpose of the work. Her father, John Burnham, had been five times mayor of the town, an alderman and member of parliament for the borough, and her husband, John Kempe, to whom she was married at twenty or 'sumdele mor', was a freeman of the borough. Margery was thus well born in her community and passed from a respected father to a husband whose career could have been expected to take a similar course. For some fifteen to sixteen years she performed the functions of a married woman, bearing fourteen children. After a harrowing first pregnancy she had hallucinatory experiences, but recovered and led a worldly life in 'pompows aray', trying to outdo her social peers. To raise money for this she tried brewing and later milling – using a horse and male servant – but failed with both. Her husband's requests to her to be more moderate fell on deaf ears, but eventually tiring of this giddy materialism she took up contemplation and yearned for a celibate life. With her customary excess, she took this too to extremes, spending hours in church and sobbing convulsively. Eventually her husband agreed to her celibacy, provided she paid his debts before going to Jerusalem on pilgrimage. The religious side of Margery's life will be treated in chapter 5; here it suffices to say that her secular story may be rather more typical. Vying with each other in such status symbols as fashion has always been a temptation to comfortably off, under-occupied women, though both sexes were restrained in the Sumptuary Laws of 1363 and their subsequent updatings. How many servants the Kempes kept is unknown. Margery had 'maydens and kepars' while out of her mind, and must have had help in bringing up numerous children. Later on, Margery shouldered the burden of caring for her husband in his last illness, and has left a graphic description of the constant washing with an incontinent invalid.[47] She was obviously practical as well as visionary, and although her career included signs of the stand-offishness demonstrable by mayors' daughters and freemen's wives, she was not incapable of physical hard work 'at the wash and at the wring'.

Glimpses of other aldermanic wives and daughters appear in their civic capacity at feasts, or rituals, in their pious capacity in their parish churches, and in their social connections and economic standing in their families' wills. Parliament in 1402 and 1406 narrowed the privilege of wearing fine fur and gold ornaments to knights and to mayors and former mayors of London, York and Bristol and their wives. At Coventry in 1474 Queen Elizabeth gave six Feckenham bucks to the mayor and his worshipful brethren, and six to the mayoress and her sisters.[48] Mayors and aldermen and members of common council had often risen through a *cursus honorum* of gild activities as gild overseers and aldermen. This level of society was generally comfortably placed and not prey to insecurity except business failure or disease.

Merchants married carefully, for marriage was 'an important means of building up one's resources'.[49] Trading widows could be courted for their assets as much as landed ones, but the lesser craftsman probably counted on his wife's help rather than her injection of capital. In terms of the woman's working day in such households, a variety of patterns may be suggested. Sometimes the woman would be left minding the shop in her husband's absence. In these circumstances she might have to accept deliveries of materials, or actually sell items to customers. In the first instance she would be most effective if she was a shrewd judge of quality and quantity, and capable of detecting any sharp practice the deliverer might be attempting. In the second she might need to know something about the product, and be psychologically persuasive to the customer about its quality and price. In both cases she had to be empowered to be effective or the transactions would not have been valid. The Hull merchant John Astlott left his fiancée his keys and business to manage when he went abroad in 1421, returning to find her parents had persuaded her to break off the marriage, and he claimed she was withholding her account of the goods sold in his absence.[50]

On other occasions the woman would be involved in the shop in her husband's presence because he was doing something else there and needed her momentarily, or because there was work enough for them both anyway. Work rhythms varied in different trades: in some the process was fairly even throughout the production, in others there were crescendos of activity and lulls – while pots baked, or iron heated or cooled. The assisting wives and daughters would have had to give priority to the urgent production processes, setting their domestic chores round these critical moments. Some wives made by-products related to their husbands' trades, for example butchers' and skinners' wives made tallow candles, and the former sausages and black puddings.

In such activities, a domestic unit of production was feasible because the workshop was in the home. The women of the house did not have to absent themselves from the hearth (or brazier) or children for long periods of time. As the continental studies have shown, as technologies became more sophisticated and distribution more ambitious, the husbands began to leave the domestic shop for an equipped workplace shared with other men, and products began to exceed the range of informal local delivery by a servant girl. Women's domestic ties prevented them joining this workforce and they were driven back to less skilled activities or put out of work altogether. None of these developments should, however, be viewed solely as the product of technology: demography also played its part. Labour was scarce after the Black Death and women could be admitted to the labour force without jeopardising male jobs. With a serious option of earning a living, they may have tended to delay marriage, which would diminish their fertility. Given the excess of females over males in towns after the plague, some never could marry. These factors, besides renewed plagues (increasingly an urban phenomenon), held back population growth, perpetuating the conditions. The high point of female economic activity in York was the second to fifth decade of the fifteenth century, according to Goldberg. But there were recessions in the fifteenth century and, as demands fell, women were forced into marginal and ill-paid jobs to protect male employment.[51] This seems to have been happening in England in the later fifteenth century, as far apart as Bristol and York, without needing technology and capitalised manufacture and distribution to account for it.

There remain for consideration other urban housewives whose trade was independent of their husbands' trades, and wives of journeymen who did not work at home in their own shop. Where did these women work and at what? In fiction, Chaucer's Wife of Bath was a skilled clothmaker, surpassing Flemish standards, he says, though this may be an ironic comment.[52] She had married five husbands, and contemplated a sixth. Her fifth and current husband, Jankyn, an ex-Oxford clerk twenty years her junior, does not sound like a fellow weaver. So the Wife of Bath had held to her trade and changed husbands, a nice literary inversion of the more normal pattern, which is shown in another literary figure, Rose the Regrator in *Piers Plowman*. Wife to Covetousness, who apparently was trained in drapery, she is represented as a weaver of woollen cloth, a brewer of ale for sale and a huckster.[53] This suggests amateurish dabbling in any profitable trade to hand, and no commitment to any organised craft (or standards, in Rose's case). This was probably the pattern of work among journeymen's wives too.

Service, essentially 'live-in', was a significant occupation for women in medieval towns. The proportion of servants to all poll tax payers was higher in towns than in the countryside, being, in 1377, 17.1 per cent in Carlisle, 22.8 per cent in Hull, but 10 per cent in rural Rutland. Furthermore, the service sex ratio (number of male servants to 100 female servants) in households in the countryside was higher – 161.9 in Rutland (excluding Oakham), 119.1 in Hull, 113.2 in Carlisle.[54] Some of the town servants, of both sexes, had migrated there from the countryside and young women were more mobile than young men in this regard. On admittedly slender evidence, Goldberg suggests many girls migrated in their early teens.[55] Migrants lived first in poorer suburban districts, sharing accommodation in cheap tenemental property if they did not get into service which took them to the wealthier parishes. Categorising servants as individuals living with their employers, contracted by the year, they comprised 20 to 30 per cent of the urban population, but only about 10 per cent of the rural one, and about a third of urban households employed them. Women servants were more likely to be found in certain types of household, most often in mercantile and victualling households, least often in metalworking. In York in 1381 45 per cent of women servants were employed by mercantile traders and 23 per cent by victuallers.[56]

Employers and servants came together through a variety of introductory circumstances including kinship, trade connection and neighbourhood proximity, besides hiring fairs. Girls entered service at about twelve, staying into their mid-twenties, and boys until a year or two older. Most finally left service to marry.[57] During their service they might move in search of better conditions or stay several years. The service term was properly a year and the contract was enforceable at law. From an analysis of thirty cases of excess wages paid to servants in Oxford in 1391–2, a mean wage of 4s 10d for females and 13s 2d for males emerges, and Goldberg thinks generally male wages were about twice the female rate. Female servants may often have worked simply for their food, lodging and clothes.[58]

Goldberg urges us to realise that master–servant relations were not essentially exploitative or antagonistic. Servants were often of a similar social class to their employers, and went on to keep servants themselves. Not infrequently they were related. Bequests to servants suggest some benevolence: but they might be conscience money. A York draper, John Stranton, a widower at the time of his death, left his servant Maud More ten marks and some household goods, with ten marks to the child with whom she was pregnant.[59] Undoubtedly servants' conditions were worse than those of their employers. Thrupp remarked that a wealthy mercer of Edward IV's day who had only one chamber for himself, his wife and seven children, must have consigned his three servants to sleeping in the clothes cupboard or a little room under the gallery of his hall.[60]

The female servants in urban craft households, like their masters' wives and daughters, probably mixed domestic and trade tasks. Mercers, drapers, tailors and cordwainers might all utilise female employees' skills with a needle. Girls worked for bakers, and as chambermaids and tapsters. Dyers employed them to wash cloth before dyeing. Many must have served as shop assistants –

one York cause paper shows a woman helping to weigh candlewick being purchased, and another helping with delivery to the customer's home; later the first servant was sent to demand payment.[61]

Other types of service were rather differently organised, and much more gender specific. Women had a monopoly of wet-nursing and midwifery, and were also specialists in general nursing of the sick. In the thirteenth century the authorities tried to ban Christian women serving Jews as nurses or domestic servants.[62] The sick-nurses and midwives presumably attended most patients in the patient's own home, though some staff were employed in institutional hospitals. One would love to know more about the sister at St Leonard's Hospital, York described in an ordinance of 1276 as '*medica*'.[63] Wet-nurses might take the child to their own home. Other carers for young children would live with the family. Few urban families had a staff of specialists, however. Thrupp suggests the majority of London merchants probably had no more than one or two servants, but the great houses would need five or more, with the women and girls acting as children's nurses and personal maids.[64] One service which was frequent, but obscure in practice, is laundry work. Laundresses are identifiable, but where they actually worked less so. Did they go a regular round of clients, washing in the clients' homes? Did they take washing in? Or take it away and wash on the river bank? Goldberg notices the regular employment of one at St Leonard's Hospital in York, but only an institutional employer would have sufficient work to keep a laundress fully employed, and he suggests elsewhere that laundering was probably only a part-time occupation in most cases.[65]

Midwives form perhaps the most interesting group. Theirs was an important and skilled job. The practitioners must have ranged from skilled and knowledgeable women with a reasonably scientific attitude (given prevailing beliefs) to old women who had survived many childbirths themselves and could cope in uncomplicated circumstances. At Nuremberg in the late fifteenth and sixteenth centuries there was a properly organised profession with four-year apprenticeships and textbooks (showing the practitioners must have been literate),[66] but there is no evidence of any such excellent system in England. Midwives or midwifery do not even feature in Goldberg's index. They presided over a critical moment. It was essential that they were physically able to act sensibly in crises. They had to be morally irreproachable since the baptism of infants incapable of survival was entrusted to them. There had to be no suspicion of them helping to 'lose' unwanted children. Midwives, because of Christ's nativity, do appear in art, but rarely doing anything useful. The pictures usually have Mary and a fully clad baby, safely delivered. Where midwives had to be respectable, prostitutes, by definition, were not. Consequently, although a non-judgemental society may require them to be viewed as providing a form of service, they will here be considered in the section of this chapter dealing with crime and poverty, with which they were often associated.

Women in the urban community

As earlier remarked, all urban government and administration was firmly in men's hands. There were no women mayors, aldermen or council members, and no women executive officers such as chamberlains. In the craft gilds, wherein office holding was in many places a prerequisite stepping stone to civic office, the officials were normally male. Two exceptional situations are frequently cited, one relating to a gild council and one to processes of quality control. The first is the case of Marion Kent, widowed in 1468, who continued her late husband's business in York, and served on the council of the York mercers' gild in 1474–5.[67] The other is an incident from London in 1423, where the keeper of the assay of oysters had farmed his office to women of Queenhithe, but 'that women should have such things in governance' was deemed contrary to the worship or good name of the City of London, because they could not effectively suppress the frauds of the trade.[68] There are other relevant illustrations: David Palliser cites the case of a York mayor's widow in 1487 continuing his ironmongery business, and describes her as 'even eligible for office in the ironmongers' gild', and in Southampton in 1503, the women who packed wool for shipment were told to choose two of their number annually to be wardens of their company.[69] It is still clear, however, that women's participation in craft gild organisation and quality control was exceptional.

So women had no 'civic capacity' in the urban community and no 'committee level' involvement in their associations. But English medieval mercantile and craft gilds were not on their professional side exclusively male trade unions, nor on their social side 'men only' clubs. Their ordinances dealt with women both as practising members of the craft and as the assisting wives and daughters of members. Many ordinances of craft gilds refer to sisters. On the social side, the women were not excluded from the feastings, and they were eligible for the charitable support services provided by the gild. On the religious side they participated in gild ceremonials and rites such as members' funerals. The Norwich carpenters' ordinances offer relevant examples. All the brothers and sisters had to assemble yearly the Saturday after the Ascension 'in cause of deuocioun', and the next day process with candles and torches; any brother or sister dying outside Norwich was to have funeral support, and any brother or sister falling into mishap or poverty (by God's sending or worldly chance, not by folly or riotous living) was to have a farthing a week from each brother and sister.[70] Some gilds apparently set aside particular facilities for women, though it is open to interpretation whether providing a ladies' chamber was a refined facility to protect ladies from the embarrassments of fraternity socialising, or a provision to remove them from the scene and reduce their influence.

On their social and religious side, the craft gilds were akin to the purely social and religious gilds, but these latter had no mercantile or craft control. Membership of the craft gild was therefore necessary for professional reasons, whereas membership of the social or religious gilds was voluntary, variously for religious devotion, social insurance, or for status. 'The whole and sole cause' behind the Paternoster Gild at York was the maintaining of the paternoster play, and the 'main charge of the gild is to keep up this play, to the glory of God, the maker of the said prayer, and for the holding up of sins and vices to scorn'.[71] The gild of Killingholme in Lincolnshire met many contingencies:

> if a brother or a sister is unlucky enough to lose a beast worth half a mark, every brother and every sister shall give a half penny towards getting another beast. If the house of any brother or sister is burnt by mishap, every brother and every sister shall give a half penny towards a new house ... if the house of any brother or sister is broken into by robbers, and goods carried off worth half a mark, every brother and every sister shall give a half penny to help him.[72]

The Corpus Christi Gild in York was of high social standing, enrolling Richard duke of Gloucester and his wife among its members.[73] The gild book of the Holy Trinity Gild at St Botolph's Aldersgate, London, founded in 1369 and rededicated in 1374, lists 530 men who joined between 1374 and 1415, and 1443 to 1445, and 274 women, mostly the wives of craftsmen entering with their husbands, but a few alone.[74] The ordinances of the gild of St Mary at Beverley (E. R. Yorks.), founded in 1355, allowed the older brothers and sisters an assenting voice in the election of the alderman and stewards, apparently without discrimination.[75]

The craft gilds were gilds of employers, and the recognition of status rubbed off on gildsmen's wives. Within the gilds, the officers had status, which again their wives enjoyed. The lack of distinction between gild and borough aldermen which has been noticed in Chaucer's Prologue to the *Canterbury Tales* is not particularly significant because in many boroughs entry to the borough hierarchy was a progession from gild hierarchy. Chaucer's five craftsmen – a haberdasher, carpenter, weaver, dyer and tapestry weaver – wore one livery. Since they could not have been members of one craft gild, this indicates their association was not craft related. But each was 'shaply for to been an alderman', and their wives were enthusiastic for the status:

> It is ful fair to been ycleped 'madame,'
> And goon to vigilies al bifore,
> And have a mantel roialliche ybore.[76]

Thrupp notes that the wives of London aldermen 'seized upon the title of Lady, which was used by the wives of knights and esquires, and clung to it to the end of their lives, even when widowed and remarried to men who held no office'.[77] Women were not left out of social events. The 1494 ordinances of the gild of St Katherine at Stamford (Lincs.) ordained a feast the Sunday after St Katherine's day, when the brethren and sisters should come to their gild hall and there dine together. The tariff was 4*d* for a man and his wife, and for any single person, priest, man or woman 2*d*.[78]

Medieval borough charters did not grant privileges to all the inhabitants of the town. There was a distinction between the so-called freemen, burgesses or citizens of the borough, and the rest. Those admitted to the freedom enjoyed the right to trade retail, exemption from tolls, the right to take apprentices and in theory a voice in urban government. The unenfranchised laboured under trading disadvantages, for example having to pay for licences to trade. There is no evidence that women were anywhere barred wholly from these urban franchises, but their take-up rate was minimal. The York records from 1272 to 1500 register 142 women, about one per cent of all admissions.[79] At Norwich only four women are recorded as admitted to the franchise in the later Middle Ages, and in Exeter Kowaleski thought women were barred, except for the very rare widow.[80] Freedom was acquired through successful completion of apprenticeship, patrimony and purchase, which explains the low female entry. Few women were apprenticed, few women took the patrimonial route and purchase was beyond many – who could, however, raise piecemeal funds to buy a licence to trade. Although the wives of freemen do not seem to have been automatically enfranchised, they seem to have shared the status, and widows stepped up either legally or in effect. The court of aldermen in 1465 declared it ancient custom that widows of London freemen, married to and living with them at the time of their death, were recognised as freewomen of the city while they lived sole in the city, remaining a widow. Apparently there are hardly any references in London records to women who were not widows being admitted to the freedom.[81] In York, Goldberg identifies the 'labour-employing classes' with the enfranchised, identifying many of the heads of households with servants in 1377 with freemen or their widows.[82]

Women's standing in the community was affected by the legal customs of that community and the way these were operated. It is clear women had no participation in the definition of the customs, nor in the staffing of the courts which enforced them. However, the London *Liber Albus* did allow women to wage law (that is, clear themselves by producing in court a specified number of compurgators or oath helpers) with either men or women.[83] Customs varied considerably. Burghal tenure was a form of socage tenure and lands so held could be freely devised like chattels. So there is less significance to patterns of landed inheritance in towns. Nevertheless, in London, the husband could not alienate land which belonged jointly to himself and his wife without her consent in the Hustings Court. The London widow was entitled to a third (if there were children) or half (if there were not) of her husband's real estate as dower, but goods were of greater significance than land in towns, and she was bound to receive, absolutely, a third or half of his movable goods on the same principle. On remarriage, she forfeited her freebench home, but not the share in lands and tenements which provided her with income.[84]

In London and other towns married women could elect to trade as *feme sole* – an independence for them which was probably rooted in saving their husbands from liability for their debts. In Exeter, it is clear husbands were willing to sue for debts due to their wives, but glad to see them sued sole for their own debts.[85] When cases reached court, Kowaleski finds males secured more favourable verdicts than females, as both plaintiffs and defendants, in debt cases, in Exeter. Women plaintiffs were three times more likely to be fined for false complaint, and males 7 per cent more likely to have plaints against them dropped, though males were 5 per cent more often guilty. However, Kowaleski believes the courts seemed prejudiced against women plaintiffs, but favourably disposed to defendants.[86] Women's fines and amercements were often condoned, whether out of general sympathy or because they were known to be worse off as individuals is not clear.

Compared with the mass of rural women, urban women seem to have been marginally advantaged. But the ones so far considered have been the better-placed ones. What about women of the urban underclass?

Women of the urban underclass: poverty, prostitution, crime and charity

In a society where some female servants worked merely for their board and clothes, and wage rates for females lagged well behind those paid to male servants, a town's women in service were not well off. But others were worse off. Goldberg specifically makes the point about young female immigrants to towns living at first in the poorer suburban districts 'unless reasons of service or marriage dictated otherwise'.[87] Though servants might be left to sleep in cupboards, at least they were under their employer's roof, in the salubrious parts of town, for the most part.

Humble spinsters were a poor and exploited class. Pieceworkers, they were cheated by employers using false weights. Spinning with a distaff needed little capital investment; spinning with a wheel was more productive but required capital purchase or possibly renting of the equipment. Where women were solely dependent on spinning to support themselves, their position was not enviable, and the use of the term 'spinster' for single women indicates that this was their characteristic employment. Patricia Cullum, commenting on employers' bequests to spinsters, writes: 'these women, although living and working independently, were in need of charitable support due to the low level of their wages'.[88]

Poll tax and rental evidence shows that women, whether occupationally spinsters or not, tended to congregate in poor parts of the town. Widows and other single females were driven to find accommodation in cheap tenements or cottages. In York, eighteen of the twenty-five tenants of one group of properties owned by the Vicars Choral in 1399 were female, and there were concentrations of women in the Ouse Bridge rentals in Micklegate, Hamerton Lane and Rotten Row.[89] This imbalance of the sexes was not a phenomenon restricted to the Middle Ages. Olwen Hufton invented the phrase 'spinster clustering' for women living in twos and threes and fours to rent cost-sharing accommodation in the eighteenth century.[90] The clusters consisted of proportionately high concentrations of female-headed households, and households of women sharing houses. The topography of prostitution followed much the same economic geography.

In York, Goldberg noted 'large numbers of prostitutes . . . associated with a group of cottages owned by the Vicars Choral on the corner of Aldwark and St Andrewgate'. Rents there were low, at 4s to 6s per annum in the later fourteenth and fifteenth centuries.[91] It is observable in several towns that the haunts of prostitutes were often close to major religious houses, and clearly clergy were not infrequent clients as well as being landlords.

Goldberg believes that few Englishwomen practised prostitution as a profession, but that some were forced into it from time to time. Presentments of them often show low-status occupational bynames, such as spinster, kempster etc. A few towns tried to regulate prostitution – for example Sandwich (Kent) and, especially, Southwark (Surrey), 'the one well-documented instance of legal brothels' – but this regulation was nothing like as total as on the Continent; compare Otis's work on Languedoc towns.[92] Some towns tried to shut prostitution out beyond their walls and jurisdiction, for example Coventry in 1445 and Leicester in 1467, while at Hull the borough leased land just outside the walls, and town walls and towers, to prostitutes in the 1490s. Other boroughs imposed fines on prostitutes, which became the policy at Winchester and was operative at Exeter.[93] The York prostitutes were generally obscure people and moved around frequently. Joan Cryspyn was presented for fornication between 1440 and 1452 variously resident in Goodramgate, Aldwark and Swinegayle. Several York prostitutes were called Scott, and migrants generally seem more than proportionately represented among them. Clients included clergy, and married and unmarried men. Actual brothels can be identified, some under female management, and procuresses were plentiful. Kowaleski found 32 per cent of brothel keepers in Exeter's court records were female.[94]

If women were forced into casual prostitution when other conditions were bad, one might expect an increase of this in the later fifteenth century, as they were denied access to other employment in recessionary times. Certainly borough concern about prostitution seems to have sharpened up then, for example at Nottingham (1463), Leicester (1467) and Coventry (1492). Goldberg links the later fifteenth-century burgeoning of charitable bequests of dowries for poor maidens with an awareness of the single woman's problems.[95] Such dowries were earlier an institutional provision. The monopolistic gild of Berwick-upon-Tweed provided, apparently in 1283–4, 'if any brother die, leaving a daughter true and worthy and of good repute, but undowered, the gild shall find her a dower, either on marriage or on going into a religious house'. From the Welsh Marches, Ludlow's Palmers' Gild returns of 1388–9 similarly provided:

> if any good girl of the gild, of marriageable age, cannot have the means found by her father, either to go into a religious house or to marry, whichever she wishes to do; friendly and right help shall be given her, out of our means and our common chest, towards enabling her to do whichever of the two she wishes.[96]

Marriage or religion patently were seen as safer situations for women than secular spinsterhood, and it was a pious deed to put as many as possible in the way of either escape route. However, not a high proportion of town girls entered convents, so marriage and servanthood should be regarded as the more realistic alternatives.

Goldberg suggests the exigencies of their regular employment may have forced some occupational spinsters to resort to theft and prostitution, pointing to early sixteenth-century Quarter Session evidence from Norwich. Women described as spinster were presented at Nottingham for receiving goods and for petty theft. What Goldberg calls the 'sub-economy of crime and prostitution' sucked in those at the bottom of the urban heap: Margaret Mason, a known Hull prostitute, was fined in 1485 for receiving stolen goods. In Exeter Kowaleski found prostitution the most common 'alternative occupation' for female servants, and noted women presented in court as receivers, petty criminals and brothel keepers.[97] Women's activities in petty crime were similar to those of their rural counterparts and need not be repeated here.

What does need treatment here is the imprisonment of women, for most medieval gaols were in towns. This is not an aspect of women's history which has attracted much attention. Hanawalt's study of the female felon in the fourteenth century revealed one woman to every nine men coming up through gaol delivery rolls in three counties, Norfolk, Yorkshire and Northamptonshire, 1300–48.[98] Most medieval imprisonment was pending trial, like modern remanding in custody; a sentence of imprisonment as a punishment was not the normal pattern. Periodically a commission of gaol delivery was appointed to try prisoners in a gaol, releasing those acquitted and fining or hanging those convicted, depending on the seriousness of the crime, regardless of sex. (For treason, only, were the death penalties different – men were drawn and quartered, women burnt at the stake, and it was treason for a woman to kill her husband, and for a man to kill his lord.) Convicted women facing the death penalty who claimed to be pregnant were examined by a jury of matrons and allowed to live in gaol to give birth. Becoming pregnant in gaol was not uncommon – men and women were sometimes imprisoned together in common cells, and there was the possibility of rape by male gaolers. Hanawalt cites the case of Matilda Hereward of Brandiston, Northamptonshire, who was found to be pregnant on each occasion in a series of gaol deliveries between June 1301 and January 1303, when there is a gap in the records.[99] Margery Kempe, imprisoned by order of the mayor at Leicester, hearing the gaoler had nowhere to put her unless among the men, successfully pleaded not to be put there so that she might keep her chastity.[100] York was more sensitive, with a women's division in the civic prison at Ouse Bridge, the woman kidcote, wherein each woman prisoner was left 3*d* by John Newton (d. 1442).[101]

Charity towards the poor in medieval England included the giving of alms on a regular basis – such as weekly doles to individuals; as a single gift – of money doles, food or clothing, as part of the obsequies for the dead; and also the provision of hospitals and almshouses. Such activities are recorded in wills and institutional statutes and ordinances. More obscure is the amount of charity performed informally and impulsively: kitchen-door handouts of surplus food and casual giving to beggars in the street. In the Catholic Middle Ages, the motivation towards such good deeds was the believed benefit to the soul of the giver and/or the soul(s) on whose behalf the gift was made. Cullum points to the teaching of the Seven Works of Corporal Mercy: giving food to the hungry, drink to the thirsty, shelter to the stranger, clothing to the naked, visiting the sick, comforting prisoners and burying the dead. She cites the lesson in the Last Judgement play in the York Cycle that charity performed to 'lest or moste' was the equivalent of doing it for Christ. The morality play *Everyman* (early sixteenth century) had a similar message.

However, there was creeping into charity before the Reformation the rather more Protestant idea of selecting the 'deserving' poor to receive charity. Hence most of the social and religious gilds formed insurance groups selectively to benefit their own provident members in hard times, sometimes specifically defined as those arising from act of God or worldly misfortune, not folly. The outcome of this was that the underclass, by and large, received help only from casual donors, or from those of such saintly disposition that they could identify with anyone as a child of God. The Corpus Christi Gild of Walden in Essex which paid for burial of poor strangers, among other good deeds, was unusual.[102] Selective charity must have made the urban squalor difficult to get out of, and dire to fall into from perilous respectability just the other side of the divide.

Where the sex of charitable recipients was specified, female beneficiaries were usually widows or unwed maidens, or poor spinsters or other servants who had worked for the benefactor. In York, Roger Burton (d. 1392) left 40s to the poor and widows bedridden in York; Richard Wartre (d. 1458) left 12d to each poor woman or widow with a child or children in St Saviour's parish.[103] The selectivity can be seen in the Cambridge Holy Trinity Gild's poor relief in the 1389 gild return: it offered 7d a week, and a gown and hood to any brother or brother's wife in penury (through mishap, not by fault), adding: 'his wife shall be treated in the same way after his death, so long as she does rightly and is not remarried'.[104] Poor maidens' dowries were for 'good girls'. The rehabilitation of prostitutes and criminals was not so popular a cause.

Sheltered housing was available in almshouses and hospitals, but not all this relief was as 'charitable' as one might suppose. Certainly some of the inmates bought their way in, with a cash payment which bought them a certain level of care, 'upmarket retirement care for the well-off elderly', as Cullum has described in the case of the large St Leonard's Hospital, York.[105] In York, all of the maisonsdieu received women, and one in St Andrewgate took them exclusively, as St Nicholas and the Ouse Bridge maisondieu came to do respectively in the 1380s and somewhere between 1433 and 1445. St Leonard's itself consistently supported more women than men in the infirmary in 1461–3. Cullum posits 'a pattern of feminisation of the inhabitants of a significant number of maisonsdieu' during the fifteenth and sixteenth centuries, which she thinks almost certainly reflects a 'feminisation of poverty' during that period, as economic depression and increasing gild regulation to protect male jobs squeezed women out of work.[106] There were of course always specific women's needs and the charities of Richard Whittington (d. 1423) included a refuge for unmarried mothers at Southwark.[107] Maternity and orphan care was not, however, as institutionalised in England as it was becoming in the different social milieu of fifteenth-century Italian cities.

Conclusions

Towns were more sophisticated organisms than villages or manors and they evolved varied rules to suit their own requirements. Under these rules women as widows or heiresses benefited from generally less constrained inheritance conditions in regard to property, and widows benefited from a certain amount of protection to their craft livelihood on the deaths of their husbands. Married women (and their husbands) benefited wherever the town gave them the choice, or required them, to take *feme sole* status with regard to their trading activities. The woman who was single because she never married was not so well placed and if her only remunerative work was as a spinster or kempster she was likely to lead a poverty-stricken life in a poor part of the town.

Conditions were not static in the medieval towns and although there is little sophisticated economic evidence before the thirteenth century, it is obvious that the later Middle Ages witnessed some particularly significant changes for women. After the Black Death there was a shortage of labour and a rise in wages, stimulating demand for goods and services, and women began to consolidate their role in the economy, eventually beginning to take formerly male jobs, without apparent male resentment. Their acceptance is acknowledged in gild and borough regulations. During a period of almost a century they had some realistic possibilities of earning their own living respectably, and outside pressure to get them married or consigned to conventual life decreased. Some may have deferred marriage, enjoying the independence, or at least may have ceased to rush into matrimony because the alternative was so appalling. Ideas of medieval women enjoying independence may seem anachronistic, but Chaucer's Criseyde, in her widowhood, counts as a blessing 'I am myn owene womman.'[108] In the later fifteenth century it seems these opened doors were being pushed back on women's faces. Recession was bringing protectionist policies to the fore in always male-dominated gilds. Technology and changing trade patterns were taking work from the craftsman's workshop away from the family unit and therefore from its women.

Even the high point of female economic activity, placed in York around 1410–50, was not as glowing as the apparent employment opportunities might suggest. Work always tended to be gender specific: the woman had the less prestigious handling of raw material, men the more prestigious finishing processes and the merchandising on any big scale. It was the women who were always expected to be flexible, changing trades and crafts as circumstances changed, while the men stuck to one line. So women's 'always precarious hold on the labour market', in Goldberg's phrase,[109] was easily pushed aside and their economic potential marginalised. By the end of the period urban women were being faced with the stark alternatives of marriage or perpetual servanthood. This chapter clearly illustrates that the urban scene was a much more sensitive barometer than the rural one to the economic standing of women in the later Middle Ages.

Notes

1   P. J. P. Goldberg, 'Female labour, service and marriage in the late medieval urban north', *Northern History*, XXII, 1986, p. 19.

2   P. J. P. Goldberg, *Women, Work and Life Cycle in a Medieval Economy: women in York and Yorkshire* c. 1300–1520, Oxford, 1992, p. 31; Goldberg, 'The public and the private: women in the pre-plague economy' in P. R. Coss and S. D. Lloyd (eds.), *Thirteenth Century England*, III, 1989, p. 85.

3   Goldberg, *Women Work and Life Cycle*, pp. 17, 333, 200; C. Phythian Adams, *Desolation of a City: Coventry and the urban crisis of the late middle ages*, Cambridge, 1979, pp. 87–8, 327.

4   Goldberg, *Women, Work and Life Cycle*, p. 26; C. M. Barron and A. F. Sutton (eds.), *Medieval London Widows, 1300–1500*, London, 1994, p. xxxiii; Goldberg, 'Women in fifteenth-century town life', in *Towns and Townspeople in the Fifteenth Century*, ed. J. A. F. Thomson, Gloucester, 1988, p. 109.

5   C. Roth, *A History of the Jews in England*, 3rd edn 1964, p. 30.

6   R. H. Hilton, *The English Peasantry in the Later Middle Ages*, Oxford, 1975, pp. 76, 82, 85, 90.

7   P. J. P. Goldberg, 'Female labour', p. 28.

8   M. Kowaleski, 'Women's work in a market town: Exeter in the late fourteenth century', in B. A. Hanawalt (ed.), *Women and Work in PreIndustrial Europe*, Bloomington, 1986, p. 146.

9   J. M. Bennett, 'Medieval women, modern women: across the great divide', in D. Aers (ed.), *Culture and History 1300–1600: essays in English communities, identities and writing*, London, 1992, pp. 147–75.

10 M. K. Dale, 'The London silkwomen of the fifteenth century', *Economic History Review*, IV, 3, 1933, p. 324.

11 *Ibid.*, pp. 326–7.

12 *Ibid.*, pp. 325–6. Female apprenticeship was not common in medieval London, however, and the silk apprentices are exceptional, D. Keene, 'Tanners' widows, 1300–1350', in Barron and Sutton (eds.), *London Widows*, p. 4.

13 C. Barron, 'The "Golden Age" of women in medieval London' in *Medieval Women in Southern England*, Reading Medieval Studies XV, 1989, p. 39.

14 *Ibid.*, p. 40.

15 *Ibid.*, p. 40.

16 T. Smith and L. T. Smith (eds.), *English Gilds*, Early English Text Society, 1870, p. 382.

17 Dale, 'Silkwomen', p. 335.

18 *Ibid.*, p. 332.
19 Goldberg, *Women, Work and Life Cycle*, pp. 104–18.
20 Goldberg, 'Female labour', p. 34.
21 *York Memorandum Book I 1376–1419*, ed. M. Sellars, Surtees Society, CXX, 1912, pp. 243, 114; Smith, *English Gilds*, p. 180. The Lincoln ordinances seem to have been officially sealed in 1337, and the gild had been founded in 1297, which is the date Eileen Power gives for this particular ordinance, *Medieval Women* (ed. M. M. Postan), Cambridge, 1975, p. 60.
22 Smith, *English Gilds*, p. 329. Craftsmen were limited to three servants and an apprentice at most, unless licensed for more, *ibid.*, p. 315.
23 P. J. P. Goldberg, 'Women's work, women's role in the late medieval north', in *Profit, Piety and the Professions*, ed. M. [A.] Hicks, Gloucester, 1990, p. 44.
24 Goldberg, *Women, Work and Life Cycle*, pp. 127–9. According to Abram, blacksmith women sometimes paid less quarterage, 'Women traders', *Economic Journal*, XXVI, 1916, p. 284; C. Barron, 'Johanna Hill (d. 1441) and Johanna Sturdy (d. *c.* 1460) bell founders', in Barron and Sutton (eds.), *London Widows*, pp. 99–111.
25 E. Veale, 'Matilda Penne, skinner (d. 1392–3)', *ibid.*, pp. 48–9; Goldberg, *Women, Work and Life Cycle*, pp. 129–34.
26 D. Hutton, 'Women in fourteenth-century Shrewsbury', in L. Charles and L. Duffin (eds.), *Women and Work in Pre-Industrial England*, London, 1985, pp. 93–7; A. V. C. Schmidt, *William Langland: the vision of Piers Plowman*, London, 1978, p. 49.
27 Barron, 'Golden Age', p. 47; see also R. H. Hilton, 'Lords, burgesses and hucksters', *Past and Present*, 97, 1982, pp. 3–15.
28 Kowaleski, 'Women's work', p. 148.
29 C. Dyer, *Standards of Living in the Later Middle Ages: social change in England c. 1200–1520*, Cambridge, 1989, p. 230.
30 S. Wright, 'Churmaids, huswyfs and hucksters: the employment of women in Tudor and Stuart Salisbury', in Charles and Duffin (eds.), *Women and Work in Pre-Industrial England*, p. 106.
31 Goldberg, *Women Work and Life Cycle*, p. 99.
32 Abram, 'Women traders', p. 276.
33 Kowaleski, 'Women's work', pp. 157–8.
34 Barron, 'Golden Age', p. 47, citing Guildhall Library MS 5440, fos 105–7.
35 Hutton, 'Shrewsbury', p. 91.
36 B. Dobson, 'The role of Jewish women in medieval England', in *Christianity and Judaism*, ed. D. Wood, Studies in Church History, XXIX, 1992, p. 155.

37 Roth, *History of the Jews*, p. 115.
38 *Ibid.*, pp. 96–102; Dobson, 'Role of Jewish women', pp. 156–61.
39 M. C. Howell, *Women, Production and Patriarchy in Late Medieval Cities*, Chicago and London, 1986, pp. 87, 27–8, 94, 129, 133–4, 155, 158, 178.
40 S. L. Thrupp, *The Merchant Class of Medieval London [1300–1500]*, Chicago, 1948, p. 136.
41 A. Quiney, *The Traditional Buildings of England*, London, 1990, p. 146.
42 Thrupp, *Merchant Class*, pp. 137–8.
43 *Ibid.*, p. 142.
44 G. Chaucer, 'Troilus and Criseyde', in *The Riverside Chaucer*, ed. L. D. Benson, Oxford, 1988, pp. 490, 497, 500, 502.
45 Thrupp, *Merchant Class*, p. 132.
46 Translated by E. Power as *The Goodman of Paris* (Le Ménagier de Paris), London, 1928.
47 *The Book of Margery Kempe*, ed. S. B. Meech, Early English Text Society, 1940, pp. 6–9, 24, 180–1.
48 Thrupp, *Merchant Class*, p. 148; *Coventry Leet Book*, II, ed. M. Dormer Harris, Early English Text Society, 1908, p. 405.
49 Thrupp, *Merchant Class*, p. 105. See also C. Rawcliffe, 'Margaret Stodeye, Lady Philipot (d. 1431)', in Barron and Sutton (eds.), *London Widows*, pp. 85–98.
50 Goldberg, 'Women's work, women's role', p. 46. John sued to enforce their contract of marriage, but no sentence survives, R. H. Helmholz, *Marriage Litigation in Medieval England*, Cambridge, 1974, pp. 32–3.
51 Goldberg, 'Female labour', pp. 35–8.
52 Chaucer, 'Canterbury Tales', *Riverside Chaucer*, p. 30.
53 *Ibid.*, pp. 30–1, 105, 107, 111–12; Langland, *Piers Plowman*, p. 49.
54 Goldberg, *Women, Work and Life Cycle*, pp. 370, 372.
55 Goldberg, 'Female labour', p. 20.
56 Goldberg, *Women, Work and Life Cycle*, p. 189.
57 Goldberg, 'Female labour', pp. 21–3.
58 Goldberg, *Women Work and Life Cycle*, p. 186.
59 *Ibid.*, p. 184.
60 Thrupp, *Merchant Class*, p. 132.
61 Goldberg, 'Female labour', p. 25; *Women Work and Life Cycle*, p. 191.
62 Roth, *History of the Jews*, p. 54. There was less concern about Jews serving Christians.
63 P. H. Cullum, *Cremetts and Corrodies: care of the poor and sick*

at *St Leonard's Hospital, York, in the middle ages*, Borthwick Paper, 79, 1991, p. 13.
64 Thrupp, *Merchant Class*, pp. 151–2.
65 Goldberg, *Women Work and Life Cycle*, p. 135; 'Women's work, women's role', p. 47. St Leonard's also had a ferrywoman at one time, Cullum, *Cremetts*, p. 7.
66 M. E. Wiesner, 'Early modern midwifery: a case study', in Hanawalt, *Women and Work*, pp. 99–100.
67 Goldberg, *Women Work and Life Cycle*, p. 125. According to H. Swanson, *Building Craftsmen in Late Medieval York*, Borthwick Paper, 63, 1983, p. 29 (cited by Goldberg), Marion Kent was already trading as a merchant's widow in 1449.
68 Thrupp, *Merchant Class*, p. 173, also Goldberg, *Women Work and Life Cycle*, p. 108.
69 D. M. Palliser, *Tudor York*, Oxford, 1979, p. 150; Power, *Medieval Women*, p. 61.
70 Smith, *English Gilds*, pp. 37–8.
71 *Ibid.*, p. 137.
72 *Ibid.*, p. 185.
73 *Register of the Gild of Corpus Christi in the City of York*, ed. R. H. Skaife, Surtees Society, LVII, 1872, p. 101. Richard's wife is described, inexplicably, as Elizabeth. She was in fact Anne Neville.
74 Thrupp, *Merchant Class*, p. 36.
75 Smith, *English Gilds*, p. 150.
76 Chaucer, 'Canterbury Tales', p. 29.
77 Thrupp, *Merchant Class*, p. 18. After the death of her fourth husband, Adam Bamme, Margaret née Stodeye chose to style herself Lady Philipot, reverting to her title from her second husband, Sir John: Rawcliffe, 'Margaret Stodeye', in Barron and Sutton (eds.), *London Widows*, p. 97.
78 Smith, *English Gilds*, p. 189.
79 Goldberg, 'Female labour', p. 32.
80 Goldberg, *Women, Work and Life Cycle*, p. 51, n. 22; Kowaleski, 'Women's work', p. 146.
81 Barron, 'Golden Age', pp. 39, 44, 45.
82 Goldberg, *Women Work and Life Cycle*, p. 162.
83 Barron, 'Golden Age', p. 52, n. 27.
84 *Ibid.*, pp. 38, 41. See also Barron and Sutton (eds.), *London Widows*, *passim*.
85 Kowaleski, 'Women's work', p. 146.
86 *Ibid.*, pp. 150–1.
87 Goldberg, 'Female labour', p. 20.
88 Goldberg, *Women, Work and Life Cycle*, pp. 119, 145; H. C.

Swanson, *Medieval Artisans: an urban class in late medieval England*, Oxford, 1989, p. 31; P. H. Cullum, ' "And Hir Name was Charite": charitable giving by and for women in late medieval Yorkshire', in *Woman is a Worthy Wight: women in English society* c. *1200–1500*, ed. P. J. P. Goldberg, Stroud, 1992, p. 197.

89 Goldberg, *Women Work and Life Cycle*, p. 313.
90 O. Hufton, 'Women without men: widows and spinsters in Britain and France in the eighteenth century', *Journal of Family History*, ix, 4, 1984, p. 361.
91 Goldberg, *Women Work and Life Cycle*, p. 151.
92 R. M. Karras, 'The regulation of brothels in later medieval England', *Signs*, 14, 2, 1989, pp. 405, 410; L. L. Otis, *Prostitution in Medieval Society: the history of an urban institution in Languedoc*, Chicago, 1985.
93 K. J. Allison, 'Medieval Hull', in Victoria County History, *York, East Riding*, I, 1969, p. 75.
94 Goldberg, *Women Work and Life Cycle*, pp. 151–5; Kowaleski, 'Women's work', p. 154.
95 Goldberg, *Women Work and Life Cycle*, pp. 155–7.
96 Smith, *English Gilds*, pp. 340, 194.
97 Goldberg, *Women, Work and Life Cycle*, pp. 119–20; 'Female Labour', p. 36; Kowaleski, 'Women's work', p. 154.
98 B. A. Hanawalt, 'The female felon in fourteenth-century England', in S. M. Stuard (ed.), *Women in Medieval Society*, Philadelphia, 1976, p. 126.
99 Hanawalt, *ibid*., pp. 135–6; Hanawalt, *Crime and Conflict in English Communities 1300–48*, Cambridge, Mass. and London, 1979, p. 43.
100 *Book of Margery Kempe*, p. 112.
101 Cullum, 'And Hir Name', p. 195.
102 E. Rickert, *Chaucer's World*, ed. C. C. Olson and M. M. Crow, London and New York, 1948, p. 351, cited in Cullum, 'And hir name', p. 196, where the impression is incorrectly given that this was the sole dedication of the fraternity.
103 Cullum, 'And hir name', p. 198.
104 Smith, *English Gilds*, p. 267.
105 Cullum, *Cremetts*, pp. 6, 7, 8, 20.
106 Cullum, 'And hir name', pp. 199–200.
107 J. Imray, *The Charity of Richard Whittington*, London, 1968, p. 2.
108 Chaucer, 'Troilus and Criseyde', p. 499.
109 Goldberg, *Women Work and Life Cycle*, p. 347.

4

Women of the landholding classes: queens, noblewomen and gentlewomen

Although statistically a smaller group than the women of the agricultural countryside and towns, the women of the landholding classes came from better-recorded strata of society in the Middle Ages, and have received a good deal of attention in consequence.

By the later Middle Ages women of these classes embraced wide ranges of economic and social standing, yet the tiers in landed society overlapped, and movement between them was constant. At the pinnacle of society, the royal family, from the twelfth century to the end of the fifteenth, refreshed itself each generation with foreign blood. No English king was married to a wife from the British Isles between Henry I's marriage to Matilda of Scotland in 1100 and Edward IV's to Elizabeth Woodville in 1464. (The Black Prince's marriage to Joan of Kent in 1361 and Henry Bolingbroke's to Mary Bohun in 1380 would have produced English-born queens, however, had the Black Prince lived to succeed Edward III, and had Mary not died before her husband's assumption of the throne.) The English nobility, and the Welsh and Scottish royal dynasties, did not climb up into English royalty by providing brides for heirs to the throne, but the English royals spread themselves outwards into them, by the marriages of daughters, younger sons and bastard children. In particular this is observable in the large family of Edward I by his successive wives, Eleanor of Castile and Margaret of France, but it also occurred in less prolific generations, creating a wide royal cousinship. As a result there were women whose place was clearly in the aristocracy, but who moved in royal circles. Elizabeth de Burgh (b. 1295) is an obvious example. Daughter of Gilbert de Clare earl of Gloucester and his second wife Joan of Acre, a daughter of Edward I, Elizabeth married three times, bearing a child to each of her husbands: John de Burgh (d. 1313) eldest son of the earl of Ulster, Theobald de Verdun (d. 1316) and Roger Damory (d. 1322). Her only son succeeded to the Ulster earldom but was murdered young, leaving as sole heiress his daughter Elizabeth countess of Ulster, who married Edward III's son Lionel, thus reconnecting the royal link. The older Elizabeth's two daughters married members of the parliamentary peerage, and her household accounts reveal her lavish entertainment of royalty, higher and lesser nobility, clergy and officials.

While heirs to the throne regularly married foreign wives, the aristocracy did this rather less consistently, and decreasingly so in the fourteenth and fifteenth centuries. Less than three years before his death in 1324, Aymer de Valence, earl of Pembroke, married Marie de St Pol, whose widowhood was adversely affected when hostilities between England and France made it impossible for her to uphold cross-Channel interests unscathed. The childless Marie, who had lands in both countries, chose to remain in England, where she was unaffected by the confiscations suffered here by other aliens; indeed it was ultimately her French lands which she lost. Marie became a great benefactress to the University of Cambridge, as foundress and patron of Pembroke College, and sought burial at her foundation for Minoresses at Denny (Cambs.), in 1377.

The higher nobility was tied in with the royal family, but it also stretched down into the lower nobility and gentry. A wide span of relationships was created as a result of the two prolific marriages of Ralph Neville (d. 1425), first earl of Westmorland, who had twenty-three children by his successive wives Margaret Stafford, daughter of the second earl of Stafford, and Joan Beaufort, legitimated daughter of John of Gaunt duke of Lancaster. At gentry level, families were also intermarrying, and rising and falling in the social hierarchy, often by marriage. The Pastons' rise, to gentry standing in the fifteenth century and ultimately to nobility, was founded on the marriage of Clement Paston to Beatrice Goneld or Somerton, whose brother was a justice of the peace and member of parliament for Yarmouth, Norfolk, of rather better standing than Clement himself. Clement's grandson, William Paston II, a younger son, married Anne Beaufort, daughter of the duke of Somerset.

There was obviously huge disparity in birth and wealth between modestly endowed widows such as Alice de Bryene, whose income in the late 1420s approached £182 per annum, and Isabella Morley, whose estate receipts and profits of jurisdiction in 1463–4 were about £170, and great ladies such as Elizabeth de Burgh, with an income of £2,500–3,000 per annum, Margaret of Brotherton, whose income in 1394–5 was over £2,839, and Lady Margaret Beaufort, whose revenues in 1495–6 were about £2,200.[1] But viewed from the eyes of their tenantry and tradespeople, the lives of these women had common features which differentiated them from women below their ranks. The common denominator was feudal landholding with concomitant lordship connections.

The feudal classes held their lands from the crown or from an intermediate lord. At each tenant's death, the heir had to be identified and formally admitted. Primogeniture awarded the patrimonial estates to the eldest son. If there was no son and only a single daughter, she was sole heiress, but if there were several daughters, by around 1135 they were treated as coheiresses.[2] Henceforth partition had to be effected, unless the estate became entailed to the nearest male heir. If a tenant died leaving an under-age heir or heiress(es), his or their wardship was the feudal overlord's, and the ward's marriage was usually under the same control. As the overlord of all tenants-in-chief (for their mesne lands as well as their holdings *in capite*), the king had many wardships and marriages, and generally sold these to the highest bidders. The guardian was then free to negotiate the wards' marriages, but often had personal dynastic designs, so many heirs and heiresses found themselves betrothed to their guardians' children, as did John Mowbray, later duke of Norfolk, and Richard Plantagenet, later duke of York, wards of Ralph Neville; they married his daughters Katherine and Cecily. Life expectancy being hazardous, even a younger daughter could end up sole heiress, so her marriage could turn out a better bargain.

The women of these classes were born into families whose resources were in land, and they lived by demesne produce, sale of surplus, rents, fees and profits of justice. In 1435–6 the yields from the estates of Anne Stafford, then perhaps the wealthiest woman in England, can be analysed as 37 per cent rent, 52 per cent farms, 6 per cent casual yearly issues and 5 per cent court perquisites.[3] In such families marriages of children were matters of family policy and enterprise, rather than of free attraction and affection. Children could be betrothed young, though canon law did not allow marriage below the age of seven, and marriages between that age and puberty, twelve for the girl and fourteen for the boy, were supposed to be reviewed then and confirmed as agreeable to the couple or publicly disavowed. The haste was to tie up eligible heirs and heiresses, and the marriages were in the nature of investments and business partnerships. The families negotiated over the heads of the youngsters involved.

The bride's family had to provide a dowry, in money or land, and land assigned as *maritagium* (marriage portion) reverted to the grantor if the grantees left no children. The groom provided dower to cushion his wife's widowhood for life; normally this was a third of his lands but the nature of the allocation varied at different times. In the years up to 1200 the dower was a formal grant, at the church door at the time of the marriage, of a nominated property or one-third of the lands held in free tenure at that time by the husband. Magna Carta (1217, 1225 versions) defined dower as a third of the lands the husband ever held in his lifetime, unless the wife had been dowered with less at the church. By the late thirteenth century dower was allocated from the land held by the husband on the day of his death.[4] By this time, it was becoming common in landed families for the husband's family to settle estates jointly on the married couple, and the wife held on to such jointure if she survived the husband. From the tenant-in-chief's point of view, dower and jointure lands escaped the unwelcome attention of royal custodians during a minority, but whereas the minor heir did come of age and take up his inheritance, no heir could enter dower and jointure lands until the death of any surviving dowagers.

In the nobility, Katherine Neville survived her first husband John Mowbray, duke of Norfolk, by fifty-one years, outliving son, grandson and great-granddaughter. The Clifford estates were briefly supporting three successive dowagers between 1391 and the end of 1393, the widows of the fourth, fifth and sixth lords.[5] In the gentry, Agnes Paston survived her husband William Paston I by thirty-five years, and outlived her eldest son John Paston I by thirteen; John had his anticipable inheritance delayed by the survival of his mother, his wife's mother and his wife's grandmother. In turn, his wife Margaret survived him by eighteen years, outliving her son John II.[6] Dower and jointure protected the wife in widowhood, but the widower in some cases had rights: if a child of the marriage was born alive, whether or not child or mother survived, the husband gained life interest in the mother's lands. This probably lay behind Edmund Tudor's hasty marriage and impregnating of Margaret Beaufort, who bore Henry Tudor at thirteen in 1457, but if this was a calculated risk by Edmund, it backfired, as he died in the sixth month of the pregnancy.

Thus far in this chapter, marriage has been treated as a civil contract and a tool of dynastic aggrandisement. It was, however, also a matter of canon law and a sacrament. By 1100 the church was tightening its grip on marriage, and becoming the sole authority for judging matrimonial cases. Twelfth-century society, which was feudal, military and essentially patriarchal, seems to have accepted the church's control because of the need to define legitimate hereditary succession.[7]

From the beginning of the twelfth century the church offered a public ceremony of marriage, consisting of the exchange of words of consent, and the assignment of dower at the church door, followed by a nuptial mass in the church. Individual archbishops of Canterbury ordered that the celebration of marriage should be public (1175), and that it should follow three publications of banns in church (1200). Marriages not publicly solemnised in the face of the church (*in facie ecclesiae*) were deemed illegal, but not thereby necessarily invalid. Mary O'Regan points to 'several medieval cases in which the ecclesiastical courts (the proper forum) decided against a later, solemnly performed marriage ceremony, followed by consummation, in favour of a prior, informal, unconsummated marriage *per verba de praesenti*'.[8]

For a valid, indissoluble, marriage the church insisted that there should be no impediment of consanguinity or affinity between the contracting parties, who should be free, as individuals, to marry, and that the consent of the couple should be genuine on both sides. If these conditions were fulfilled, marriages contracted in secrecy in any surroundings could be as valid as those contracted publicly in the presence of a priest and other witnesses. There were two ways of creating such a valid marriage: by exchange of vows, even privately, in the present tense (*verba de praesenti*), even if not followed by cohabitation, and by intercourse following an earlier exchange of vows in the future tense (*verba de futuri*). Secret marriages were not uncommon, and some certainly led to later dispute. In the Middle Ages the church courts were the resort of far more people trying to enforce a marriage contract than petitioning for nullity.[9]

In the propertied classes, with so much at stake, self-interest might have been expected to have dictated a more considered approach to matrimony, but there are examples of the clandestine wedding at all levels. Edward IV landed his heirs in dire trouble after his death in 1483 because of his own matrimonial past. It was alleged that he had been pre-contracted to Lady Eleanor Butler before his (therefore bigamous) marriage to Elizabeth Woodville. The truth has never been satisfactorily resolved – both parties to the alleged pre-contract were dead when it was raised – but the argument in 1483 shows that such an allegation could be serious, and Edward's behaviour had laid him open to such charges. His marriage to Elizabeth Woodville was itself concealed at the time, and apparently took place without banns, in a private house, hardly *in facie ecclesiae*,[10] though a priest, his assistant, the bride's mother and two gentlewomen were said to have been present. At gentry level, the secret marriage of Sir William Plumpton and Joan Wintringham led to thirty years of litigation (see below). Perhaps the best-known example is the marriage of Margery Paston to Richard Calle in 1469. The bishop of Norwich tried to break their betrothal, but had to admit defeat in face of its technical validity. Here the motive is clear: the couple betrothed themselves indissolubly in secret because they foresaw Margery's family's opposition.

Besides the problem of clandestinity, there were problems arising from the degrees of consanguinity and affinity constituting impediments to valid marriage. These degrees were reduced in 1215 from seven to four. The prohibition of in-marrying was necessary since the material interests of any powerful family could have worked towards incestuous marriages to keep land from passing to outsiders. However, what the church could rule on it normally could dispense from, and dispensations could be sought for marriage within the prohibited relationships. The nobility and upper gentry are the ones who could be expected to make use of dispensations, to further dynastic policy and because they could afford the procedure. Helmholz notes that papal dispensations are rarely cited in cases involving ordinary people in the consistory courts.[11] One dispensation granted by the pope in May 1477 allowing the marriage of the daughter and heir of the deceased duke of Norfolk with Edward IV's younger son, reveals both the relationship and the age of the couple: it was a dispensation for Richard and Anne, who were described as infants, 'who have completed their fifth and fourth years of age respectively, to contract espousals forthwith, and as soon as they reach the lawful age to contract marriage, not withstanding that they are related in the third and fourth degrees of kindred'.[12] Richard's grandmother and Anne's great-grandmother were sisters. The church did not regard marriage under seven as valid: the necessary free consent could not be meaningfully given by young children. But this infant couple nevertheless married in St Stephen's Chapel, Westminster on 14 January 1478. The ceremony was performed by the bishop of Norwich, and the bride was led to the altar for the nuptial mass by the king, who gave her away. Anne died in November 1481, two years before the disappearance of her husband, one of the 'Princes in the Tower'. The case is as blatant an example of child marriage as one could find at any date, and it is late in the fifteenth century, and not an isolated example, as will become clear below.

Divorce as such was unknown, but a marriage could be annulled, or end in separation. A declaration of nullity could be obtained from the church courts on certain grounds – the most frequent method was by arguing the existence of an earlier clandestine marriage.[13] Other grounds included consanguinity (which was the ground for Louis VII's 'divorce' from Eleanor of Aquitaine, and for King John's from his first wife Isabella of Gloucester, but was not a common cause of annulment), impotence (which was the ground on which Maud Clifford initiated the annulment of her marriage to John Neville, Lord Latimer[14]), duress and the infancy of the parties. Some of the allegations were undoubtedly fraudulent, and witnesses perjured. Separation acknowledged the existence and validity of the marriage bond but allowed the couple to live henceforth apart, in cases such as adultery, heresy, apostasy and cruelty; most cases were brought on grounds of cruelty.[15] The church courts seem to have handled the business before them flexibly and expeditiously. Undoubtedly marital disagreements must have brought individual heartbreak. It is pleasing to see that some couples who later discovered technical impediments were discreetly allowed to legitimise their position in such a way as to avoid local scandal.[16]

[126]

The landed woman's world was thus one of widely known and practised inheritance customs and rules, normally lived out in circumstances reasonably acceptable to society, but exploitable at times to the lengths of abduction of heiresses or their unwilling incarceration in convents. When Ralph Stafford abducted Margaret Audley she had an income potentially at least twenty times his own.[17] All women of the landed classes lived under the same conventions, honoured or breached. Dower was important to the widows of kings, earls, lesser lords, knights and gentry. The production of a legitimate heir throughout these ranks could not be jeopardised by questionable paternity, so the woman's chastity was the more closely watched. Widowed mothers had to do their best to protect the inheritance from kings, feudal overlords, and grasping relatives. They lived in a world which, compared with other women's, had distinctive common threads from queen to countess to lady of a small manor. As Rowena Archer puts it: 'virtually all women of property could expect to exercise a measure of administrative responsibility wherever and whenever the need arose'; in fact 'no undertaking that might normally be deemed the responsibility of men should lie outside the purview of wives, sisters or mothers'.[18]

Subdividing this class into royalty, nobility and gentry edges the discussion towards the later Middle Ages when these classifications fit. The term 'gentry' as a social classification is only a sixteenth-century usage, though this is not to deny the earlier existence of a local non-noble landholding class. After the Norman Conquest, society was stratified by tenure, with tenants-in-chief and subtenants, and the levels interwove. Many of the Domesday subtenant class became the knightly families of the thirteenth and later centuries, and the less clearly definable squirearchy and gentry, both later terms. Yeomen, another later term in its meaning of small landholders, are generally classed beneath the gentry, the relevant distinction being that they tilled their own land – they did not belong to the governing classes. Not only did individual families rise and fall socially over two or three generations, but the whole structure of society shifted over time, with definitions emphasising birth, military service and landed income predominating at different periods. Landholding women in England were never the equals of men when the honours were being given for military service, but they could pull their birthright, and when they did come by vast estates and profits, they ran them on the same lines as the men of their class, with the same kinds of staff.

The numbers of women in the landholding classes were comparatively small at any one time. There was only one queen consort, though there could be a queen dowager, and Joan of Navarre (d. 1437) survived into her (step) grandson's reign. The displaced Anglo-Saxon landholders (of both sexes) in Domesday Book are variously estimated at 4–5,000, but it is clear now that some of them formed a smaller group of overlords (including a minority of women). The dominant barons in 1086 (not exclusively male) numbered about 170, over half holding land worth less than £100 per annum; even if these did not replace several thousand thegns but rather their overlords (a group more like their own in number), the Anglo-Saxon aristocracy must still have been three or four times more numerous than its Norman supplanters, since most 1086 tenants-in-chief had more than one antecessor.

After the Conquest, the 170 main tenants gradually polarised so a baronage or peerage emerged at the top, shading down to landowners of the classes later called knights, esquires and gentlemen. By 1200 there were about 160 barons with lands worth £200 per annum, and in the thirteenth century an estimated 300 families in an upper stratum of society. By the early fourteenth century a new criterion offers itself, the parliamentary peerage, fossilising by writs of summons to a group of known size, approximately sixty to seventy. Within this group came earls and the later gradations of dukes (1337), marquesses (1385) and viscounts (1440). By 1436 earls had incomes of over £2,000 per annum and other peers mostly £300–1,300.[19] These individuals had mothers, some had wives and daughters. Primogeniture prevented nobility multiplying in each generation in England, but it did not prevent landholding classes spreading. However, since the supply of land was finite, this meant that estates fluctuated in size with fragmentations and agglomerations.

Knights appeared in Domesday Book as undertenants or household knights, but the class later rose in status. Military service had been allocated in the late eleventh century to provide an army of about 5,000 knights, but though the 1166 *Cartae Baronum* reveals how tenants-in-chief had made enfeoffments above or below their quota, by the thirteenth century there were insufficient knights, and kings began distraining landholders of above a certain annual landed income to undertake knighthood: in 1242 the qualifying amount was land worth £20 a year, held by military or socage tenure; by the end of the century the figure was £40. Thus can be seen the flexibility of social classes: in Anglo-Saxon times a ceorl who prospered and acquired land and authority could become a thegn, in the thirteenth century the landholder worth £20 a year could be forced to become a knight (or pay a fine).

It is difficult to estimate the size of the gentry class in the later Middle Ages. Christopher Given-Wilson estimates 9–10,000 gentry families in the fifteenth century: a quarter were gentry of county standing, or upper gentry, three-quarters merely 'parish gentry' or lower gentry.[20] Such is the group reviewed in this chapter: small, select and privileged, the governing class. It is not surprising that the womenfolk were better recorded than most, and some, for example Isabella de Fortibus (de Forz) and Margaret Paston, have become perhaps too prominently known, being credited with more typicality than can be proven.

The women of the landholding classes are most objectively seen in archival sources, in estate records, including charters and financial accounts, and in wills and correspondence, and this evidence is weighted towards the later part of the period. A few major women landholders headed estate administrations which have left copious records, among them Isabella de Fortibus, Elizabeth de Burgh, Anne countess of Stafford, her daughter-in-law Anne Neville duchess of Buckingham, and Margaret Beaufort countess of Richmond and Derby. Charter evidence, mainly from after 1200, shows us landholding women, often in association with husbands and heirs, granting land, and many women of these classes were associated with religious foundations especially of the chantry kind. But neither in estate administration nor in their land grants were women doing anything inherently different from the activities of their menfolk, nor were they doing it differently. Running an estate efficiently, and making one's land transactions watertight, were not gender-specific tasks, and to achieve either, both sexes tended to need male stewards, clerks, auditors, councillors and legal experts.

The evidence from wills, mainly from after 1300, is a little more gender specific for two reasons. Firstly, a married woman could only make a will with her spouse's approval, a condition which did not apply to his testamentary power. Partly for this reason, most female testators were widows. Secondly, women's bequests tend to be heavily domestic in colour. It is mainly women's wills that go into details of bedhangings, furnishings, dresses, robes and personal jewellery, often bequeathed to other women, whereas the male will of the same class will concentrate on horses, armour, plate and money bequests. Lady Alice West's will, proved in 1395, disposed of a hierarchy of bedding, and also books, Lady Peryne Clanbowe's in 1422 of plate and gowns, Sir Roger Salwayn's in 1420 of horses and armour.[21]

In the surviving correspondence, largely from the fifteenth century, some women's letters are gender coloured, but most are not. Cosy requests for oranges, frieze for the children's clothes and the odd comment about pregnancy must be balanced against hard-headed reports of writs issued, juries nobbled, arms procured (and used) in defence of the manor house, and the unwillingness of tenants to pay rents. Men writing to women are often penning business rather than domestic matters, but men writing to men can relate domestic affairs. Letters written between women are fairly rare. One of the most famous of the domestic news letters in the Paston collection is Elizabeth Clere's letter to John I concerning the proposed match between Elizabeth Paston and Stephen Scrope, and Elizabeth's treatment by her mother.[22]

Landholding women appear more than others in government archives, for example in judicial records (cases of novel disseisin and dower) and inquisitions post mortem. In dower-related actions stepsons emerge, not surprisingly, as the widow's most predictable adversary.[23] As landholders in their own right women attracted the attention of tax collectors. In the Income Tax of 1436 Anne Stafford's income was assessed at £1,958, apparently reasonably.[24]

Outside of archival sources, landholding women appear fleetingly in narrative sources: chronicle, biography and fiction. Chronicles were mainly the product of religious houses, and of authors who had little personal experience of women and much exposure to antifeminist texts. Not surprisingly, when such chroniclers find a queen positively impressive in some way, they often qualify the individual example with the reminder of its rarity in the sex. Thus the author of the *Gesta Stephani* described King Stephen's wife Matilda of Boulogne as a woman of subtlety and a man's resolution, and Richard of Devizes, writing of Eleanor of Aquitaine, called her 'an incomparable woman, beautiful yet gracious, strong-willed yet kind, unassuming yet sagacious (which is a rare combination in a woman)'.[25] Chroniclers could be positively vitriolic to queens: Matthew Paris, who seldom wrote approvingly about anyone, from the safety of the next reign, described John's queen Isabella of Angouleme as 'an incestuous and depraved woman, so notoriously guilty of adultery that the king gave orders for her lovers to be seized and throttled in her bed'.[26] In chronicles the appearance of women other than queens tends to be impersonal – a patron's lady is accorded due reception on visiting a religious house, but her personality remains hidden. She may earn the writer's approval by contributing to the church's fabric or treasures by gift of money, land or a relic, or by adding her influence to obtain favour from a superior, king, bishop or pope. The Cistercian house of Waverley, Surrey, near to the Montfort castle at Odiham, had a good relationship with the family. In 1245 Countess Eleanor (Henry III's sister), described in the Annals as 'our most sincere friend', visited Waverley with her 'very pious husband, Simon de Montfort earl of Leicester, their two sons, Henry and Simon, and three ladies in waiting'. Eleanor gave the abbey a precious altar cloth and money, and helped it acquire some lands. 'She attended the sermon in chapter, the procession and high mass.'[27] Occasionally a sheer Jezebel had to be denounced: Jennifer Ward cites the instance of Adam of Usk's such handling of Joan Beauchamp, lady of Abergavenny.[28]

There are no biographies of Englishwomen of these classes, but some appear in biographies of their husbands. The wife and daughters of William the Marshal earl of Pembroke (d. 1219) are presented as a loving and united family. On the Marshal's death-bed he asked his wife to kiss him – 'dear love, come and kiss me; it will be for the last time'. Husband and wife wept at this, and the countess and her daughters had to be taken grieving from the scene.[29]

In narrative fiction the class is represented by kings', earls' and knights' wives, paramours and household damsels. The life style portrayed is usually unrealistic in detail, but the setting is distinctly aristocratic. Literary sources are attractive, but their interpretation is open to the changing fashions of literary criticism. The link between landholding women and literature is less controversial if we turn from the content to the inspiration and encouragement of writers. Women were perhaps surprisingly early patrons of writers. Constance FitzGilbert, wife of a Lincolnshire landholder, secured through her husband the loan of a book, probably to be identified with Geoffrey of Monmouth's *History of the Kings of Britain* (*c.* 1136), from Walter Espec at Helmsley, and had it translated into Norman French in the later 1130s by Geoffrey Gaimar. Matthew Paris (d. 1259), the St Albans chronicler, wrote Anglo-Norman lives for women: of St Edmund Rich for Isabel countess of Arundel, and of Edward the Confessor for Queen Eleanor. Robert Grosseteste (d. 1253), bishop of Lincoln, devised a practical estate manual for the countess of Lincoln. Geoffrey Chaucer was a page in the household of Elizabeth countess of Ulster in the 1350s. John Lydgate (d. 1449) composed many minor religious works for women patrons. Margaret Beaufort influenced Caxton's publications, and had her own translations printed.

In art, this is the class of women appearing in finery in Books of Hours and on tapestries of outdoor scenes in hunt and garden. These social classes were armigerous, and female alabaster effigies are likely to be from these levels, whereas monumental brasses can spread down to merchants.

The plentiful evidence about women of the landholding classes needs critical appraisal, which it has not always received in the past. Well-known individuals must not be interpreted as typical of their position or period. The lure of Eleanor of Aquitaine as a queen, Eleanor de Montfort as a countess, Margaret Paston as a country housewife and Margaret Beaufort as a pious bluestocking must be resisted. Each has her claim to fame, but it is more important to place them in context with many others. After generalising about the common conditions pertaining to the lives of these women, it is now proposed to separate them to focus on illustrable areas: the unique position of successive queens and their influence; the life cycle of noblewomen, and the position of the gentry women, which may be seen to parallel the noblewomen's on a lesser scale.

Queens

At the top of the hierarchy came the king's wife, the queen. Anne Crawford, writing in 1981, regarded the choice of a suitable wife as the single most important decision ever made by a medieval king, a view reiterated in her book *Letters of the Queens of England 1100–1547* (1994), a far more significant treatment of queens than its limited title suggests.[30] Queens' roles were inevitably circumscribed by convention, but individuals made some mark. The queen's prime function was to bear a suitable heir. Pauline Stafford's comment that no wife who failed to conceive could ever feel entirely safe,[31] was made of early medieval kings' wives, but is of course best illustrated in the reign of Henry VIII. Primogeniture in royal succession only really solidified in England in the early thirteenth century – as late as 1199 John's succession elbowed out Arthur of Brittany, the son of John's predeceased older brother. The first post-Conquest English succession crisis caused by failure of a royal male heir created an unfortunate precedent. Henry I was strong enough to make his baronage swear to accept his daughter Matilda, the widowed German empress, remarried to Geoffrey of Anjou, but in 1135 his nephew Stephen seized the throne and a civil war ensued. The Empress Matilda lost the war, but her dynasty won the peace; by the treaty of Winchester in 1153 it was her son by Geoffrey who was acknowledged heir to the throne, not Stephen's surviving son William. Henry II's own wife played a characterful role. Eleanor of Aquitaine attracted a lot of attention then and since as a clever, masterful woman and inspirer of courtly literature. She certainly ran the gamut of twelfth-century female experience. Heiress to Aquitaine, and granddaughter of a troubadour count, she was snapped up at about fifteen by the French king Louis VII and bore him two daughters. Failing to bear a male heir, and suspected of infidelity when accompanying her husband on the second crusade, Eleanor was 'divorced' by the king in 1152. She promptly brought her inheritance to Henry of Anjou, about eleven years her junior, and bore him five sons and three daughters. Though eminently satisfactory as a producer of heirs, she failed to satisfy her younger husband sexually and was virtually imprisoned by him in her later years, while he disported with his mistress, fair Rosamund Clifford. Over her offspring Eleanor's influence was politically pernicious, encouraging her sons to rebel against their father, in England and on the Continent.

Another rather extraordinary queen was Isabella, 'the she-wolf of France', wife of Edward II, who played with fire and escaped lightly. Alienated from her apparently homosexually inclined husband, she fled to France with her lover Roger Mortimer, and invaded England in 1326 with him, driving Edward from the throne. The young king Edward III was able to emerge from the tutelage of his mother and her paramour within three years, executing Mortimer and relegating Isabella to dowered comfort; she lived on until 1358. Edward's own wife, Philippa of Hainault, is presented as a much more popular figure, but it is hard to judge whether this was because of her own peacemaking and pleasant personality (consider the image presented by her countryman and one time household clerk Froissart, of her appealing to Edward to soften his treatment of the Calais hostages[32]), or because of the opportunities of the times (Welsh, Scottish and French wars inspired greater travels on campaign and the queen was seen by far more people in the country at large), or because of the increasingly chivalric interests of chroniclers and other writers.

From Bede's day to the Conquest, and less frequently beyond, some widowed queens retired into nunneries. Eleanor of Provence retired to Amesbury in old age, professing as a nun in 1284. The widows of Henry IV and Henry V caused stranger problems. Joan of Navarre was imprisoned by her stepson Henry V for suspected sorcery, probably to deflect her dower income into the king's coffers. (The English queen's dower was instituted before the Conquest and in the fourteenth century was normally a charge of about £4,500 per annum. Unlike other dowers, although the queen's provided her with an income in widowhood, it came into effect immediately, supporting her household while the king lived.) Henry's own wife, Katherine of Valois, presented an acute problem as a youthful widow disinclined to a life of chastity. Legislation was passed curbing her chances of remarriage; however, she bore the obscure Welsh squire Owen Tudor four children in circumstances which were not generally known, and are best described as secret marriage.[33]

Henry VI's queen, Margaret of Anjou, is portrayed as a termagant in the traditional interpretation of fifteenth-century history. In her case perhaps desperate straits inspired extraordinary remedies. Margaret was unpopular as the personification of what seemed to some a shameful and shady peace with France. Given this unpromising start, she found herself married to probably the least able personality of all England's kings. Just when at length her pregnancy seemed to offer better prospects, her husband's mind gave way and she had to endure the duke of York's promotion to regent. Her son's birth gave her a purpose to fight for his succession, but when Margaret took steps to rally a party, her factional favour was held against her. Ultimately she lived to see her son killed in his teens and her husband dead in suspicious circumstances in captivity. Hers was a melancholy tale, and surely a case where a royal couple suffered from being unsuited to conventional requirements: had he been impulsive, determined and provocative and she the nonentity all might have been well.

The next queen of England, Elizabeth Woodville, was so ill-qualified for the post that it is generally assumed Edward IV let passion override political calculation in marrying her at all. Eldest daughter of Sir Richard Woodville, later Earl Rivers, and his higher-born wife, Jacquetta of Luxemburg widow of the duke of Bedford, Elizabeth was a previously married woman, with sons. Unpalatably for a Yorkist queen, she was the widow of a Lancastrian participant in the Wars of the Roses, Sir John Grey of Groby. She bore Edward IV the requisite sons and daughters, but the promotion of her family, the Woodvilles, aroused great resentment among the older nobility, and this had a divisive effect at Edward IV's death in 1483, leading to a final outburst of the civil wars and bloodletting. The political posturings of the early Tudor period make it difficult to judge Elizabeth Woodville's own role, but her career was not enviable. She was in sanctuary when her eldest son, Edward V, was born, during the Lancastrian re-adeption of 1470–1, and took refuge again when Richard of Gloucester seized this son and imprisoned his uncle, Earl Rivers, prior to usurping the throne. Quite what she hoped to salvage for her daughters from either Richard III or Henry Tudor is unclear, still less how. But her eldest daughter, Elizabeth of York, lived through dangerous times to become Henry VII's queen, and ancestress of the Tudor dynasty.

Elizabeth of York makes an appropriate final illustration of a medieval queen, for her primary function was transmission of throne-right by blood, with the secondary one making peace between warring factions. She died in childbed after the birth of her sixth child, Catherine, in 1503. As her accounts 'are full of repayments to her ladies for gambling debts settled, sometimes using her winnings',[34] the playful habits of royalty as well as the conventional responsibilities of this queen may be seen.

All in all, it appears that the medieval queen of England was principally a breeding animal and desirably of good stock, in terms of both health and status. Most outlived their husbands. The queen had normally been a first-time bride: the Black Prince's marriage to Joan of Kent in 1361 was a little risky because of her chequered matrimonial history, though she was Edward I's granddaughter. Elizabeth Woodville was also a widow, but the lowliness of her birth and greed of her relatives gave offence. A few other kings married widows, especially as second wives when they already had heirs by the first. Diplomatic marriages were frequent in royalty, but this suggests optimism triumphing over precedent, for successful marriages long outlasted their short-term and soon irrelevant motive, as in the case of Edward III and Philippa of Hainault, and unfortunate ones long attracted opprobrium from the political overtones – as with Henry VI and Margaret of Anjou.

Outside the immediate function of royal wife and mother, circumstances might offer a queen the chance to be particularly influential in the public sphere, for example as a cultural patron and model of piety. Henry I's wife Matilda is an early example of both. Crawford claims that it is clear from her few surviving letters 'that Matilda displayed a scholarship rare among laymen and quite exceptional among laywomen'. However, it is difficult to substantiate this claim as the letters would have been written by a clerk, as Crawford admits, and the argument that 'the tone suggests that they were quite closely dictated by Matilda' can be no more than a matter of opinion.[35] There are other indications of this queen's literary and pious tastes however. It appears that it was at her behest that the longer *Life of St Margaret* (her mother) was written (in Latin), and the Anglo-Norman *Voyage of St Brendan* was composed for her.[36] Crawford tells of Matilda's daily visits to Westminster Abbey; she was founder of Holy Trinity Priory, Aldgate, London (1107), and the hospital of St Giles in the Fields, and Baker calls hers 'a formidable personality and a restless piety'.[37]

Wace dedicated his *Brut* to Eleanor of Aquitaine, who is portrayed as an arbitress of courtly love in western European culture. Later, Queens' College at Cambridge reflects the patronage of three unequal successors, Margaret of Anjou, Elizabeth Woodville and Anne Neville (wife of Richard III), but this seems a clear case of it being the appropriate charitable fashion of the day, not an equally genuine interest of each individual. Anne of Bohemia's painters are credited by Susan Bell with revitalising English art at the end of the fourteenth century; Crawford denies any overt trace of Bohemian artistic influence attributable to the queen or her immediate household, but Gervase Matthew noted a suggestion that the illuminations of the *Liber Regalis*, a manuscript on coronation rites, 'were the work of a Bohemian in the queen's service; certainly they reflect Luxemburg standards of taste and have no English precedent'.[38]

Queens could hardly, however, be role models, for their unique position was not one to be emulated. Moreover, they could hardly be models for other women at all because only a comparatively small circle of women saw them in action. The modern intense media interest in the royal family makes it necessary to emphasise how totally irrelevant to the lives of most medieval English people their royals were, hence it was not widely known that Henry VI's widowed mother had borne four other children!

In terms of influencing their subjects, therefore, queens were not as important as might be thought; it must have been their influence on their husbands which had more significance in practical terms. There was a long tradition of queens as interceders in politics. Crawford tells us that Matilda's intercession was begged for by the clergy in 1105, and 'she burst into tears but said she could not intervene', Philippa's pleas for the Calais burghers are well known from Froissart, and Richard II's queen Anne of Bohemia was humiliated when her pleas to the Appellants in 1387, for the life of Sir Simon Burley, were overruled.[39] The queen's influence on the king has to be at root a matter of personality – both the queen's influence and the king's receptiveness – it was never constitutionally regulated. Current convention must also have played a part, in defining the areas in which a queen might be expected to involve herself, and those where her involvement would be totally unexpected and, if attempted, unwelcome.

Noblewomen

Noblewomen would not, probably, have modelled themselves on queens but they did have similar experiences on a more private scale. This can surely be illustrated from the exceptional career of

Margaret Beaufort, Henry VII's mother, who was one of the most influential 'queen mothers' of the Middle Ages (or of any period), but who came to this role not as a retired queen, but as a promoted countess.

As the main conditions of the noblewoman's existence, the inheritance rules, marriage customs and widows' entitlements against which she lived out her life, have already been indicated, it is proposed in this section not to dip into these areas in categories for illustrable examples but to follow through the woman's life cycle, which is actually, because of the availability of evidence, more clearly illustrated in this class than for the peasant and lesser landowning classes more commonly studied in cyclical study by anthropologically or sociologically minded historians.

It is for the noblewoman that there is the best chance of knowing the precise date of an individual's birth. Margaret Beaufort's, on 31 May 1443, was entered in a Book of Hours which she inherited from her mother, and left to her chapel in Westminster Abbey.[40] Noble infants were generally wet-nursed and reared within the family household until adolescence by governesses, maids and tutors. Noble boys passed from the hands of women to male tuition traditionally round seven, though individual experiences varied. The girls remained in the care of women, having a less formal education than their brothers. Royal and high aristocratic households did have mistresses for their girls: Nicholas Orme cites Cecilia of Sandford who was mistress to Eleanor, King John's youngest daughter, and later to Joan de Mountchesney.[41] John of Gaunt first employed Katherine Swynford as governess to his daughters Philippa and Elizabeth, later making her his mistress and finally his third wife. Orme suggests the mistress was 'likely to have provided general teaching on dress, behaviour, singing and dancing, with technical help from clergy in religious topics, minstrels with music and grooms with horses'.[42] This is not an academic education, but there was some support for teaching girls to read – largely for their salvation – and clearly some could. *The Book of the Knight of the Tower*, a French aristocratic work translated into English in Henry VI's reign, and translated again by Caxton who published it in 1483, a work Orme calls 'the first book on the education of women to circulate in England', though concentrating on character and behaviour rather than accomplishments, did expect the knight's daughters to learn to read, and the knight says 'as for wrytynge it is no force yf a woman can nought of hit, but as for redynge I saye that good and prouffytable is to al wymen'.[43]

Girls' education in letters was less formally organised than their brothers', and has left fewer traces. Henry Bolingbroke soon had his children exposed to the written word: primers and ABCs were bought in 1397 for his two daughters when they were aged five and two-and-a-half.[44] The Conqueror's daughter, King Stephen's mother, Adela, read Latin poetry and prose, and Henry I's wife Matilda read Latin, but there is no sign that aristocratic women knew Latin grammar after 1200, until the very end of the fifteenth century; even Margaret Beaufort had only 'a little perceiving' of it according to her confessor John Fisher.[45] Such women read French, however. Anglo-Norman was the language of the aristocracy after 1066 until into the fourteenth century; however, by the mid- to late thirteenth century it was becoming necessary to have teaching aids for French instruction. Around 1250 Walter of Bibbesworth wrote his *Tretiz de langage*, to help Denise de Mountchesney teach her children.[46] Despite her small Latin, Margaret Beaufort read French well enough to translate from it.

From their own and others' wills, we know aristocratic ladies possessed books. Lady Alice West in 1395 left all her Latin, English and French books to her daughter-in-law, and texts in specific languages can be identified passing to women and from them – Henry Lord Percy left a French bestiary to his daughter Isabella in 1349, and Sir Robert Roos a French book of ancient histories to his daughter-in-law Joan and a French *Legenda Sanctorum* and psalter to his daughter Eleanor in 1392. The same Eleanor Roos left her nephew's wife an English book called 'the first book of Master Walter [Hilton]' in 1438.[47] Aristocratic girls also learned artistic skills such as embroidery, working with the finest materials. More practically, Anne Talbot, daughter of Gilbert Lord Talbot, had a governess and a tutor, and was given practical experience in handling household money and overseeing the daily account book, between 1402 and 1411.[48]

Childhood was often disrupted by the death of a parent and remarriage of the survivor. Stepbrothers and sisters by serial marriages grew up in the same households, but primogeniture was divisive even among children of the same parents.[49] Margaret Beaufort, the only child of her mother's marriage to John Beaufort, was brought up with the children of her earlier marriage to Sir Oliver St John, apparently happily since Margaret worked an embroidery of their descent for the marriage of John St John in 1498.[50] Sometimes girls were sent to nunneries for education up to ten to fourteen, before entering a lay household.[51]

Many daughters of the nobility were initially betrothed young – Margaret herself was married at six to the seven-year-old son of the duke of Suffolk, who was her guardian, but this was dissolved in 1453 and her wardship and marriage were transferred to Edmund and Jasper Tudor. She and Edmund were married in 1455. Her most recent biographers castigate Edmund for making her pregnant too young. It was appreciated that such young pregnancies were dangerous to the mother: the marriage contract tying Elizabeth, daughter of Thomas Lord Clifford, to William Plumpton (after the death of her earlier fiancé, his brother Robert) specified she was not to be lain with until the age of sixteen.[52]

The nobility was anxious, throughout the Middle Ages, to arrange suitable marriages for its offspring. Though Sir James Holt disputes the common interpretation of the promise in Magna Carta (1215) that heirs and heiresses should not be disparaged in marriage, as then reflecting feeling against marriage to an inferior partner, there was some feeling against such alliances. Woodville brides were bestowed on English earls, with at least rumoured resentment, at the end of the fifteenth century. On the other hand some noblewomen voluntarily disparaged themselves, especially in widowhood. Joan of Acre, daughter of Edward I and dowager countess of Gloucester, willingly espoused a mere knight, Ralph de Monthermer; the duke of Bedford's widow married Sir Richard Woodville, only later made Lord Rivers by Henry VI. Even without disparagement, the pressures on couples could seem, to modern eyes, unfair. Particularly in instances where brothers married sisters, it looks like dynastic policy overruling personal inclination. John of Gaunt, after the death of Blanche of Lancaster, married Constance, daughter and heir of the murdered King Pedro of Castile, in September 1371, and the following January assumed the title King of Castile and Leon. His younger brother Edmund Langley married her sister Isabel the following July. It seems unlikely that all four parties to these arrangements were equally enchanted by their spouses.

A century later the two daughters and coheiresses of Richard

Neville, earl of Warwick, were in a vulnerable position because of their wealth and power. The elder daughter, Isabel, was married to George, duke of Clarence, brother of Edward IV, in July 1469, before her father's death at the battle of Barnet in 1471. The younger, Anne, originally betrothed to Edward prince of Wales, killed at or shortly after the battle of Tewkesbury in 1471, was pursued by Clarence's younger brother Richard duke of Gloucester, to Clarence's annoyance. They were married on 12 July 1472. The sisters' widowed mother Anne, who had brought the Beauchamp inheritance to Richard Neville, was disinherited for the brothers' benefit, and only fared marginally better under Henry VII.[53] Wealth undoubtedly created its own problems for women.

For properly negotiated marriages high prices were paid. A portion worth £1,000 was settled on Katherine Stafford in 1458 on her marriage to John earl of Shrewsbury.[54] With negotiations complete, festive celebrations were mounted to give publicity to the actual marriage. Ward tells us that when Thomas Mowbray earl of Nottingham married Elizabeth Montague, née Arundel, in 1384, celebrations at Arundel Castle in Sussex lasted over a week. Women were sentimental: Isabel countess of Warwick left her wedding gown in her will, drawn up in 1439.[55] A well-publicised wedding was helpful: Richard II's mother Joan of Kent complicated her life considerably by her clandestine marriage to Sir Thomas Holland when she was twelve, a marriage eventually upheld by the Curia in preference to her subsequent marriage to William Montague, later earl of Salisbury.

Once married, noble wives, like queens, were safest if they bore heirs. Barrenness was not ground for divorce, but it may have been a motive for seeking extrication from a marriage. *Hali Meidhad*, a letter on virginity, dating from around 1200, comments on the barren wife: 'her lord loves her and honours her less'.[56] It is impossible to tell whether childlessness was the start of the discontent in some childless marriages, or the product of it. The last earl of Warenne (d. 1347) and Joan of Bar were unhappily married, and childless, and he tried to annul the marriage on the grounds of precontract with his mistress Maud de Neirford, by whom he had several children. The marriage was upheld, however, and Joan survived to enjoy her dower.

Noble wives do not appear to have retreated into discreet privacy until late in pregnancy. In a letter of November 1472, John

Paston II reflected uneasily on his coarse jesting to the duchess of Norfolk, his patron's wife: 'they say that I said my lady was large and great and that it should have enough room to go out at'.[57] A birth, especially when an heir was needed, was a moment for publicity and celebration. Expenditure for the lying-in could extend to new furnishings, and it was useful to have witnesses about the castle or manor to testify to the heir's age in future years. The affinity felt involved: 'God send my lady of Norfolk a son, for upon that rests much matter.'[58] *The Pageant of the Birth, Life and Death of Richard Beauchamp Earl of Warwick*, which Antonia Gransden believes to have been executed between 1485 and 1490, probably for Richard's daughter Anne, Richard Neville's widow, shows his mother in bed after his delivery, with another woman holding the baby and three serving women in attendance.[59] Noble wives, like lesser ones, bore children too rapidly for their physical health, and not infrequently died young as a result. Their rapid pregnancies may have been facilitated by the practice of putting their children out to wet-nurses. Mary Bohun, who bore Henry Bolingbroke seven children, the first when she was thirteen, died in 1394 giving birth to the last at twenty-four.

During her marriage, the noblewoman generally subordinated herself to her husband's interests. In a few cases the couple ran separate household staffs, but this was not common, and most married noble households were male dominated. Kate Mertes characterises the English noble household as relatively small and constantly on the move in the period *c.* 1250 to 1380, larger and more complex thereafter, with departmentalisation and specialisation. Conspicuous consumption was a matter of policy. The most powerful ladies spent extravagantly maintaining their position. Elizabeth de Burgh entertained Edward III *en route* to Sluys in 1340; she had goldsmiths working for her, and an illuminator in her household in 1339; clothing and furs were a major expenditure.[60] Noblewomen employed more personal servants, and depended more on these for companionship, than noblemen did.[61] The noble wife, however, could take part in running the joint household, and indeed the estates, in her husband's absence on estate or other business, on royal administrative duties or on military service. The Hundred Years War presented some wives and mothers with the additional burdens of raising ransom moneys to secure their husbands' and sons' release.[62] Earlier the crusades had led to marital absenteeism. In these circumstances the wife was often involved in sanctioning administrative decisions to be effected by stewards and bailiffs.

The noblewoman's life style embraced hunting, hawking, probably less frequently attending jousts, watching plays and minstrelsy brought to the house, and acting hostess to gatherings which could be both socially and politically important in the family's advancement or maintenance of status. Religious and charitable activities were expected of them: Margaret Beaufort was an outstanding example for religious observance and benefaction but many doing more ordinary good deeds set more imitable examples. Ward tells us that Elizabeth Berkeley, whose household was about fifty strong around 1420, normally had the local parish priest to Sunday dinner.[63] Orme sees the free grammar school founded at Wotton-under-Edge (Glos.) by Lady Katherine Berkeley in 1384 as 'the archetype of the endowed schools of later times'; a century later Lady Anne Wingfield established a grammar master at Rushworth College in Norfolk in 1490 to teach the five poor boys on the foundation and eight other children.[64]

Most marriages were for life, annulment was not common. However, with short life expectancy, Christopher Brooke points out that 'till death us do part' in the Middle Ages meant ten to twelve years, and second and third marriages were common.[65] Youthful widows were commonplace in the nobility: indeed some child brides were widowed before they were properly married. At the age of nine a girl who lost her husband was eligible for dower.[66] Margaret Beaufort was widowed at thirteen, and married again within fifteen months. She lived happily, though childlessly, with Sir Henry Stafford for fourteen years; he died in October 1471 when she was still only twenty-eight, and by June 1472 Margaret was married to Lord Stanley. There was more to medieval remarriage than loneliness seeking companionship. With dower and jointure held for life, a remarrying widow brought landed wealth from an earlier husband to a later marriage. Anne Stafford, successively married to two Stafford brothers, retained a hold on over half the Stafford inheritance from the time of her second husband's death in 1403 until her own in 1438, being married in the interim to Sir William Bourchier, Count of Eu, by whom she bore sons. Anne Neville, widowed duchess of Buckingham, her daughter-in-law, held Stafford estates from 1460 to 1480 meanwhile marrying Lord

Mountjoy. Of fifteenth-century widowed English peeresses, Rosenthal finds eighty-nine of 162 did not remarry.[67] Well-founded serial marriages could persist in enhancing a widow's career, but at any point in this process the sitting husband might be the one left in life possession by courtesy of England, which allowed an heiress's widower to hold her lands for the rest of his life provided the marriage had not been childless.

It is as widows that many medieval noblewomen left their mark. Their landed wealth brought them power and prestige which they had not enjoyed separately from their husbands while mere wives. It was in their widowhoods in the thirteenth century that Isabella de Fortibus was a force to be reckoned with, and Devorguilla de Balliol in a position to develop the Oxford college whose foundation had been imposed on her husband as a penance. In the next century, the widowed Elizabeth de Burgh and Marie de St Pol founded Clare and Pembroke colleges at Cambridge, and eventually the widowed Lady Margaret Beaufort eclipsed all others, founding Christ's College in her lifetime and St John's after her death. However, perhaps not surprisingly, widows' household accounts show their establishments were among the most economical and orderly. This is not entirely a matter of necessity mothering economy: a household with a female head had less political and military expenditure to finance. Widows do, however, appear to have been the most charitably inclined.[68]

The noble widow inherited estates, ecclesiastical patronage, a household framework and servants from her husband. But she was more defenceless than her husband had been. There is a recurrent thread, in the history of this class, of widows cheated by more powerful persons. Anne Stafford was unjustly treated by Henry V when he succeeded in getting a repartition of the Bohun lands descending through Mary countess of Hereford and Eleanor duchess of Gloucester in 1421.[69] Widows of attainted nobility were apt to receive high-handed treatment. Richard of Gloucester deprived the countess of Oxford of her lands unjustly.[70] The widows' tenure of family property was a weak period when political vultures might pounce.

Safely past childbearing, and for the most part removed from political intrigue, many English noble dowagers lived to a ripe old age. Joan countess of Hereford died in 1419 after holding a third of the Bohun estates in dower for forty-six years. Margaret

Beaufort herself outlived her son. Katherine Neville, duchess of Norfolk, outlived four husbands; her sister Cecily duchess of York outlived all her sons. In their old age many of these dowagers lived in semi-conventual households, with more female servants than was usual in noble households. They looked to the future, to their grandchildren in particular, and to the past, busying themselves with tidying up family monuments and chantries. Margaret Lady Hungerford had her own ideas about the Hungerford family mausoleum, clashing in some respects with those laid down by her father-in-law.[71] For the most part these ladies thought in terms of the nuclear family, and sought to benefit the souls of direct ancestors and the material standing of direct descendants. Some made themselves ready for death, and left precise instructions as to where they should be buried (with ancestral tombs, and successive husbands, their choice might be complicated), what sort of funeral arrangements should be made and how their property should be disposed of.

Gentlewomen

From noble daughters descending in the social hierarchy, to yeomen's daughters marrying upwards, the English medieval gentlewoman mirrored many aspects of the noblewoman, deliberately. Indeed, it is common today for books and articles apparently restricted to the nobility to admit to embracing the gentry and indeed the whole class of landholders who did not till their own lands.[72]

Less is known about the details of individual lives in the gentry than in the aristocracy, but there is still plentiful if piecemeal information. Birth was just as hazardous and infant mortality little different. Edmund Paston accepted the inevitability: 'my sister is delivered, and the child passed to God, who send us his grace'.[73] Children were reared in the family household until old enough to be sent to a social superior, or at least an equal, for the household-type of education. Sir William Plumpton sought Brian Rocliffe's help in 1464 apparently for obtaining a place for his niece Isabel Marley in the household of Joan Lady Ingoldesthorpe.[74] Patently the girls' education was hardly of academic quality, but they were taught to read English, and accomplishments such as music and embroidery besides household management. At four, young Margaret Plumpton, already installed in the home of her intended future in-laws, was beginning to learn French and her psalter.[75] The necessity of reading and writing for themselves was not obvious for girls in households where clerks were at hand for secretarial work: Margery Brews' Valentine to John Paston III was actually penned by a clerk of her father's![76] Gentry women may not have been scholars, but obviously many were shrewd practical women in the experiences required of them, and in the fifteenth century increasingly able to manage the levels of literacy required for more personal religion, and reading as recreation.

Their marriages paralleled the aristocracy's in that they were matters for negotiation and family settlement, and often youthful. The sorry tale of Margery Paston's betrothal in 1469 to the family employee Richard Calle, and her family's attempt to break it, shows the intensity of their shame at the disparagement, and the bitterness was lasting. Calle, however, continued to be employed, and Keith Dockray suggests that whereas Margery was looked down on for marrying beneath her, Calle was not blamed for trying to better himself.[77] The stakes were lower than in noble alliances, but the principles were the same, as sharp practice in the Plumpton family shows well. Sir William Plumpton made an arranged marriage to Elizabeth Stapleton when he was twelve. She had a dowry of 360 marks, and died leaving him two sons and several daughters. His eldest son's widow was married to the second son, and he died in 1461 leaving two daughters. Within three years Sir William had arranged marriages for these: Margaret to John Rocliffe and Elizabeth to John Suthill. The Rocliffes and Suthills thought they were each getting one of two coheiresses. John Suthill's father, however, was sufficiently wary to insist that should Sir William produce a male heir, this heir should be given to him for wardship, and marriage to a Suthill daughter. However, Sir William was already secretly married, in the 1450s, to one Joan Wintringham, by whom he had a son Robert. He also had at least two acknowledged bastard sons, and seems to have been happy to let Joan's son appear bastard until events became too pressing. With the ecclesiastical courts pursuing him for living with Joan, he acknowledged her to be his wife in 1468, and the marriage was found valid in 1472. This made Robert the heir male, and after Sir William's death in 1480 a dispute erupted between the Rocliffes and the Suthills and Robert, which lasted thirty years.[78] Clandestine marriage was surprisingly common in the propertied classes given the problems it caused. Why couples should enter into it, except in bad faith hoping to break it more easily, is hard to imagine, though some clandestine marriages were to blur the reality of the bride's prenuptial pregnancy, or perhaps to create a marriage which the church would not at the time have allowed but might permit to continue if later presented with a *fait accompli*. An impeccably conducted ceremony and properly publicised births were as valuable to the gentry as to the nobility. All tenants-in-chief had to be able to provide necessary proof of age to succeed to their inheritance, and the variety of plausible *aides-mémoire* cited gives insight into the gentry world.

Once made, gentry marriages could be as happy or unbearable as the nobility's. The gentry may have had marginal advantage in that there were more local equals to match with, allowing perhaps more room for private manoeuvre, and more privacy in the smaller households, to allow both courtship and a less public married life. Margery Brews' mother was a helpful agent in the romance between Margery and John Paston. Arranged and youthful marriages often seem to have settled down into reasonable and affectionate companionships. Margaret Paston identified herself fully with her husband's interests, and made a brave defence of the manor house at Gresham when it was attacked by Lord Moleyns' men in 1449. Margery sent and received affectionate messages in correspondence with her husband.

Like the aristocracy, only less wealthy, gentry widows held dower and jointure lands to the detriment of heirs, and ran their own households with economy and style. *The Household Book of Dame Alice de Bryene*, a widow living in Suffolk in the teens of the fifteenth century, shows a constant stream of visitors entertained at Acton, including many ecclesiastics: two friars of Sudbury, others from Norwich, Clare, Ipswich, Colchester, Babwell and even Hereford, and numerous secular clergy, the rector of Withersfield, vicar of Acton, rectors of Lidgate and Stanstead and two priests of Slapton (Devon) where Alice's husband was buried. Many gentry widows, like aristocratic ones, remarried, creating the same accumulations of dower and multiple-parented families.

It is clear that gentry women were noblewomen writ small, and that they were conscious of this may be demonstrated from the

Paston family's anxiety to copy the aristocracy in abnormal circumstances such as mourning over Christmas.[79] Dukes, earls and
barons were legally defined and identifiable, but with gentry there
was no legal definition and a wider scale for acceptance – gentle
is that gentle does. Consequently doing the proper thing was
important, and in view of the traditional crediting of women with
the more sensitive ear to social nuance, medieval gentlewomen's
all-round emulation of the aristocracy is not surprising.

Conclusions

These landholding classes produced the famous individual English
women of the Middle Ages, those whose careers seem to belie all
that is taught about the inferiority and powerlessness of women.
In these strata, it may look as though the woman's role was quite
enviable – Power went so far as to award the lady of the upper
classes 'considerably more scope than she sometimes enjoyed at a
much later period, for example in the eighteenth and early nineteenth century'.[80] None is more familiar, or more extraordinary,
than Lady Margaret Beaufort, 'the brightest ornament of her sex
in the fifteenth century' in the words of her nineteenth-century
biographer, Caroline Halsted. Margaret's latest biographers take a
shrewder perspective, crediting her with a calculating tempera-
ment and natural astuteness, 'a veteran of bruising political bat-
tles', whose life and works show 'a constant blend of the practical
and the pious which argues at least an active and disciplined will'.[81]
Margaret suffered the disadvantages of her birth and sex, as a
valuable commodity on the marriage market. When, extraordinarily, she reached a position of influence which allowed her to act
to get her position redefined, it is interesting to see how she moved:
she was the only woman licensed to retain under fee, she was
given *feme sole* status (while still married to Stanley) by act of
parliament, and she took a vow of chastity while her husband
lived. These acts show surely the disadvantages she felt conscious
of, disadvantages under which normal upper-class women had to
carry on living. Thousands of them over the centuries undertook
their conventional roles, voicing neither enthusiasm nor protest.
Housed in comparative comfort, and buttressed, civil war conditions excluded, by a network of kin and affinities, they led a

physically less demanding life, for the most part, than the towns-women and countrywomen. Here was concentrated the conspicuous consumption of the Middle Ages, fine clothes and jewels and plate, illuminated manuscripts, etiquette and ceremony. Here can be seen what women were capable of when under minimum constraint, that is in well-provided widowhood, and it is surely quite impressive that so many emerge as patrons of literature and education and benefactresses of the church.

Notes

1   J. C. Ward, *English Noblewomen in the Later Middle Ages*, Harlow, 1992, pp. 125, 126; M. K. Jones and M. G. Underwood, *The King's Mother, Lady Margaret Beaufort, Countess of Richmond and Derby*, Cambridge, 1992, pp. 93–136.
2   J. C. Holt, 'Feudal society and the family in early medieval England: iv the heiress and the alien', *Transactions of the Royal Historical Society*, 5th series, XXXV, 1985, pp. 2, 8–19.
3   Ward, *Noblewomen*, p. 122.
4   *Ibid.*, p. 27.
5   I am grateful to Dr R. T. Spence for alerting me to this situation. G[eorge] E[dward] C[okayne] *Complete Peerage*, III, London, 1913, p. 292.
6   Ward, *Noblewomen*, pp. 37–8; C. Richmond, *The Paston Family in the Fifteenth Century: the first phase*, Cambridge, 1990, pp. 129, 185.
7   C. N. L. Brooke, *The Medieval Idea of Marriage*, Oxford, 1989, pp. 104, 142.
8   M. O'Regan, 'The Pre-contract and its effect on the succession in 1483', in *Richard III: crown and people*, ed. J. Petre, London, 1985, p. 52.
9   R. H. Helmholz, *Marriage Litigation in Medieval England*, Cambridge, 1974, p. 25.
10   O'Regan, 'Pre-contract', p. 53.
11   Helmholz, *Marriage Litigation*, pp. 85–6. The nobility and gentry tended to bring their disputes to the bishop in person or his court of audience, *ibid.*, p. 161.
12   P. Jones, 'Anne Mowbray', in Petre (ed.), *Richard III*, pp. 86–7.
13   Helmholz, *Marriage Litigation*, pp. 64–5.
14   S. Shahar, *The Fourth Estate: a history of women in the middle ages*, trsl. C. Galai, London and New York, 1990, p. 137.

15 Helmholz, *Marriage Litigation*, p. 101.
16 See examples in R. N. Swanson (ed.), *A Calendar of the Register of Richard Scrope, Archbishop of York 1398–1405*, I, York, 1981, pp. 24, 101–2.
17 C. Rawcliffe, *The Staffords, Earls of Stafford and Dukes of Buckingham 1394–1521*, Cambridge, 1978, p. 8.
18 R. Archer, ' "How ladies ... who live on their manors ought to manage their households and estates": women as landholders and administrators in the later middle ages', in J. P. J. Goldberg (ed.), *Woman is a Worthy Wight: women in English society* c. *1200–1500*, Stroud, 1992, p. 150.
19 H. L. Gray, 'Incomes from land in England, 1436', *English Historical Review*, XLIX, 1934, p. 619.
20 C. Given-Wilson, *The English Nobility in the Later Middle Ages: the fourteenth-century political community*, London, 1987, pp. 72–3.
21 F. J. Furnivall (ed.), *The Fifty Earliest English Wills in the Court of Probate, London 1387–1439*, Early English Text Society, London, 1882, pp. 4–6, 49–51, 52–4.
22 N. Davis, *Paston Letters and Papers of the Fifteenth Century*, Oxford, I 1971, II 1976, ii, no. 446. 104 of Margaret Paston's letters survive.
23 J. S. Loengard, ' "Of the gift of her husband": English dower and its consequences in the year 1200', in J. Kirshner and S. T. Wemple (eds.), *Women of the Medieval World: essays in honour of John H. Mundy*, Oxford, 1985, p. 232.
24 Ward, *Noblewomen*, p. 128.
25 A. Crawford (ed.), *Letters of the Queens of England 1100–1547*, Stroud, 1994, pp. 25, 34.
26 *Ibid.*, p. 48.
27 A. Gransden, *Historical Writing in England*, c. *550 to* c. *1307*, London, 1974, p. 414.
28 Ward, *Noblewomen*, p. 4.
29 Gransden, *Historical Writing*, p. 354.
30 A. Crawford, 'The king's burden? The consequences of royal marriage in fifteenth-century England', in R. A. Griffiths (ed.), *Patronage, the Crown and the Provinces in Later Medieval England*, Gloucester, 1981, p. 33. See also Crawford, *Letters of the Queens*, *passim*.
31 P. Stafford, *Queens, Concubines and Dowagers: the king's wife in the early middle ages*, London, 1983, p. 62.
32 J. Froissart, *Chronicles*, selected, trsl. and ed. G. Brereton, Harmondsworth, 1968, pp. 10, 106–10.
33 Crawford, *Letters of the Queens*, pp. 8–9, 111; R. A. Griffiths and

R. S. Thomas, *The Making of the Tudor Dynasty*, Gloucester, 1985, pp. 28–9; Griffiths, *Law Quarterly Review*, XCIII, 1977, 'Queen Katherine of Valois and a missing statute of the realm', pp. 248–58.

34 K. Mertes, *The English Noble Household 1250–1600: good governance and public rule*, Oxford, 1988, p. 94.

35 Crawford, *Letters*, pp. 20–1.

36 D. Baker, '"A Nursery of Saints": St Margaret of Scotland reconsidered', in Baker (ed.), *Medieval Women*, Studies in Church History, Subsidia I, 1978, p. 124; A. M. Lucas, *Women in the Middle Ages: religion, marriage and letters*, Brighton, 1983, p. 172.

37 Crawford, *Letters*, pp. 20–1; Baker, 'A Nursery', p. 140.

38 S. G. Bell, 'Medieval women book owners: arbiters of lay piety and ambassadors of culture', in M. Erler and M. Kowaleski (eds.), *Women and Power in the Middle Ages*, Athens, Gia and London, 1988, p. 177; Crawford, *Letters*, p. 104; G. Mathew, *The Court of Richard II*, London, 1968, p. 39.

39 Crawford, *Letters*, pp. 21, 104; and above, n. 32.

40 Jones and Underwood, *King's Mother*, pp. 32, 34 and plate 1.

41 N. Orme, *From Childhood to Chivalry: the education of the English kings and aristocracy 1066–1530*, London and New York, 1984, p. 26.

42 *Ibid.*, p. 27.

43 *Ibid.*, pp. 108, 157, citing M. Y. Offord, *William Caxton, The Book of the Knight of the Tower*, Early English Text Society, Supplementary Series, II, 1971, pp. 13, 122.

44 K. B. McFarlane, *The Nobility of later Medieval England*, Oxford, 1973, p. 43.

45 Orme, *Childhood to Chivalry*, pp. 160–1.

46 *Ibid.*, p. 124.

47 Furnivall, *English Wills*, p. 4; H. M. Jewell, 'The cultural interests and achievements of the secular personnel of the local administration' in *Profession, Vocation and Culture in Later Medieval England*, ed. C. H. Clough, Liverpool, 1982, pp. 135–7.

48 Mertes, *Noble Household*, p. 174.

49 *Ibid.*, p. 165.

50 Jones and Underwood, *King's Mother*, p. 31.

51 Orme, *Childhood to Chivalry*, p. 65.

52 K. Dockray, 'Why did fifteenth-century English gentry marry? The Pastons, Plumptons and Stonors reconsidered', in M. Jones (ed.), *Gentry and Lesser Nobility in Late Medieval Europe*, Gloucester, 1986, p. 65.

53 A. J. Pollard, *North-Eastern England during the Wars of the Roses: lay society, war and politics 1450–1500*, Oxford, 1990, pp. 318–21, 384.

54 Rawcliffe, *Staffords*, pp. 119–20.
55 Ward, *Noblewomen*, p. 12; Furnivall, *English Wills*, p. 118.
56 B. Millett and J. Wogan-Browne (eds.), *Medieval English Prose for Women*, Oxford, 1990, p. 31.
57 Davis, *Paston Letters*, I, no. 269.
58 *Ibid.*, no. 296.
59 Gransden, *Historical Writing in England* c. *1307 to the Early Sixteenth Century*, London and Henley, 1982, p. 312; Orme, *Childhood to Chivalry*, p. 8.
60 Mertes, *Noble Household*, p. 9; Ward, *Noblewomen*, pp. 92, 77, 83, 63.
61 Mertes, *Noble Household*, p. 43.
62 M. A. Hicks, 'Counting the cost of war: the Moleyns ransom and the Hungerford land sales, 1453–87', *Southern History*, VIII, 1986, pp. 11–31 discusses Lady Hungerford's travails in this area, which were complicated by attainders in the Wars of the Roses.
63 Ward, *Noblewomen*, p. 104.
64 N. Orme, *English Schools in the Middle Ages*, London, 1973, pp. 188–9, 268.
65 Brooke, *Medieval Idea of Marriage*, p. 262.
66 Orme, *Childhood to Chivalry*, p. 7.
67 J. T. Rosenthal, 'Fifteenth-century widows and widowhood: bereavement, reintegration and life choices', in S. S. Walker (ed.), *Wife and Widow in Medieval England*, Ann Arbor, 1993, p. 36; see also his section on widows in *Patriarchy and Families of Privilege in Fifteenth-Century England*, Philadelphia, 1991, pp. 175–256.
68 Mertes, *Noble Household*, pp. 54, 158.
69 Rawcliffe, *Staffords*, pp. 14–17.
70 *Ibid.*, p. 14; see also M. A. Hicks, 'The last days of Elizabeth, countess of Oxford', *English Historical Review*, CIII, 1988, pp. 76–95.
71 M. A. Hicks, 'The piety of Margaret, Lady Hungerford (d. 1478)', *Journal of Ecclesiastical History*, XXXVIII, 1987, pp. 19–38.
72 Thus Given-Wilson, Ward, Mertes.
73 Davis, *Paston Letters*, I, no. 397.
74 J. W. Kirby, 'Women in the Plumpton Correspondence: fiction and reality', in *Church and Chronicle in the Middle Ages: essays presented to John Taylor*, ed. I. Wood and G. A. Loud, London, 1991, p. 228.
75 *Plumpton Correspondence*, ed. T. Stapleton, Camden Society, 1839, p. 8.
76 Davis, *Paston Letters*, I, no. 415.
77 Dockray, 'Why did gentry marry?', pp. 73–4.
78 *Ibid.*, pp. 65–7.

79 Davis, *Paston Letters*, I, no. 153.
80 E. Power, 'The role of women' in *The Legacy of the Middle Ages*, ed. C. G. Crump and E. F. Jacob, Oxford, 1962, p. 410.
81 C. A. Halsted, *Life of Margaret Beaufort*, London, 1839, p. lxiii; Jones and Underwood, *King's Mother*, pp. 171, 201.

5

Women and religion

Women's classification as countrywomen, townswomen or landed women was largely dictated by birth; few careers crossed categories. But in medieval England all women were supposedly Christian, with the exception, for some two hundred years up to 1290, of the tiny Jewish population. Christianity preached a mixture of equality – 'There is neither Jew nor Greek, there is neither bond nor free, there is neither male nor female, for ye are all one in Christ Jesus' – and subordination – 'Wives, submit yourselves unto your own husbands, as unto the Lord.'[1] No woman could live in a Christian community without its view of women impinging upon her, so the church had influence on Englishwomen, whether they were personally piously inclined or not. However, the church also afforded a complete career opportunity for women, the conventual option. This chapter will deal firstly with women of the church, looking at the professed religious, communities of nuns and individual anchoresses, then at women in the church, looking at laywomen's opportunities for pious participation in religious activity, and the effect of church teaching on aspects of women's life. At the end of the chapter attention will be turned to the counterscene, heretical women (the Lollards) and witchcraft.

The remark that medieval Englishwomen were supposedly Christian was deliberately made to qualify widespread bland assumptions about female piety. Can we be convinced that sufficient attention was given to fostering the faith of the generality of women? Doubts about the depth of their exposure to early Christianity were expressed in chapter 1. In the later Middle Ages sermons reveal what was preached at women, confessors' manuals illustrate how they were guided and synodal statutes reflect on

their activities. But none of these can show how much real understanding women had, although mothers seem generally to have
been expected to instil the earliest religious education into their
children.[2] Even the tiny Jewish communities, which might be expected to have had a tighter hold on worshippers, expected less
understanding among women. Cecil Roth thought highly of the
Jewish standard of education, pointing out that women were not
overlooked in the educational system; 'nevertheless it was found
necessary to translate the domestic service on Passover Eve into
the vernacular for their benefit and that of children'.[3] After the
Reformation, Elizabethan churchmen were appalled at the ignor-
ance in both sexes in remote parts of the country, so the possibility remains that men and women living in isolated hamlets were
little touched by Christianity throughout the period, and that even
where the church had more hold, with physical presence in the
form of a stone building, and an often poorly educated clergyman,
many went along with the rituals with no great understanding.

The sources for studying professionally religious women are
quantitatively comparatively good since religious personnel had
more education and both leisure and motive to write. But these
sources were largely male produced and, it can be argued, tended
to belittle women's role, from Bede onwards. Archivally, after the
Norman Conquest, though actual foundation records remain rare,
and cartularies are rarer from female than from male houses, some
conventual institutional history can be traced for a couple of centuries before the more sophisticated records of visitations (in bishops' registers) begin to afford evidence, extending up to the
Reformation, of conditions and attitudes inside the nuns' cloisters.
By the nature of visitations, however, these sources essentially
emphasise backsliding rather than rectitude.

As early as the twelfth century, there were spiritual developments outside the convents which led to the production of both
Latin and vernacular tracts for anchoresses, and this kind of spiritual guide endured through the rest of the Middle Ages.

For the day-to-day piety of ordinary orthodox laywomen the
evidence is weighted by class. The possession of religious books
attested by wills and surviving manuscripts was limited to the
higher classes. The coming of the friars to England led to greater
popularity of sermonising, and sermons and collections of sermon
exempla in English and Latin from the mid-thirteenth century

onwards proclaim what was said to and about women in this medium. Townswomen in church did not always have their mind on the service if the literary sources tell true – nor did the clergy if Absolon, censing the wives of the parish in Oxford with 'many a lovely look on hem', is typical. (The same idea comes through to us from some of the medieval English lyrics.)[4]

By the later fourteenth century mysticism was developing a following, of both sexes, in England, and in the late fourteenth and early fifteenth centuries two remarkable East Anglian mystical women, Julian of Norwich and Margery Kempe of Lynn, ventured into authorship, despite the Pauline tradition that women should not utter in church nor teach in public. Small wonder that this insubordination led to Margery being suspected of Lollardy, and from the records of Lollard heresy trials, and the exaggerations of the Lollard danger (by its enemies), its attraction to women and their contribution to it must be analysed.

Witchcraft, wizardry, sorcery and demonism were not essentially gender specific. One of the earliest references to such practices is a ban on their practitioners entering the Christian priesthood, so patently they were male. However, medieval treatises on the subject culminate in the German Dominican Inquisitors' tract *Malleus Maleficarum* (The hammer of witches) of 1486, which saw witchcraft as a primarily female phenomenon. On the English scene it will be shown that two of the most famous accusations of witchcraft in the fifteenth century penetrated the heart of the royal family and have 'political' overtones. All in all, there is a good spread of evidence, throughout the period, concerning the varied aspects of women and religion considered here.

Women of the church: nuns

The disrupted history of Anglo-Saxon female monasticism was traced in chapter 1. In 1066 there were only nine or ten houses for women, and the number had only reached about twenty by 1130; increase in numbers was slow and lagged about a generation behind developments for men. The peak decades for the foundation of Benedictine male monasteries were 1080–1110, whereas Benedictine nunneries reached their height of foundation around 1160. Roberta Gilchrist suggests this delay may have been a product of the lower social class of their founders.[5] The pattern of royal dynastic connection and patronage, begun in Anglo-Saxon times, was maintained beyond the Conquest. Amesbury was refounded, as a Fontevraldine house, by Henry II in 1177, and still in royal favour a century later: Edward I's daughter Mary took the veil there in 1285, and her grandmother, Eleanor of Provence, had become a nun there in 1284.[6]

Sally Thompson's recent study of the founding of English nunneries after the Norman Conquest has disclosed that the origins of many of these houses are obscure. Some apparently grew out of informal groups of recluses; others split off or were deliberately distanced from men's religious communities. The development of the priory at Markyate, a few miles north-west of St Albans, embraces both features: an eremetical group originally gathered round a hermit, Roger, involvement with the Benedictine house of St Albans and establishment on land owned by the canons of St Paul's London. Considering the evidence for the linkage of women's institutions to houses such as St Albans, Peterborough and Westminster, and for monks' or canons' residence in women's communities, for example at Stixwould (Lincs.) in the twelfth century – indeed canons and brothers were still to be found at Swine (E. R. Yorks.) in the 1260s, with walls separating the sexes – the supposedly distinctive 'double orders' of Fontevrault and Sempringham look now less extraordinary. During the twelfth century a relatively free partnership between the sexes in religion gave way to stricter segregation to avoid scandal. The Cistercians were initially hostile to women and only reluctantly acknowledged women's houses in the later thirteenth century: far more nunneries claimed to be Cistercian than Cîteaux itself ever recognised. The Premonstratensians initially welcomed women but later distanced them. Nuns still needed male priests and some houses had male priors (uneasily yoked with prioresses); many houses were put in the temporary care of *magistri* (masters) or *custodes* (guardians) to administer their financial affairs, but this died out in the later Middle Ages. Archbishop Romeyn of York put the nunneries of Sinningthwaite, Wilberfoss and Arthington under the guardianship of the rectors of Kirk Deighton, Sutton on Derwent and Kippax, and made the vicars of Thirkleby and Bossall successively masters of Moxby.[7] So although the nunnery offered a complete women's world, it was one long overshadowed by men.

There were at least 142 English nunneries by the third quarter of the thirteenth century; few were added thereafter. Sharon Elkins estimates that approximately 120 new communities for religious women were established in the twelfth century, mostly after 1130. By 1200, 3,000 women could be accommodated. Elkins calls the twelfth century 'the apex of enthusiasm for women's religious life in England'.[8] Though local accessibility varied – there were no women's houses in twelfth-century Lancashire or Westmorland, and only one each in Cheshire and Shropshire – developments certainly brought a new element of choice for the intending nun, bringing new affiliations, particularly the Gilbertine, Cistercian, Fontevraldine and Premonstratensian orders. Gilbert of Sempringham established seven women at Sempringham (Lincs.) in 1131; when he died in 1189 he left the single largest organisation of female religious in England. There were nine monasteries for both sexes, and four for men alone; in the double houses the normal ratio was two women to every man.[9] North of the River Welland, the Gilbertines were a dominant force regionally. Important friends of Gilbert, from the king and archbishop of York to the prior of Bridlington (E. R. Yorks.), wrote to Pope Alexander III in the late 1160s defending his order and testifying to complete segregation within it. These defensive letters to Alexander III were prompted by a lay brothers' revolt at Sempringham, which raised the matter of moral lapses arising from the proximity of nuns and canons, and occurred soon after a series of events (probably in the early 1160s, at Watton in the East Riding of Yorkshire) centring on a love affair of a nun and a brother, described by Ailred of Rievaulx in a single-surviving twelfth-century manuscript source.[10]

After the tightening of segregation, late medieval nunneries may have been less scandalous but their condition was hardly enlightening or fervent. Many houses, especially north of the Thames, were small and not particularly efficiently managed, though recent research, such as Graves's study of Stixwould, shows houses were more efficiently run than Eileen Power's picture suggested.[11] Meagre endowments limited resources. The 1535 valuations reveal the poverty of the nunneries. The value per inmate of just over 50 per cent of the nunneries was under £5, and no nunnery was worth more than £30, whereas most male houses were in the £10 to £25 range, and a small peak exceeded £50 rising to £70.[12] Not surprisingly, recent study of nunneries' layout has revealed their spatial and architectural inferiority compared to men's houses.[13] With most medieval houses for women small and relatively poor, it seems that their recruitment came from lower social classes than before the Conquest, so a choice of career which had been limited to royal and aristocratic girls in Anglo-Saxon England was extended to daughters of small landowners and merchants, and, via the lay sisters, to rather poorer women. Marilyn Oliva's recent research on office holding in the eleven female monasteries in the diocese of Norwich between 1350 and 1540 suggests that more English nuns were then coming from middling and lower ranks of society than from the aristocracy and upper gentry. Oliva estimates that only 1 per cent came from the aristocracy, about 15 per cent from the upper gentry, 64 per cent from the lower or parish gentry, 16 per cent (mostly at Norwich's Carrow) from urban families and 4 per cent from the substantial freeholders or yeomen. The percentages from the different social origins holding office were almost identical. Interestingly, in the Norwich diocese at this period none of the aristocratic nuns served as abbesses, prioresses or in other office. Recruitment to the community, as well as office holding in it, varied from convent to convent, the richest, Campsey Ash (Suffolk), producing the majority of the upper gentry office holders.[14] Oliva's study has revealed a flexible career ladder in these houses: abbesses and prioresses almost always rose to office after a grounding in lower administrative posts.

Overcrowding and demands of hospitality outstripped resources. The nunneries' educational standards were low, and there were no longer nuns respected for Latin scholarship as in Anglo-Saxon times. The twelfth-century nuns of Barking who translated Latin lives of Edward the Confessor and St Catherine of Alexandria into French showed more skill than most. Archbishops Giffard and Newark wrote to the nuns of Swine in Latin, in 1268 and 1298 respectively, but even knowledge of French declined in fourteenth-century convents, and in the fifteenth and sixteenth centuries bishops sent their injunctions to nunneries in English.[15] Significantly, nuns wrote no chronicles, and the books in most houses were only service books. The role of convents in educating girls seems to have been exaggerated.

Episcopal visitations, designed to unearth what needed correction, discovered nuns interested in possessions, clothes and appearance, indulging in sleep and comfort and going out from their cloisters, and apt to squabble and tell tales. In 1489 Archbishop Rotherham wrote to the prioress of Nunappleton (W. R. Yorks.) that no sister 'use ye alehouse nor ye waterside'.[16] Power thought most houses had a sinner at some time: youthful vow taking did not always hold. The unchaste nun of Watton interviewed by Ailred of Rievaulx in the twelfth century had been an oblate at the age of four, far too young for any aptitude or vocation to have been considered. In 1442 the prioress at Catesby (Northants) reported to Bishop Alnwick that Isabel Benet had conceived a child by a sometime chaplain. She admitted misbehaviour, but denied the identity of the partner, and apparently cleared herself by compurgation. The departing bishop left Isabel as one of two nuns who were to receive the priory's money as the prioress had proved so incompetent. These two treasurers were next in trouble for refusing to give up private chambers, and more startlingly still, Dame Isabel was reported to have spent a night dancing and playing the lute with the Austin friars of Northampton, and the next night similarly with the friars preacher.[17]

Most nuns doubtless kept their vows of chastity, and virginity had a tremendous hold over the medieval Christian imagination. In the twelfth century, Christina of Markyate, or her biographer, was obsessed with hers, interpreting her defence of it, perhaps seen as a guarantee of her freedom, as the cause of extraordinary determination in others to violate it. The story of Christina's outwitting Ranulph Flambard's attempt to seduce her leads to the comment: 'the only way in which he could conceivably gain his revenge was by depriving Christina of her virginity, either by himself or someone else', and the tale of Christina's determined resistance of her betrothed suitor Burthred contains her mother's astonishing reaction: 'in the end she swore that she would not care who deflowered her daughter, provided that some way of deflowering her could be found'.[18] Christina, though she was sensitive to sexual temptation, was able to preserve her virginity by private action, but tales spread in the Middle Ages of individuals and communities going to extraordinary lengths including sacrificial mutilation *en bloc*, and suicide, to avoid sexual intercourse. As Jane Schulenburg points out, such stories, true or false, testify to obsession with sexual purity and acute fear of rape.[19]

The vulnerability of Anglo-Saxon cloistered women to abduction and rape was noted in chapter 1; later, politics became another complication: Henry I wished to marry Matilda, daughter of Malcolm Canmore and (St) Margaret of Scotland, of the Old English royal dynasty. Matilda had worn the veil under her aunt Christina. It seems that both she and the top churchmen wanted her out of the cloister to be queen. So she put forward an explanation of having only worn the veil to escape Norman lust and to please her aunt, and of being personally uncommitted and tearing it off in private. Still later the last surviving child of King Stephen, Mary of Blois, left Romsey where she was abbess to marry Matthew of Boulogne in 1160. Whether the marriage had been forced or voluntary is not known. Later still nuns presented temptations even to religious men: it was the chaplain who was the seducer at the nunnery of Moxby in the North Riding of Yorkshire in 1325.[20] So one can understand why women who wished to be chaste were obsessed by fear of rape or seduction, and it has long been obvious why churchmen laid such stress on virginity not only for women but most obviously for them – as a way of cooling sinful sexual passion. Virginity was the superlative form of chastity, but as the most recent editors of the Middle English tract *Hali Meidhad*, described by its translators as 'a form of preaching by written instruction' comment, 'virginal habit of mind is even more important than literal intactness', so the tract warns true virgins not to develop pride in their state – 'a modest wife or a meek widow is better than a proud virgin'. *Hali Meidhad* describes virginity as the queen of heaven, the one loss which cannot be recovered.[21]

Women of the church: recluses

The solitary life was deemed holier than the regulated life of the cloistered community, but it was much riskier for a woman to undertake such a comparatively unprotected life. Ann Warren's recent work on anchorites and their patrons has shown nevertheless that documented English anchoritism was a vocation always biased towards women, though in varying proportions. She calculates that there were five female anchoresses to every three male anchorites in the twelfth century, four to every one in the thirteenth, five to every two in the fourteenth, five to three in the fifteenth, and three to two in the sixteenth, before the ending of the option in 1539.[22] One of the earliest traceable careers of a woman drawn to the more solitary life is that of Eve of Wilton, who left her English abbey at the age of twenty-two to be enclosed at St Laurent de Tertre in Angers; two years later Goscelin wrote the *Liber Confortatorius* (Letter of comfort) to her, which is dated to 1082–3. From a poem written in Eve's praise *c.* 1125 after her death, it seems she had already withdrawn from the main communal life into a small cell at Wilton before taking the still more striking step.[23] It was not uncommon for monks to move, with their abbots' approval, from regular monasticism into an eremetical option. Christina of Markyate's spiritual director, the hermit Roger, was still a St Albans monk, obedient to his abbot though living in a hermitage. But the women anchoresses were more often ex-laywomen than ex-nuns, although ex-nun anchoresses were regarded as the more holy ideal.

Christina's biography reveals some surprising features in the early twelfth-century situation. With the help of a hermit, Edwin, who had consulted the archbishop of Canterbury, Christina escaped her parents' custody and lived for two years with an anchoress, Alfwen, at Flamstead (Herts.), there 'putting on the religious habit'. Alfwen was under the protection of the hermit Roger, Edwin's cousin, and Roger, when first approached about Christina, expressed strong disapproval of dissolved marriages. When her husband Burthred came looking for Christina, Alfwen told him, 'it is not our custom to give shelter to wives who are running away from their husbands'.[24] These episodes suggest the eremetical life was under some pressure from wives seeking refuge and that its propounders had to be careful not to tangle with broken marriages. At Flamstead Christina lived a pious life, 'her reading and singing of the psalms by day and night' tormenting the devil. The *Life* glosses over why, after two years, it became necessary for her to go elsewhere, but it does tell us that Roger had her cell brought near to his in spite of Alfwen's opposition. This indicates that there was some communication between Roger and Alfwen on the subject, perhaps via one of Roger's servants. Roger, we are told, resolved not to see or speak to Christina 'in order that there might be no excuse for Alfwen to accuse him before the bishop of being a cause of dissension'.[25] Events rapidly took a different turn with Christina soon hidden under his roof in a minute room off his cell, both afraid that 'if by chance Christina were found in his company she might be snatched away on the orders of the bishop and handed over to her husband to do as he liked'.[26] As these extracts show, the biographer keeps up a clever interweaving of his heroine's innocence contrasted with what any reasonable worldly reader might well suppose to be going on. Later her husband released Christina from her marriage vows, and Archbishop Thurstan of York interviewed Christina at Redbourn and sent her back to Roger. After Roger's death, Thurstan found her a protector who was soon inflamed by the devil with other than chaste and spiritual affection, and Christina herself suffered impure thoughts. But lust was overcome, and around 1130 Christina made a monastic profession at St Albans to Bishop Alexander of Lincoln. By 1145 the Markyate community had become a regulated priory, but Christina's career continued to teeter on the brink of scandal: her biographer writes, concerning her influence on Abbot Geoffrey of St Albans, 'the abbot was slandered as a seducer and the maiden as a loose woman'.[27]

The manuscript of Christina's life is fourteenth-century and incomplete, but the original biographer was apparently a St Albans monk who knew Christina and talked with her. She was a revered figure and ended her career in a regular community as prioress of Markyate. But for about twenty years she had lived in less regular religious associations, some of which undoubtedly could have given rise to scandal, and all of which show that in the early twelfth century the eremetical life was far from solitary.

Anchoresses never were entirely solitary, for those entombed in their narrow cells needed at least one servant to communicate with the outside world, fetch food and water, and perhaps to restrict visitors' access to them. Sometimes several lived together – the early thirteenth-century *Ancrene Wisse* (Guide for anchoresses) was composed for three, who lived together with a couple of maids and a kitchen boy. Christina's biography represents her first diocesan bishop, Robert Bloet of Lincoln, as a bribable persecutor of her, but he must have found her a somewhat wayward daughter. Episcopal supervision of anchorites and anchoresses became routine: the bishop was supposed to investigate a would-be recluse's personal suitability, the financial viability of the proposal, and the suitability of the proposed site, and supervise the proper enclosure of the recluse. Giffard's register in 1267 looked into the morals of a would-be anchoress at Hedon, and Romeyn's records the licence of one at North Cave in 1286, to give examples.[28]

A number of religious tracts began as writings for specific female recluses known to the authors. Besides Goscelin's already mentioned *Liber Confortatorius*, Ailred of Rievaulx's letter to his sister, *De Institutiis Inclusarum*, c. 1162, the *Ancrene Wisse*, originating in the West Midlands c. 1220, Richard Rolle's *Form of Living* and Walter Hilton's *Scale of Perfection* (both fourteenth-century) were all for such recipients. They recommend moderation and silence. The recluse was confined in order to contemplate God, to channel energies inwardly, to meditate. Though isolated for these purposes, recluses remained in the community visibly in their anchorages, through which only windows (desirably not to be open too often) gave them physical visibility. As they were for the most part dependent on alms, they could not be too contemptuous of those whose goodwill they required: they repaid material aid with spiritual, praying and sometimes counselling. Anchoresses came from all social groups and widely varied education. They were supported by all classes from the royal family to aristocracy, gentry, merchants, churchmen and institutions. Warren notes that Julian Lampett, anchoress at Carrow Priory (Norwich) for at least fifty-six years, attracted specific bequests from sixty-seven persons in the period 1426–81, including nineteen clergy, twenty-two merchants and their wives, and seventeen gentry.[29] An earlier Julian of Norwich was the anchoress visited by Margery Kempe. This Julian (b. c. 1342) was the first author to write theology in English, in the short and long texts of her *Revelations of Divine Love*. Benedicta Ward has recently challenged the assertion that Julian was a nun, arguing that she had probably been a widowed wife and mother, and should not be classed in 'the little world of professionally religious people'.[30] As Warren points out, anchoritism was central to the varied trends of medieval religion, reflecting the asceticism of the twelfth century, the absorption of large numbers of women in the thirteenth, mysticism in the fourteenth and austerity in the fifteenth.

Women in the church: pious laywomen

The professionally religious women so far observed may be regarded as building upon conventional piety and taking it further. Christina of Markyate's parents, in taking the girl to St Albans Abbey, obviously never intended to plant aspirations to a life of religious chastity in her head. But Christina, on the morrow of her St Albans visit, on the way home, took herself to church and vowed herself to God, subsequently having her vow confirmed by a canon of Huntingdon, Sueno. In their efforts to persuade her instead 'to become the mistress of a house', her parents had her lectured by the prior of Huntingdon and brought before the bishop of Lincoln. Clearly this early twelfth-century daughter of a well-to-do (but in origin Anglo-Saxon) Huntingdon family was brought up to practise her religion in a very positive and selective way, free to betake herself to churches and spiritual counsellors of her choice. In this she may have been unusually free for a young woman, but it is also clear that she was not expected to resist the authoritative advice of the local prior and diocesan bishop, and it is as she begins to emerge as abnormally obstreperous in her determinations that she leaves the mould of normal filial behaviour. Eventually of course she crossed the divide into professional religion.

It is difficult to define what constituted normal lay piety in the Middle Ages. It seems generally agreed that the majority of people did not attend daily mass, but that attendance on Sundays and feast days was expected. Actually within church, Margaret Aston believes 'women seem always to have formed a major part of congregations', but they were often segregated, either women on the north side and men on the south, or in an east/west divide, women furthest from the altar.[31] The laity normally only communicated (in bread) once a year, at Easter, and annual confession was thought sufficient by many. Ordinary Christians fasted on Fridays and in Lent, paid tithes (grumblingly) and had their children baptised. After the coming of the friars in the thirteenth century there was a growing demand for sermons, and preaching took on a higher profile than the confession. The basic knowledge expected of Christians was the Apostles' Creed, the Ten Commandments, the Lord's Prayer and the Ave, of which the Creed and Lord's Prayer were probably the best known. To participate in more than these activities was to show particular fervour.

There were no doubt many medieval laywomen, and indeed laymen, who were in effect religious professionals manqués, whose inclination was for a more religious life than circumstances permitted. The best-known women in this category are naturally the socially high-class ones, who were most able to fund their inclinations and leave evidence behind. The most obvious example is

Lady Margaret Beaufort. In 1499, during the lifetime of her last husband, the earl of Derby, she took a vow of chastity, and with his permission set up an independent household at Collyweston (Northants), where he, however, was a regular guest. The establishment went into mourning at his death in 1504, but she was not an executor of his will. Bishop Fisher tells us she rose at 5 a.m. to hear four or five masses, and her day included private prayers, reading and meditation, and public services in her chapel.[32] At Christ's College Cambridge, which she founded *c.* 1504–6, she had a suite of rooms available, one with a window looking into the college chapel. Some of the images and statues in her own chapel passed to her colleges. She had particular devotion to specific feasts and was recognised by the pope as the English patron of the feast of the Holy Name of Jesus. She possessed religious books, joined religious gilds and confraternities, supported religious orders, founded professorships of theology at both universities, was behind the foundation of two Cambridge colleges, and was a sponsor of Caxton as a political and religious publisher. There would be enough here to cast Margaret as a kind of secular abbess, but in fact this piety was only one facet of her remarkable experience-steeled character. Her recent biographers quote with approval Bernard André's comment on her: 'steadfast and more stable than the weakness in woman suggests'.[33]

Margaret Beaufort was a survivor, whose political wiliness, physical energy and application were amply passed to some of her descendants. Her piety, however, though long famous, was perhaps at the time one of her less remarkable features. Cecily Neville, mother of Edward IV and Richard III, has been presented as another early riser for religious devotions, who similarly occupied her day, at any rate latterly, with prayers and meditations and services. As a university college foundress, and patron, Margaret Beaufort followed in the footsteps of Devorguilla Balliol, Elizabeth de Burgh, Philippa of Hainault, Marie de St Pol and Margaret of Anjou and her successors. Margaret Beaufort differed only in scale, being in a position to achieve, and involve herself, more than they.

Below royalty and the major aristocracy were a lower aristocracy and gentry where wives and daughters also had some funds to spare. Michael Hicks has recently investigated female piety in these classes in his study of Margaret Lady Hungerford.[34] Such ladies normally had household chaplains who officiated in private chapels or oratories on the family estates. In their wills, primers and psalters, portable breviaries and chapel furnishings are frequently mentioned. Margaret, wife of William de Thorp, knight, left her psalter in 1347 to the chapel of Thorp 'to serve there while it lasts'; Agnes widow of John de St Quentin left a missal to the high altar of Sigglesthorne church in 1404; Margaret wife of William Plays, knight, left her best primer to her daughter Elizabeth Hastings, and all her books with chalice, vestments and altar cloths to John Fervour, chaplain, in 1440.[35] Besides officiating in a priestly capacity, many household chaplains acted as secretaries, counsellors and schoolmasters. Margaret Paston, particularly in her widowhood, leaned on Sir James Gloys, the family chaplain, to the annoyance of other members of the family – John III called him 'the proud, peevish and evil disposed priest to us all'.[36] Gloys seems to have had some hold over Margaret, whereas one might expect that domestic chaplains had to humour their employers: this would not make these clergy much more subservient than the normal parish clergy, however, for many clerical livings were appointed to by the locally influential family, though as conscience about lay presentation grew in the twelfth century, many advowsons had been given to ecclesiastical patrons.

The Pastons had quite a network of ecclesiastical personnel connected to them; having their own chaplain did not stop them relating to other, beneficed, clergy. The family presented, or partly presented, to more than twenty livings in Norfolk in the fifteenth century.[37] In Norwich itself, the Pastons attended St Peter Hungate, where Walter was buried, and John was attacked at the cathedral door in 1452.[38] A well-placed family had a number of 'tame' clerics who could ill-afford to annoy the members of the family by reproach or reproof. The reinforcement of the bonding recurred through anniversaries or more frequent commemorative masses. The vicar of Paston celebrated mass every Friday for the souls of William and Agnes Paston, and exhorted parish prayers for them every Sunday.[39] Physical memorials to the dead, monuments and brasses, decorated with effigies and/or armorial bearings, reminded landed families of their dynastic situation whenever they entered their churches, and every generation there were more funerals. Though Gloys appears frequently in the Paston correspondence in various business capacities not spiritual ones, the nature of the correspondence would encourage this emphasis.

Below the gentry, families did not have private chaplains and were thrown back on the normal public services of local churches. The wives and daughters of these families would have less time or money to devote to religion, and less easy familiarity with the local clergy, whom they probably held in some awe, though clerical poverty caused many rural churchmen to level down to their parishioners and till their own glebe. There is very little evidence of the pious aspirations of the women of the rural tenantry. In English sources there is neither a Montaillou of scandalous liaisons, nor a Joan of Arc of innocent youthful piety. However, it is startling to see Henry of Birkenshagh, vicar of the prebend of Barnby on the Marsh, presented to the justices of the peace in 1362 for wounding and ill-treating Emma wife of Arnold Cliff of Howden, Margaret widow of Thomas Whitsed, and Alice Daughdoghter, two on the same day.[40]

In towns, there is indirect evidence from literature, archival sources and topography. Churches in urban parishes were closer together, and if the town also housed one or more of the friars' orders, there was further choice. These churches all offered their own daily services and some were busy with additional commemorative masses. Larger parish churches might contain extra altars or even chantry chapels, and urban cathedrals many more. There was concern that Christian ears might be assailed in some towns by overloud worship from the Jewish synagogues, where these were allowed, and more alarming contamination might be voluntarily entered into: the bishop Richard Swinfield excommunicated Christians who attended a Jewish wedding in Hereford, against his prohibition, in 1286.[41]

Townsfolk, however, had worldly calls on their time and purses. It was on a holiday that the carpenter's wife Alison went to church in Oxford in Chaucer's 'The Miller's Tale', not on a normal working day, and there she was censed by the amorous parish clerk Absolon.[42] In real life, as far as this is filtered through her collaborative autobiography, Margery Kempe, ever prone to excesses, set a far sterner example:

> sche was schreuyn sum-tyme twyes or thryes on þe day . . . sche ʒaf hir to gret fastyng & to gret wakyng; sche roos at ij or iij of þe clok & went to cherch & was þer in hir prayers on-to tyme of noon and also al þe aftyrnoon.[43]

This was before her boisterous sobbings and mortifications, and English and foreign pilgrimages, marked her out as quite beyond normal or even fervent piety, but it is useful information that these facilities were there for a woman of Lynn's burgess class. Later Margery claimed that Christ commanded her to abstain from eating flesh, and to receive the sacrament every Sunday and meditate daily after six. She becomes a useful illustration of the confusions in an undisciplined enthusiast, seeing biblical visions and believing herself married to the Godhead in a ceremony in the apostles' church at Rome. 'I take þe, Margery, for my weddyd wyfe, for fayrar, for fowelar, for richar for powerar' said God to her, before heavenly witnesses.[44] Margery was excessive by nature, but she was only an exaggeration of the hysterical delusions any fervent, illiterate but impressionable woman could fall into, left too much to her own unbridled imagination, with the raw material of church imagery and ritual as inspiration.

At the more normal level, in the towns, the gild involvement in religion invited participation by the gild sisters. Gilds commonly had a patron saint and celebrated his or her festival. Rich gilds had their own chaplains and chapels, or at least altars, poorer gilds raised funds to pay for a service in the local church. The gild members often paid specific sums, including designated fines, for wax for candles, sometimes of specified weight. As noted earlier, they formed burial clubs to assist at members' funerals. The overall impression in the gild ordinances is concern to do the proprieties correctly, and this embraces variously processing, attending mass and making offerings (and fining absentees), and providing the appropriate candles or lights. As souls were equal, the brothers and sisters enjoyed equality in this sphere. The specific gild prayers of the St Christopher Fraternity in Norwich, which had women members, are printed in *English Gilds*.[45]

Women do not, generally, appear to have taken active part in the gild performance of Corpus Christi plays. The evidence about the Chester Wives' pageant is late and imprecise, for they could have taken responsibility for the play without acting in it themselves. The banns, indeed, only say, 'The worshipful wives of this town / Find of our Lady the Assumption; / To bring it forth they are ready [bowne] / And maintain with all their might.'[46] Women may well have had a hand in the supporting work, for example in the wardrobe department, and they certainly would have participated as audience. The Coventry smiths in 1487 rewarded one Mistress Grimsby for lending her 'gear' for Pilate's wife.[47] Gilds were institutional providers of charity, and the sisters of the gild had to contribute their dues, as shown in chapter 3. There could of course be a strong religious motivation behind private charitable acts, and almsgiving was particularly enjoined upon women, as Cullum's work shows.[48]

Women and the church: the effect of church teaching

It was shown in chapter 1 that the church brought its own rules on sexual activity and marriage. In the twelfth century the definition of marriage by the church, and its supervision of both the ceremony and the pertaining jurisdiction, became stronger, with the support of the landholding classes. Though this tended to create conditions which people could follow to ensure that they were likely to be found to be properly married on any subsequent investigation, dynastic interests kept up a perpetual pressure to ensure loopholes to enable escape especially from barren marriages. Only surprisingly late did marriage by a priest, inside a church, become a legal necessity, but from the twelfth century, church courts had the monopoly of matrimonial litigation. The flexibility of the conditions within which marriage was valid was one of the problems: eighty-nine of 122 marriages investigated in the Ely consistory court 1374–82 involved real or alleged clandestine, but not necessarily invalid, unions.[49] The Council of Trent declared marriages not solemnised by a priest invalid (1563), but it was 1753 before parliament made this statutory in England and Wales.

The church courts, from the levels of rural deans, archdeacons and bishops to popes, handled sexual morality and matrimonial cases. Judging by the fines imposed, fornication (sexual intercourse between two unmarried people) was seen as less serious than adultery (sexual intercourse between two parties, one of them married to someone else), and multiple offences most serious. Both sexes were liable to summons, but there is obviously room for concern over double standards, evidenced as early as Archbishop Theodore's *Penitential*. Georges Duby argues that patriarchal feudal society was keen to keep the wife's reproduction uncontaminated to pass on the inheritance, whereas the husband's siring of bastards did not endanger the estate, so the laity condemned adultery more in the woman.[50] In practical terms, however, wherever extra-marital sex led to pregnancy, the woman was far more easily identified for condemnation. Church courts affected medieval women by having jurisdiction over marriage, and over sexual misconduct and other misbehaviour such as breach of contract and slander.

Church teaching heavily emphasised the submissive role deemed appropriate to women, and their mischievous tendencies if left unchecked. A religion polarising Mary and Eve could do no other. Adam was created before Eve, and she was taken out of man. Weaker than Adam, Eve was tempted first, precipitating the Fall. Eve could thus be blamed and women seen as the origin of all evils. The elevation of Mary did not rehabilitate her sex as much as the constant recrimination of Eve depressed it, for Mary's example was seen as too pure to be successfully emulated, whereas Eve's was seen as all too easily followed. The cult of the Virgin Mary was exceptionally developed in Anglo-Saxon England, and was rapidly advanced after the Norman Conquest. This accompanied the according of growing significance to earthly queens in England. Eileen Power that believed that the cult of the Virgin and the cult of chivalry went together, but Penny Gold makes less of both developments.[51] Great leavening of the position of ordinary women cannot be attributed to the cult of Mary because she was too holy to be sullied as a role model.

A religion administered by men easily leaned to unbalanced views, whether misogynistic, indifferent, or sympathetic. Women were seen sometimes as dangerous temptresses whose company should be shunned by holy men, sometimes as weak-willed vacillating creatures, easily misled and needing strict supervision for their own good, and sometimes as delicate merciful peacemakers who needed protection in an evil world. None of these perspectives allowed women to develop without interference. The misogynist view told them they were inherently sinful, daughters of Eve, as good as lost. It suspected their motives and application and scorned their efforts. Women were constantly preached at to dress more plainly, and eschew hair dyes and cosmetics. The indifferent view simply disregarded women, or made sublime assumptions of what they should feel and do, based on masculine premises and emotions. The protective view, though more kindly meant, was similarly suffocating. Even this is an anachronistic remark, for far from being suffocated, women were hardly expected to need to breathe.

The overall effect of church teaching therefore was constraining, though there is disagreement over the way this developed. Caroline Bynum believes that late medieval preaching was moderate, enhancing the role of laity, women and marriage, a cosy domestication against which the more exuberant women mystics reacted.[52] Susan Stuard, however, believes that as the Middle Ages progressed, the place of women in ecclesiastical opinion fell: the Gregorian reform of the late eleventh century led to increased separation of the sexes, and the ecclesiastical hierarchy grew more remote from women and comprehended them less easily.[53] Did ecclesiastical constraints make heresy more attractive to women?

Orthodox contemporary male writers regarded heresy as wicked and dangerous in either sex. Modern feminist opinion finds it interesting that at various times and places heretical religion seems to have been less constraining to women than orthodox religion. The established church, acting on the assumption that women were inferior in mental facility as well as in physical strength and legal capacity, prescribed a repressed role for women. Women reacted in various ways. Some responded with saintly resignation, obeying their spiritual advisers, concentrating on their relationship with God, cutting themselves off as much as possible from worldly mental baggage. Some responded with eccentric determination, standing up to ecclesiastical superiors and carving out for themselves an unconventional active life based on their own convictions. The vast majority, one suspects, lived a life of busy practicalities, participating in local church activities without analysing what they were doing or why. Some enjoyed sexual flirtation or wilder passion with the local clergy. Others rebelled, and joined medieval England's heretical group, the Lollards.

Heretics and sorcerers: Lollards

England was remarkably free from popular heresy until the later fourteenth century, when the movement known as Lollardy emerged. Lollardy owed its origins to an expert theologian, John Wyclif (*c.* 1330–84), who had evolved, in the rarefied atmosphere of Oxford University, radical views challenging the existing visible church of his day. Wyclif was a predestinarian, believing that the true church was the body of God's elect. He believed lordship was founded on grace, so could only be truly enjoyed by the elect. Individual popes, cardinals and priests might not be in a state of grace, so Scripture was the better authority. Priestly absolution, penance and excommunication became unnecessary additional practices, for the priest might in fact be one of the damned, and the individual should be able to contact God without other human mediation. Ultimately Wyclif came to challenge transubstantiation. While his radicalism was contained in academic circles, its dangerousness was also confined, though the authorities did move to check both Wyclif and his followers in the early 1380s. Thus far few women had been exposed to the new ideas, which escaped into extra-mural circulation through small numbers of renegade priests, and began to spread in the country at large in the 1380s. Early Lollard communities sprang up in the Welsh Marches, at Bristol, in Leicester, Northamptonshire and Buckinghamshire. Some knights of Richard II's court were attracted to Lollardy and presented livings to heretical priests, but when the Lollard knight Sir John Oldcastle actually involved himself in rebellion in 1414, the propertied classes who had flirted with Lollard views shrank back from so alarming a connection.

After 1414, therefore, Lollardy was a factor only in lower urban and rural society, and it is here that it can be identified and its attraction to women probed. In his analysis of surviving Norwich heresy trial records from 1428–31, Norman Tanner identified fifty-one men and nine women defendants. Among the latter was Hawise Moone, wife of Thomas Moone of Loddon, whose English confession of her heresies is printed in Tanner's book.[54] She confessed that she had been homely and privy with known named heretics, and had concealed and comforted them, hearing from them in 'scoles of heresie' a comprehensive list of heresies. These included that the sacrament of baptism in water in church was but a trifle, as was extreme unction, that episcopal confirmation was unnecessary, and that confession need only be made to God, as no priest had power to remit sin or absolve a man from it. No man need do any penance a priest imposed, and after the sacramental words at mass there remained only material bread. The pope was Antichrist; only the holiest and most perfect on earth was truly pope,

[173]

and those called priests were lecherous, covetous and false deceivers of the people. Consent between man and wife should be sufficient for the sacrament of matrimony, without contract of words or solemnisation in church. Men may withhold tithes and offerings from priests and give them to the poor; temporal men may take possessions from men of the visible church and give them to the people. It was no sin to do contrary to church precepts, and every man and every woman in good life without sin was as good a priest as any priest, pope or bishop. Censures, sentences and cursings of the church should not be feared; men should not swear, nor kill, even by the process of law. Men need not fast and should not go on pilgrimages, or worship images of the crucifix or saints, and should pray only to God. All these errors and heresies Hawise confessed and abjured, swearing not to hold them again. Many of the other heretics, male and female, made similar declarations, in English or Latin. Some are phrased truculently: at the depositions against her at her second trial, Margery wife of William Baxter of Martham, whose husband used to read the law of Christ to her and her maid Johanna from a book, secretly, in a chamber at night, was said to have declared that her husband was the best doctor of Christianity.[55]

Of Tanner's nine women Lollards, Margery Baxter was the wife of a wright, Sybil Godsell the wife of John Godsell of Ditchingham, Matilda Fleccher the wife of Richard Fleccher of Beccles, Hawise Moone wife of Thomas Moone, whom Tanner believes to have been a shoemaker, Katherine Wright wife of Roger Wright of Shottesham, Johanna Weston wife of John Weston of Norwich, and Katherine Hobes wife of Thomas Pert. Only two of the nine were apparently single women, Isabella Chapleyn of Martham, whose penance was reduced because of old age, misery and impotence, and Isabella Davy, described as daughter of Richard Davy of Toft. Three of the husbands were separately tried: John Godsell, Richard Fleccher and Thomas Moone, and Margery Baxter's husband was clearly implicated.[56] Obviously some Lollard women had Lollard husbands, and it is not known in these cases which of the couple was converted first, or the more influential. In the much later case of Agnes Grebill, burnt as a Lollard in Kent in 1511, it is known she had been led into heresy first, some quarter of a century earlier, and then influenced her husband and sons. Individual wives converted husbands to heresy in the Chilterns and East Anglia in the early sixteenth century.[57] Presumably there were households where one spouse inclined to orthodoxy and the other to heresy. Tanner observes that the women were sentenced to the same kinds of punishment as the men, but on the whole seem to have been treated more leniently. Claire Cross suggests under a dozen women were burnt as relapsed heretics, though there is plentiful evidence of relapse. This mildness may have sprung from contempt as much as from compassion: higher clerics tended to underestimate the influence of women on the spread of Lollardy.[58]

Most of Hawise Moone's heresies were common among the East Anglian heretics tried in her period, whose opinions were fairly extreme. There is no particular gender significance. The belief that she as a woman gained least by accepting, was that consent without church solemnisation or contract sufficed to make a valid marriage. This 'Casanova's charter' was also accepted by Margery Baxter, Sybil Godsell, Matilda Fleccher and Isabella Chapleyn, while Katherine Wright denied holding opinions against five identified sacraments including matrimony. Isabella Davy believed priests should be allowed to take wives, and nuns husbands, a belief shared by some of the men. It is ironic that Lollard women, often deemed less constrained in their religion, should have accepted the weakened 'alternative matrimony', since the church's concern to regulate marriage, building on mutual consent as the essential foundation, is often held up as asserting equality of the sexes, thereby improving the lot of women.[59] From the Norwich heresy trials, one would not suspect that Lollardy had any particular attraction for women, but other aspects of the heresy suggest that it may have done. As Margaret Aston phrases it, 'unorthodoxy offered women outlets for religious activity that were not found in the established church'.[60]

The established church was, as we have seen, male dominated, and any sect which demoted popes, bishops and priests and moved in the direction of a priesthood of all believers made it easier to allow women, or logically more difficult to deny them, the same equality. Similarly, if the Bible were to be opened up, in translation, for all believers to read, literate women would be on the same level of access as literate men. It was radical enough, and too much for conservatives, if women were to be found reading, learning and communicating the Gospels. Thomas Hoccleve (d. 1426) criticised women making arguments in Holy Writ 'though their wit be thin', and told them to sit and spin and 'cackle' of some-thing else, 'for your wit is all too feeble to dispute it'.[61] It was much more startling where women were positively seen as priests or potential priests, an issue which has still much dispute in it today. Walter Brut, a heretic from Hereford diocese, argued that in theory women had the power and authority to preach and make the body of Christ and bind and loose, at the same time, however, denying the sacrificial nature of the mass performed by either sex.[62] The midwife's emergency powers of baptism in the absence of a cleric had long been accepted, but could be used as a battering-ram against a normally male monopoly; if a woman could baptise in one circumstance, effectively, why not in others, and why could she not administer other sacraments? William White, a Lollard missionary originally from Kent, believed the power of binding and loosing granted to priests did not exceed that granted to other perfect men or women. His disciples Margery Baxter, Sybil Godsell and Hawise Moone were all specific that faithful men and women were all good priests but, as already indicated, the Lollard priest's role was less sacramental and more of a preach-ing ministry, so women's participation in it would not have ac-knowledged a consecrating power for them. Evidence of women allegedly celebrating mass is much rarer, and it is not clear whether the individuals involved were common Lollards or unique eccen-trics. But the raising of even the possibility that they might do it cannot be denied: hence the reaction attributed to John Swetstock in the early fifteenth century – 'Take thee to thy distaff; covet not to be a priest or preacher.'[63]

However, not all women desired to become, or to be ministered unto by, women priests, then or now. Lollardy's appeal to women was probably not in offering them so extreme an ambition, but in pronouncing more generally religious and educational equality. Claire Cross calls Lollardy 'a family sect', and argues that women may have achieved in it a degree of participation greater than any they had previously attained in the orthodox church in England.[64] Married couples are quite a feature of disclosed Lollardy, in Kent, East Anglia, Coventry, the Chilterns and London. William and Joan White from Kent had stirred up the Norwich heretics men-tioned earlier; he was a Wyclifite university man and lapsed cleric, burnt as a relapsed heretic in Norwich in 1428, but his wife also spread his beliefs. The Moones had received them, and their daughter could read English books, and Cross believes almost certainly did so to illiterates in the group.[65]

The Lollards placed heavy emphasis on reading religious works, and Lollard scriptoria produced texts for circulation. When the heresy hunt began in Coventry in 1511, Alice Rowley prudently destroyed many of her books, though she was apparently illiterate herself; her husband read St Paul's epistles to her.[66] However, when confronted by the officers of orthodoxy it paid Lollard suspects to claim to be illiterate. The mere possession of religious books in English was dangerous. Records from the Chiltern heresy proceedings in 1521 show what Cross calls 'the eager participation of the local women in teaching lollardy, acquiring lollard books, learning lollard tracts by heart and demonstrating their dislike of catholic ceremonies'.[67] There is plentiful evidence of women teaching men as well as other women. The daughter of John Phip of Hughenden (Bucks.) made an interesting saving clause in her claim that 'she was as well learned as was the parish priest, in all things, except only in saying mass'.[68] The Chiltern Lollard women possessed books, borrowed them and met to hear them discussed. One gets the impression of a fervent self-improvement society, based on religion, but surely leavening up the disputational and reasoning powers of the participants. However, there is no evidence that Lollardy attracted a disproportionately large number of women adherents, and the contrast of Lollard women as more active in their heretical beliefs than the passive role orthodox women were accustomed to in religion, though attractive as an idea, cannot really be substantiated. Identifying several Lollard women organising book distribution, and crediting them with unique authority over impressionable children as mothers and grandmothers,[69] does not prove that they were any more active in the propagation of their faith than orthodox women in theirs.

Heretics and sorcerers: witchcraft

When Egberht, the archbishop of York, thundered against sorcerers entering the Christian priesthood, in the eighth century, he was obviously thinking of males, but *Malleus Maleficarum* declared it a fact in the fifteenth century that a greater number of witches came from the female sex.

The Bible introduces Christians to Satan, wizards, familiars and divination. In Exodus, XXII, 18 it was decreed in the follow-up to the Ten Commandments, 'thou shalt not suffer a witch to live', and in his epistle to the Galatians St Paul lists witchcraft among the works of the flesh (V, 20). In Anglo-Saxon times pagan survivals as well as inversions of Christian rituals and unclear grasp of Christianity produced a thread of activity condemned by churchmen and, under their influence, law. The growing sophistication of churchmen in the eleventh and twelfth centuries did not penetrate the minds of ordinary people, and indeed while the theologians and canon lawyers pontificated, more ordinary churchmen recorded Satanic incidents with credulity and even, one suspects, relish. William of Malmesbury (d. *c.* 1143), an intelligent monastic historian, recorded the case of the witch of Berkeley, whose corpse was snatched from church by her devil master, despite the efforts of ecclesiastics.[70]

Only women, of course, were susceptible to the charge of bearing monstrous offspring after sexual intercourse with demons (*incubi*; see the beginning of the *Brut* chronicle).[71] Persons of either sex could be accused of selling themselves to the devil, sacrificing to demons, attempting divination, casting spells and generally exercising preternatural powers malevolently. Pope Alexander IV (1254–61) gave the Inquisition power to deal with witchcraft involving heresy, but the Inquisition did not exist in England. On the Continent mass persecutions began in the later fifteenth century, becoming more zealous in the sixteenth. Witchcraft was hardly a problem in medieval England, and the most famous trials have political overtones. In 1419, when acutely in need of money, Henry V arrested his stepmother Joan of Navarre on charges of sorcery, and appropriated her dower, worth 10,000 marks a year. Her confessor accused her of 'compassing the death and destruction of our lord the king'. The charges were never pressed, the three-year captivity was reasonably luxurious, and the dower, or at least its equivalent, was restored. Later in 1441 came the trial of Eleanor Cobham, duchess of Gloucester: no contemporaries suggest her trial was in origin a political attack on her husband, but political capital was made of it by his enemies. Cited with conspiring to bring about Henry VI's death, being wife of his heir presumptive, Eleanor had to face charges of sorcery, necromancy and treason. Condemned by ecclesiastical tribunal and secular inquiry, she was divorced from the duke, forced to perform humiliating public penance, and spent the rest of her life in custody.[72] Eleanor's associate Marjery Jurdane, the witch of Eye, charged with sorcery as early as 1432 and subsequently burnt at Smithfield, London, claimed she had been employed by Eleanor to concoct medicines and potions to win Duke Humphrey's affections, a level of sorcery which, in less important people, may have been relatively commonplace. Looking into the future, too, must have been frequently attempted. It was when witchcraft had treasonable or political connotations that it became more important. Joan of Arc, called in the *Brut* the witch of France,[73] was a captured enemy, but the way to be rid of her was on a heresy charge, with sorcery, idolatry and invocation of demons thrown in: 'owing to her evil reputation, she is by no means to be dealt with as a prisoner of war'.[74]

Conclusions

In the field of religion, as elsewhere, the Middle Ages has often been seen as making a division between 'private' and 'public' activity, confining most women to the former sphere. As mothers, they were credited with formative moral influence on their children and expected to exercise this responsibly, but the church allowed them only passive participation in its own rituals and no share in ecclesiastical authority. Women, however, did gain a public religious persona by entering convents and practising a professional religious life therein, and many hardy souls succeeded in the solitary religious life of an anchoress.

Until comparatively recently much of the work on this subject was largely descriptive and even anecdotal. The trend of recent scholarship has been much more analytical, fitting the phenomena of nuns, anchoresses, pious dowagers, and heretics and witches into their appropriate and inter-relating backgrounds, and looking harder at the prejudices in the sources. It is now more possible to see how, and when, specific practices among pious women captured the imagination of the times, winning financial support, and when this dropped away. This leaves us far better informed than the chronologically vague treatment of late medieval nunneries by Power, and the generalised portrayal of the pious gentlewoman handed down in popular books about medieval women. Lollard women have also come into their own.

Recent study of religious opportunities for women has pointed specifically to gender-related characteristics, architecturally, economically and emotionally. Unlike men's houses, the architecture of women's houses reflected the layout of the manor, with moats, courtyards and pentices. Comparatively poorly endowed, women's houses tended to be less self-sufficient than men's, and sited in marginal or isolated places, a physical espousal of poverty and isolation which could also be symbolic. Emotionally, religious women inclined to particular devotion to the Passion and the Crucifixion, and denigration of the body, a feature also discussed in recent studies of holy anorexia. Despite poverty, women's houses were more consistent almsgivers. Local study has also been able to unearth a few informal communities of religious women in East Anglia, variously described as 'women dedicated to chastity' and 'sisters under religious vow', in receipt of bequests which testify to their being perceived as religious beneficiaries.[75] There was clearly in East Anglia a wider variety of religious life styles than has generally been supposed, and in the Norwich diocese the conventional convents prove to have operated a career structure based on merit not birth.

Notes

1 Galatians, III, 28; Ephesians, V, 22.
2 D. M. Webb, 'Woman and home: the domestic setting of medieval spirituality', in W. J. Shiels and D. Wood (eds.), *Women in the Church*, Studies in Church History, XXVII, 1990, p. 161.
3 C. Roth, *History of the Jews in England*, Oxford, 3rd edn 1964, p. 125.
4 'The Miller's Tale', Canterbury Tales, *The Riverside Chaucer*, ed. L. D. Benson, 3rd edn, Oxford, 1988, p. 70; see for example R. T. Davies (ed.), *Medieval English Lyrics*, London, 1963, no. 73.
5 R. Gilchrist, *Gender and Material Culture: the archaeology of religious women*, London and New York, 1994, pp. 40–1, 61.
6 S. Thompson, *Women Religious: the founding of English nunneries after the Norman Conquest*, Oxford, 1991, p. 122.
7 E. Power, *Medieval English Nunneries c. 1275 to 1535*, Cambridge, 1922, p. 231, citing *The Register of John le Romeyn*, I, [ed. J. Raine

jun.], Surtees Society, CXXIII, 1913, pp. xii, xiii, 86, 234, 125, 157, 180.

8 S. Elkins, *Holy Women of Twelfth-Century England*, Chapel Hill and London, 1988, p. xiv.

9 *Ibid.*, pp. 125–6, 90.

10 G. Constable, 'Ailred of Rievaulx and the nun of Watton: an episode in the early history of the Gilbertine Order', in D. Baker (ed.), *Medieval Women*, Studies in Church History, Subsidia I, 1978, pp. 205–26.

11 C. V. Graves, 'Stixwould in the market place', in *Medieval Religious Women I Distant Echoes*, ed. J. A. Nichols and L. T. Shank, Cistercian Studies lxxi, 1983/4, pp. 213–36.

12 Gilchrist, *Gender and Material Culture*, pp. 43–4.

13 R. Gilchrist, ' "Blessed art Thou among Women": the archaeology of female piety', in *Woman is a Worthy Wight: women in English society c. 1200–1500*, ed. J. P. J. Goldberg, Stroud, 1992, pp. 212–26; R. Gilchrist and M. Oliva, *Religious Women in Medieval East Anglia: history and archaeology c. 1100–1550*, Norwich, 1993, pp. 24, 45; Gilchrist, *Gender and Material Culture*, passim.

14 M. Oliva, 'Aristocracy or meritocracy? Office-holding patterns in late medieval English nunneries', in Sheils and Wood (eds.), *Women in the Church*, pp. 200, 199.

15 J. Wogan-Browne, '"Clerc u lai, muïne u dame": women and Anglo-Norman hagiography in the twelfth and thirteenth centuries', in C. M. Meale (ed.), *Women and Literature in Britain 1150–1500*, Cambridge, 1993, pp. 67–73; Power, *Medieval English Nunneries*, pp. 247–8.

16 Power, *Medieval English Nunneries*, p. 389.

17 J. A. Nichols, 'Medieval Cistercian nunneries and English bishops', in *Medieval Religious Women, I*, pp. 237–9; A. H. Thompson (ed.), *Visitations of Religious Houses in the Diocese of Lincoln*, II, Lincoln Record Society, XIV, 1918, pp. 47, 50.

18 C. H. Talbot (ed.), *The Life of Christina of Markyate*, Oxford, 1959, pp. 43, 73–5.

19 J. T. Schulenburg, 'The heroics of virginity: brides of Christ and sacrificial mutilation', in M. B. Rose (ed.), *Women in the Middle Ages and Renaissance*, University of Syracuse, 1986, pp. 58–9.

20 Elkins, *Holy Women*, pp. 2–3, 212; Power, *Medieval English Nunneries*, p. 447.

21 B. Millett and J. Wogan-Browne (eds.), *Medieval English Prose for Women*, Oxford, 1990, pp. xv, 39, 11.

22 A. Warren, *Anchorites and their Patrons in Medieval England*, Berkeley and Los Angeles/London, 1985, pp. 19–20.

23 Elkins, *Holy Women*, p. 26.

24 Talbot, *Christina*, p. 95.
25 *Ibid.*, p. 101.
26 *Ibid.*, pp. 103–7.
27 *Ibid.*, p. 175.
28 *Register of Walter Giffard, lord archbishop of York, 1266–79*, [ed. W. Brown], Surtees Society, CIX, 1904, p. 108; *Register of Romeyn*, p. 196.
29 B. Millett, ' "Women in No Man's Land": English recluses and the development of vernacular literature in the twelfth and thirteenth centuries', in Meale (ed.), *Women and Literature*, pp. 86–103; Warren, *Anchorites*, pp. 283–4.
30 B. Ward, 'Lady Julian of Norwich and her audience: "Mine even-Christian" ', in G. Rowell (ed.), *The English Religious Tradition and the Genius of Anglicanism*, Wantage, 1992, p. 50.
31 M. Aston, 'Segregation in Church', in Sheils and Wood (eds.), *Women in the Church*, pp. 263, 237–45.
32 M. K. Jones and M. G. Underwood, *The King's Mother, Lady Margaret Beaufort, the Countess of Richmond and Derby*, Cambridge, 1992, p. 175.
33 *Ibid.*, p. 1.
34 M. A. Hicks, 'The piety of Margaret, Lady Hungerford (d. 1478)', *Journal of Ecclesiastical History*, XXXVIII, 1, 1987, pp. 19–38.
35 *Testamenta Eboracensia*, i, nos. 28, 232, 188.
36 N. Davis (ed.), *Paston Letters and Papers of the Fifteenth Century*, I, Oxford, 1971, no. 353.
37 H. S. Bennett, *The Pastons and their England*, Cambridge, 1968, p. 215.
38 Davis (ed.), *Paston Letters and Papers*, I, nos. 405, 40.
39 Bennett, *Pastons*, p. 223.
40 B. H. Putnam (ed.), *Yorkshire Sessions of the Peace, 1361–64*, Yorkshire Archaeological Society, Record Series, C, 1939, p. 41.
41 Roth, *History of the Jews*, pp. 59, 77.
42 *Riverside Chaucer*, Miller's Tale, p. 69.
43 *Book of Margery Kempe*, ed. S. P. B. Meech, Early English Text Society, 1940, p. 12.
44 *Ibid.*, pp. 17, 87. C. W. Bynum, in *Holy Feast and Holy Fast: the religious significance of food to medieval women*, Cambridge, 1987, has recently drawn attention to the significance of feasting and fasting as a religious feature especially in women's lives, and has examined details of many holy women in medieval Europe whose passion for the eucharist and contempt for worldly food brought them into conditions now associated with eating disorders.
45 T. Smith and L. Toulmin Smith (eds.), *English Gilds*, Early English Text Society, 1870, pp. 22–3.

46 Modernised text based on P. Happé, *English Mystery Plays*, Harmondsworth, 1975, p. 46.
47 W. Tydeman, 'Costumes and actors', in P. Happé (ed.), *Medieval English Drama*, London, 1984, p. 180.
48 P. H. Cullum, ' "And Hir Name was Charite": charitable giving by and for women in late medieval Yorkshire', in Goldberg (ed.), *Woman is a Worthy Wight*, pp. 182–211.
49 M. M. Sheehan, 'The formation and stability of marriage in fourteenth-century England: evidence of an Ely register', *Medieval Studies*, XXXIII, 1971, p. 249.
50 S. Hollis, *Anglo-Saxon Women and the Church*, Woodbridge, 1992, p. 59; G. Duby, *Medieval Marriage: two models from twelfth-century France*, trsl. E. Forster, Baltimore and London, 1978, p. 7.
51 E. Power, 'The position of women', in C. G. Crump and E. F. Jacob (eds.), *The Legacy of the Middle Ages*, Oxford, 1962 reprint, p. 404; P. S. Gold, *The Lady and the Virgin: image, attitude, and experience in twelfth-century France*, Chicago and London, 1985, chapters 1 and 2.
52 Bynum, *Holy Feast, Holy Fast*, pp. 240–1.
53 S. M. Stuard (ed.), *Women in Medieval Society*, Philadelphia, 1976, pp. 8–9.
54 N. P. Tanner (ed.), *Heresy Trials in the Diocese of Norwich, 1428–31*, Camden 4th Series, XX, 1977, pp. 138–44.
55 *Ibid.*, p. 48.
56 *Ibid.*, pp. 47, 176.
57 C. Cross, ' "Great reasoners in Scripture": the activities of women Lollards 1380–1530', in *Medieval Women*, ed. D. Baker, pp. 364, 374.
58 *Ibid.*, p. 379.
59 For example by Duby, *Medieval Marriage*, p. 17.
60 M. Aston, 'Lollard women priests?', *Journal of Ecclesiastical History*, XXXI, 4, 1980, p. 441.
61 *Ibid.*, p. 443.
62 *Ibid.*, pp. 444, 453; see also A. Blamires (with K. Pratt and C. W. Marx), *Women Defamed and Women Defended*, Oxford, 1992, pp. 250–60.
63 R. M. Haines, ' "Wilde wittes and wilfulnes": John Swetstock's attack on those "poyswunmongeres" the Lollards', in C. J. Cuming and D. Baker (eds.), *Popular Belief and Practice*, Studies in Church History, VIII, 1972, pp. 152–3.
64 Cross, 'Great Reasoners', p. 360.
65 *Ibid.*, pp. 362–3.
66 *Ibid.*, p. 366.
67 *Ibid.*, p. 369.

68 *Ibid.*, p. 371.
69 *Ibid.*, p. 378.
70 William of Malmesbury, 'History of the Kings of England', in *Church Historians of England*, ed. J. Stevenson, London, 1854, pp. 196–7.
71 *The Brut, or the Chronicles of England*, I, ed. F. W. D. Brie, Early English Text Society, 1906, p. 4.
72 A. R. Myers, 'The captivity of a royal witch: the household accounts of Queen Joan of Navarre, 1419–21', *Bulletin of the John Rylands Library*, XXIV, 1940, pp. 263–84; R. A. Griffiths, 'The trial of Eleanor Cobham: an episode in the fall of Duke Humphrey of Gloucester', *ibid.*, LI, 1969, pp. 381–99.
73 *Brut*, II, 1908, p. 439.
74 D. Rankin and C. Quintal (eds.), *The first biography of Joan of Arc*, Pittsburgh, 1964, p. 43.
75 Gilchrist and Oliva, *Religious Women, passim*.

6

Conclusions

It was remarked in the Introduction how well this subject illustrates changing historiographical approaches dictated by changing interests in subsequent generations. As times change, what people want to know about the past changes too. The study of medieval women has made enormous strides in the last quarter century because so many new questions have been asked.

Moreover, these questions are being asked of a wider range of source material and with the aid of techniques taken from social and even medical sciences. In the overall study of medieval history, not just of its womenfolk, and not only in England, reliance on chronicles, statutes and charters has given way to the probing of archival material such as tax records and court records. Archival sources are undoubtedly preferable material for historical sociological research, for whereas chronicles were selective narrative, and statute and charter were proclamations of theoretical rights and privileges, the archival records are more impersonal and certainly offer more opportunities for quantitative research.

Historians in England are only just becoming aware of the potential value of poll tax records of 1377–81 in studying economic, social and demographic aspects of English society.[1] Much more than a head count, the poll tax information permits analysis of different household structures in town and country, and within the countryside, in arable and pastoral regions. Similar research has already been undertaken using appropriate continental sources. The Florentine *catasto* of 1427, covering the city and its *contadi*, provided the evidence analysed by David Herlihy and Christiane Klapisch-Zuber in their book on Tuscans and their families.[2] In Florence and Pisa in 1427 the sex ratios were 117.6 and 112.3, but in English (and north-west European) towns low sex ratios are found among the adult population, although underenumeration would be more likely to skew women's totals than men's.[3] Quantitative research on such sources is likely to increase with the growing accessibility of electronic databases.

Many editions of court rolls have been published in England, for manorial jurisdiction, eyres and assizes and justices of the peace, but because most were published before the rise of interest in women, although they are perfectly adequate scholarly editions, their introductions lack the gender analysis which would now be welcome. The published medieval Wakefield court rolls, for example, are now supporting research on women, but sparse comments on women were written in their editorial introductions.[4] In the Yorkshire peace rolls edited by Bertha Putnam, many women appear accused of labour offences, and the range and nature of their offences deserves to be highlighted, but there is no reference to them in the introduction, where women only appear by inference in the count of instances of rape.[5] From these and other edited peace rolls it appears this well-quarried evidence should be re-examined to reveal answers to new questions. The general execution of the labour laws is well enough understood, but further study of cases could be rewarding. For example, in the area of excess wages, seven Yorkshire spinsters (all acquitted) were alleged to have taken 18*d* to spin a stone of wool, where they used to take 12*d*, a rise of 50 per cent; another, also acquitted, allegedly took 2*d* to spin a pound of yarn, where she formerly took 1*d*, a rise of 100 per cent. Two other women, one described as webster, formerly taking 2*d* for weaving five ells of cloth, were said to be taking one halfpenny per ell, a rise of 25 per cent; they too were acquitted.[6] These entries prompt the questions: how often are old and new rates of pay specified, how often were women acquitted, and what were the equivalent rates – of pay and acquittal – for men? Penn has shown parity of pay between the sexes for harvestwork from labour cases, and found women to be mobile workers too.[7] This class of records is capable of revealing more about medieval women's employment than it has yet done; Dyer comments 'the female contribution to the labour force deserves our attention'.[8]

Even more diverse information should prove available in English church court records, a comparatively neglected source, recently described as 'a rich store for legal and social historians for years to come'.[9] In connection with marriage litigation both Helmholz and Goldberg have indicated, for example, some of the unusual settings of marriage contracts recollected by witnesses, casting incidental light on living conditions and servants' recreational activities. Research on church court records will doubtless be productive. It was, after all, from an inquisition register of the bishop of Pamiers that the seminal study of Montaillou was based.[10] Records of an inquisition into Cathar heresy revealed a rich haul of incidental information about the community's roving shepherds, domineering matriarchs, randy priest and promiscuous chatelaine.

Leaving records aside, there is welcome development in the application of medical science to archaeology. The recent revelation of the women of Wharram Percy's post-menopausal osteoporosis has medical repercussions both for them and ourselves. Virulent plagues were noticed and recorded by contemporary chroniclers, but research into more ordinary diseases and causes of death reveals more about normal conditions in the Middle Ages. Again English research is paralleled on the Continent. Study of skeletal remains in Denmark has revealed that in the Viking period 75 per cent of the women lived to at least the age of thirty-five, which indicates a dramatic reduction in the proportion dying between the ages of twenty and thirty-five, compared with the pre-Viking period.[11]

The ages of menarche and menopause were placed by Hildegard of Bingen in the twelfth century at fifteen and fifty,[12] giving women a similar fertility span to today, but canon law permitted women to be married at twelve. The dangers of youthful pregnancy were known to contemporaries and some marriage agreements restrained intercourse until the girl reached sixteen; study of the Welsh tractate on the law of women (the oldest text of which is mid-thirteenth-century, but incorporates archaic material) indicates girls were expected to be kept chaste between twelve and fourteen.[13] Documentation of actual births is limited to individual upper-class examples, but average family size has been estimated from court rolls at Halesowen. Despite warnings about sin, birth-control practices were known and attempted.[14] Midwifery and early childcare seem to have been more efficiently organised on the Continent, as shown by Merry Wiesner's study of early modern midwifery in Nuremberg, and Leah Otis's work on municipal wet-nurses in

Montpellier. (Otis is better known for her work on prostitution in Languedoc, where it was much more institutionalised than in England.)[15]

Gynaecology apart, women's working lives have also been studied in European cities as well as English ones. In Montpellier in the expansionist years 1293–1348 K. L. Reyerson finds 'the prestigious occupations of the mercantile elite were male oriented', and women's trades were largely related to the traditional women's work of providing food, clothing and ornament.[16] Martha Howell's *Women, Production and Patriarchy in Late Medieval Cities* was cited in capter 3.[17] North European towns are closer parallels to English towns than those of the Mediterranean in terms of household structure, industrial occupation and legal heritage, so the women's roles are different for example in Italy. England did not share in the continental beguinage movement, though the nearest reflections of it seem to be located in East Anglia, which had contact with the cities of the Low Countries, where the beguines (members of lay sisterhoods dedicated to a hardworking austere religious life but not bound by strict vows) emerged in the twelfth and thirteenth centuries.

The single most stimulating influence on the last twenty-five years of work on women has been the impact of feminist confidence in the subject. Questions no longer have to be asked defensively, and many avenues of research have been opened up in England and Europe. It is surely reasonable to want to know what women's life expectancies were and if these changed. As Herlihy points out, the duration of women's lives deeply affects their social position and experience.[18] It must be asked if there is any suspicion of selective female infanticide, and sometimes the evidence looks positive, as Emily Coleman found on estates of St-Germain-des-Prés in the ninth century.[19] Allowing girls to survive may have helped the eleventh-century population increase, and the sex ratios of the later Middle Ages, particularly bearing in mind the likelier underenumeration of women, make it clear girls were generally being let live.

In addition to using traditional source material in their search for more information about medieval women, medievalists have also attempted to use more obscure material, and even to squeeze significance out of silence itself. Brigitte Bedos Rezak has attempted to assess feminine power by the study of sigillography, and Alan

Stahl has looked at coinage in women's names.[20] Jane Schulenburg has pulled out ideas of female sanctity, and expounded on saints' lives as a source for women's history.[21] There has been an increased interest in medieval writing aimed at women, as well as attempts to identify works which might have women authors, and this has led to the welcome publication of translated anthologies such as *Medieval English Prose for Women* edited by Bertha Millett and Jocelyn Wogan-Browne (1990), and Alcuin Blamires' *Women Defamed and Women Defended* (1992). Sarah Lawson's translation of Christine de Pisan's *The Treasure of the City of Ladies* (1985) makes easily available an essential text from a remarkable woman addressing a female audience.

The European dimension has been alluded to in this conclusion to show that work proceeds widely, and that the study of medieval women is by no means insular. There are greater differences across medieval European cultures than within England, even Britain, itself (where regional diversities are noticeable enough), nevertheless, across north-western Europe similar patterns of change in the eleventh century and in the fourteenth and fifteenth have been postulated. The militarisation of society in the mid-eleventh century, furthered by the Normans, and the contemporary reform of the church on lines which separated its male elite from easy communication with women, are argued to have had a generally depressing effect on the status of women. Economic expansion occurred widely before the early fourteenth-century famines and mid-century plague, and the consequent population drop seems to have created outlets for women in trade and to have improved their legal standing in commercial centres. By the end of the fifteenth century trade practices favourable to men were squeezing women out and opportunities were being cut back. This general outline is by no means unchallenged, but individual case studies still support it.

It certainly must not be imagined that medieval women progressed steadily towards emancipation, or struggled to recover a chimerical golden age. Conditions changed in different places at different times. Though the study of medieval women has made many exciting discoveries, two very solid achievements promise to have far-reaching effect on the way history will be studied in the future. One is the discrediting of any chronologically vague and implicitly static 'identikit' picture of medieval women, and the

[189]

other is the rejection as inadequate of any interpretation of overall social history which disregards women. Barbara Hanawalt wrote in 1987: 'a characteristic of the new social history is that women are now always included'.[22] This is a remarkably recent development, and needs to be consolidated.

Notes

1 P. J. P. Goldberg, 'Urban identity and the poll taxes of 1377, 1379, and 1381', *Economic History Review*, 2nd series, XLIII, 2, 1990, pp. 194–216.

2 D. Herlihy and C. Klapisch-Zuber, *Tuscans and their Families: a study of the Florentine catasto of 1427*, New Haven, 1985.

3 *Ibid.*, p. 154, table 5.4.; Goldberg, 'Female labour, service and marriage in the late medieval urban north', *Northern History*, XXII, 1986, p. 19, and 'Urban identity', pp. 197, 200–1.

4 H. M. Jewell, 'Women at the courts of the manor of Wakefield, 1348–50', *Northern History*, XXVI, 1990, p. 61; S. J. Stratford, 'Women before the customary courts: the manor of Wakefield 1274–1352', unpublished M.A. dissertation, University of York, 1994.

5 B. H. Putnam, (ed.), *Yorkshire Sessions of the Peace 1361–4*, Yorkshire Archaeological Society, Record Series, C, 1939.

6 *Ibid.*, pp. 69, 71, 53.

7 S. A. C. Penn, 'Female wage-earners in late fourteenth-century England', *Agricultural History Review*, XXXV, 1987, pp. 9–10, 11.

8 C. Dyer with S. A. C. Penn, 'Wages and earnings in late medieval England, evidence from the enforcement of the labour laws', in Dyer, *Everyday Life in Medieval England*, London, 1994, pp. 167–8.

9 R. H. Helmholz, *Marriage Litigation in Medieval England*, Cambridge, 1974, p. 7.

10 E. Le Roy Ladurie, *Montaillou: Cathars and Catholics in a French village, 1294–1324*, trsl. B. Bray, Harmondsworth, 1980.

11 J. Jesch, *Women in the Viking Age*, Woodbridge, 1991, p. 13.

12 M. W. Labarge, *Women in Medieval Life: a small sound of the trumpet*, London, 1986, pp. 24–5.

13 M. E. Owen, 'Shame and reparation: woman's place in the kin', in D. Jenkins and M. E. Owen (eds.), *The Welsh Law of Women*, Cardiff, 1980, p. 48.

14 P. P. A. Biller, 'Birth control in the west in the thirteenth and early fourteenth centuries', *Past and Present*, 94, 1982, pp. 3–26.

15 M. E. Wiesner, 'Early modern midwifery: a case study', in B. A. Hanawalt (ed.), *Women and Work in Pre-Industrial Europe*, Bloomington,

Indiana, 1986, pp. 94–113, and L. L. Otis, 'Municipal wet-nurses in fifteenth-century Montpellier', *ibid.*, pp. 83–93; also Otis, 'Prostitution and repentance in late medieval Perpignan', in J. Kirshner and S. Wemple (eds.), *Women of the Medieval World*, Oxford, 1985, pp. 137–60 and *Prostitution in Medieval Society: the history of an urban institution in Languedoc*, Chicago, 1985.

16 K. L. Reyerson, 'Women in Business in Medieval Montpellier', in Hanawalt (ed.), *Women and Work*, pp. 11–44.

17 See too Howell, 'Citizenship and gender: women's political status in northern medieval cities', in M. Erler and M. Kowaleski (eds.), *Women and Power in the Middle Ages*, Athens, Gia and London, 1988, pp. 37–60.

18 D. Herlihy, 'Life expectancies for women in medieval society', in R. T. Morewedge (ed.), *The Role of Women in the Middle Ages*, London, 1975, pp. 1–22.

19 E. Coleman, 'Infanticide in the early middle ages', reprinted in S. M. Stuard (ed.), *Women in Medieval Society*, Philadelphia, 1976, pp. 47–70.

20 B. Bedos Rezak, 'Women, seals and power in medieval France 1150–1350', in Erler and Kowaleski, *Women and Power*, pp. 61–82, and 'Medieval women in French sigillographic sources' in J. T. Rosenthal (ed.), *Medieval Women and the Sources of Medieval History*, Athens, Gia and London, 1990, pp. 1–36; A. Stahl, 'Coinage in the name of medieval women', *ibid.*, pp. 321–41.

21 J. T. Schulenburg, 'Female sanctity: public and private roles *c.* 500–1100', in Erler and Kowaleski, *Women and Power*, pp. 102–25, and 'Saints' lives as a source for the history of women 500–1100', in Rosenthal, *Medieval Women*, pp. 285–320.

22 B. Hanawalt, 'Golden ages for the history of medieval English women', in S. M. Stuard (ed.), *Women in Medieval History and Historiography*, Philadelphia, 1987, p. 14.

Further reading

Introduction

D. Baker (ed.), *Medieval Women*, Studies in Church History, Subsidia I, 1978.

J. M. Bennett, 'Medieval women, modern women: across the great divide', in D. Aers (ed.), *Culture and History 1350–1600: essays on English communities, identities and writing*, London, 1992, pp. 147–75.

B. A. Hanawalt, 'Golden ages for the history of medieval English women', in S. M. Stuard (ed.), *Women in Medieval History and Historiography*, Philadelphia, 1987, pp. 1–24.

E. Power, 'The Role of Women', in *The Legacy of the Middle Ages*, ed. C. G. Crump and E. F. Jacob, Oxford, 1926 (reprinted 1962), pp. 401–33.

J. T. Rosenthal (ed.), *Medieval Women and the Sources of Medieval History*, Athens, Gia and London, 1990.

Chapter 1

Source material

F. L. Attenborough (ed.), *The Laws of the Earliest English Kings*, Cambridge, 1922.

A. Campbell (ed.), *Encomium Emmae Reginae*, Camden Third Series, LXXII, 1949.

J. Morris (gen. ed.), *History from the Sources* (Domesday Book published by county), Chichester, 1975–86.

D. Whitelock (ed.), *Anglo-Saxon Wills*, Cambridge, 1930.

Interpretative works

C. Fell, *Women in Anglo-Saxon England*, Oxford, 1984.

S. Hollis, *Anglo-Saxon Women and the Church*, Woodbridge, 1992.

Further reading

J. Jesch, *Women in the Viking Age*, Woodbridge, 1991.

J. Nicholson, 'Feminae gloriosae: women in the age of Bede', in D. Baker (ed.), *Medieval Women*, Studies in Church History, Subsidia I, 1978, pp. 15–29.

J. T. Schulenburg, 'Women's monastic communities 500–1100: patterns of expansion and decline', in *Signs*, Winter 1989, xiv, 2, pp. 261–92.

P. Stafford, *Queens, Concubines and Dowagers: the king's wife in the early middle ages*, London, 1983.

P. Stafford, 'Women in Domesday', in *Medieval Women of Southern England*, Reading Medieval Studies, XV, 1989, pp. 75–94.

P. Stafford, 'Women and the Norman Conquest', *Transactions of the Royal Historical Society*, 6th series, IV, 1994, pp. 221–49.

Chapter 2

Source material

H. M. Jewell (ed.), *The Court Rolls of the Manor of Wakefield, 1348–50*, Wakefield Court Rolls Second Series, II, 1981.

'Ballad of a Tyrannical Husband', in T. Wright and J. O. Halliwell (eds.), *Reliquiae Antiquae*, II, 1843 (reprinted 1966), pp. 196–9.

Interpretative works

J. M. Bennett, 'Medieval peasant marriage: an examination of marriage licence fines in *Liber Gersumarum*', in J. A. Raftis (ed.), *Pathways to Medieval Peasants*, Toronto, 1981, pp. 193–246.

J. M. Bennett, *Women in the Medieval English Countryside: gender and household in Brigstock before the Plague*, Oxford, 1987.

P. J. P. Goldberg, 'The public and the private: women in the pre-plague economy', in P. R. Coss and S. D. Lloyd (eds.), *Thirteenth-Century England*, III, Woodbridge, 1991, pp. 75–89.

H. Graham, ' "A woman's work . . .": labour and gender in the late medieval countryside', in P. J. P. Goldberg (ed.), *Woman is a Worthy Wight: women in English society c. 1200–1500*, Stroud, 1992, pp. 126–48.

B. A. Hanawalt, 'Peasant women's contribution to the home economy in late medieval England', in Hanawalt (ed.), *Women and Work in Pre-Industrial Europe*, Bloomington, Indiana, 1986, pp. 3–19.

H. M. Jewell, 'Women at the courts of the manor of Wakefield, 1348–50', *Northern History*, XXVI, 1990, pp. 59–81.

T. North, 'Legerwite in the thirteenth and fourteenth centuries', *Past and Present*, 111, 1986, pp. 3–16.

Chapter 3

Source material

M. Bateson (ed.), *Borough Customs*, II, Selden Society, XXI, 1906, pp. 102–29.

Interpretative works

C. M. Barron, ' "The Golden Age" of women in medieval London', in *Medieval Women in Southern England*, Reading Medieval Studies, XV, 1989, pp. 35–58.

C. M. Barron and A. F. Sutton, *Medieval London Widows 1300–1500*, London, 1994.

P. J. P. Goldberg, 'Female labour, service and marriage in the late medieval urban north', *Northern History*, XXII, 1986, pp. 18–38.

P. J. P. Goldberg, 'Women in fifteenth-century town life', in J. A. F. Thomson (ed.), *Towns and Townspeople in the Fifteenth Century*, Gloucester, 1988, pp. 107–28.

P. J. P. Goldberg, 'Women's work, women's role in the late medieval north', in M. [A.] Hicks (ed.), *Profit, Piety and the Professions*, Gloucester, 1990, pp. 34–50.

P. J. P. Goldberg, *Women, Work and Life-Cycle in a Medieval Economy: women in York and Yorkshire c. 1300–1520*, Oxford, 1992.

B. A. Hanawalt, 'The female felon in fourteenth-century England', in S. M. Stuard (ed.), *Women in Medieval Society*, Philadelphia, 1976, pp. 125–40.

M. C. Howell, *Women, Production and Patriarchy in Late Medieval Cities*, Chicago and London, 1986.

D. Hutton, 'Women in fourteenth-century Shrewsbury', in L. Charles and L. Duffin (eds.), *Women and Work in Pre-Industrial England*, London, 1985, pp. 82–99.

R. M. Karras, 'The regulation of brothels in later medieval England', *Signs*, Winter 1989, xiv, 2, pp. 399–433.

M. Kowaleski, 'Women's work in a market town: Exeter in the late fourteenth century', in B. A. Hanawalt (ed.), *Women and Work in Pre-Industrial Europe*, Bloomington, Indiana, 1986, pp. 145–64.

M. Kowaleski and J. M. Bennett, 'Crafts, gilds and women in the middle ages: fifty years after Marian K. Dale', *Signs*, Winter 1989, xiv, 2, pp. 474–88.

Further reading

Chapter 4

Source material

A. Crawford (ed.), *Letters of the Queens of England, 1100–1547*, Stroud, 1994.

M. K. Dale and V. B. Redstone (eds.), *The Household Book of Dame Alice de Bryene*, Suffolk Institute of Archaeology and Natural History, 1931.

N. Davis (ed.), *Paston Letters and Papers of the Fifteenth Century*, Oxford, 2 vols., 1971–6.

Interpretative works

M. K. Jones and M. G. Underwood, *The King's Mother: Lady Margaret Beaufort, Countess of Richmond and Derby*, Cambridge, 1992.

J. S. Loengard, '"Of the gift of her husband": English dower and its consequences in the year 1200', in J. Kirshner and S. F. Wemple (eds.), *Women of the Medieval World*, Oxford, 1985, pp. 215–55.

P. Stafford, *Queens, Concubines and Dowagers: the king's wife in the early middle ages*, London, 1983.

S. S. Walker (ed.), *Wife and Widow in Medieval England*, Ann Arbor, 1993.

J. C. Ward, *English Noblewomen in the Later Middle Ages*, Harlow, 1992.

Chapter 5

Source material

S. P. B. Meech (ed.), *The Book of Margery Kempe*, Early English Text Society, 1940.

B. Millett and J. Wogan-Browne (eds.), *Medieval English Prose for Women*, Oxford, 1990.

C. H. Talbot (ed.), *The Life of Christina of Markyate: a twelfth-century recluse*, Oxford, 1959.

Interpretative works

S. K. Elkins, *Holy Women of Twelfth-Century England*, Chapel Hill/London, 1988.

R. Gilchrist, *Gender and Material Culture: the archaeology of religious women*, London and New York, 1994.

R. Gilchrist and M. Oliva, *Religious Women in Medieval East Anglia:*

[195]

Further reading

history and archaeology c. 1100–1540, Studies in East Anglian History, I, Norwich, 1993.

W. J. Shiels and D. Wood (eds.), *Women in the Church*, Studies in Church History, XXVII, 1990.

S. Thompson, *Women Religious: the founding of English nunneries after the Norman Conquest*, Oxford, 1991.

A. K. Warren, *Anchorites and their Patrons in Medieval England*, Berkeley and Los Angeles/London, 1985.

Chapter 6

Source material

Christine de Pisan, *The Treasure of the City of Ladies*, trsl. S. Lawson, Harmondsworth, 1985.

Interpretative works

P. P. A. Biller, 'Birth control in the west in the thirteenth and early fourteenth centuries', *Past and Present*, 94, 1982, pp. 3–26.

P. S. Gold, *The Lady and the Virgin: image, attitude, and experience in twelfth-century France*, Chicago and London, 1985.

D. Herlihy, 'Life expectancies for women in medieval society', in R. T. Morewedge (ed.), *The Role of Women in the Middle Ages*, London, 1975, pp. 1–22.

E. Le Roy Ladurie, *Montaillou: Cathars and Catholics in a French village, 1294–1324*, trsl. B. Bray, Harmondsworth, 1980.

M. Schaus and S. M. Stuard, 'Citizens of no mean city: medieval women's history', *Journal of Women's History*, VI, 3, Fall 1994, pp. 170–98.

S. M. Stuard (ed.), *Women in Medieval Society*, Philadelphia, 1976.

Index

Personal names are indexed where the reference is to the person in his or her own right. They are not indexed where they appear in the text merely descriptively. For example, 'Emma of Normandy, successively wife to Æthelred II and Cnut' (p. 30) is indexed under Emma, but not also separately under Æthelred and Cnut. Figures in **bold** type refer to principal entries.